ALABAMA

GEORGIA

Jacksonville

Tallahassee

St. Augustine

Pensacola

Panama City

Apalachicola

Apalachicola

Apalachee Bay

Suwannee

FLORIDA

Waccasassa Bay

Withlacoochee

Epinephelus Striatus

Tampa

St. Petersburg

Sarasota

Peace

Port Charlotte

Caloosahatchee

Fort Meyers

Naples

THE EVERGLADES

Miami

Pomatomus Saltatrix

Cape Sable

FLORIDA KEYS

Dry Tortugas

Key West

STRAITS OF FLORIDA

CANCER

Havana

YUCATÁN

CHANNEL

Cancún

N

Coba Ruins

Cozumel

W

E

S

JOHN A WILSON

GULF
COAST
COOKING

An oysterman and his wife work the reefs beyond Cedar Key.
A shrimp boat waits out the off-season at Apalachicola (previous page).

Editing by Alison Tartt

Special Editorial Assistance by Jean Hardy

Food Styling by Julie Hettiger

Calligraphy by Jeff Jeffreys

Map Illustration by John Wilson

Design by Barbara Jezek

Gulf Coast

COOKING

SEAFOOD FROM THE FLORIDA KEYS TO THE YUCATÁN PENINSULA

by Virginia Elverson

With an Essay by John Graves

Photography by Bob Parvin

Food Photography by David Crossley
and Bill Pogue

Gulf of Mexico

SHEARER PUBLISHING

FREDERICKSBURG, TEXAS

For Robin Elverson,
who enthusiastically tasted
and critiqued dozens of these briny
concoctions with nary a complaint.

Library of Congress Cataloging-in-Publication Data

Elverson, Virginia T.
Gulf coast cooking : seafood from the Florida Keys to the Yucatan
Peninsula / [Virginia Elverson].
p.   cm.
Includes index.
ISBN 0-940672-56-1
1. Cookery (Seafood)   2. Cookery, American.   3. Cookery,
Mexican.
I. Title.
TX747.E48   1991
641.6'92—dc20   91-11257
CIP

ISBN 0-940672-56-1

Published in 1991 by:
Shearer Publishing
406 Post Oak Road
Fredericksburg, TX 78624

Production by Mandarin Offset, Hong Kong

Printed in Hong Kong

Lacy palms form abstract patterns on the white sands of this Florida beach.

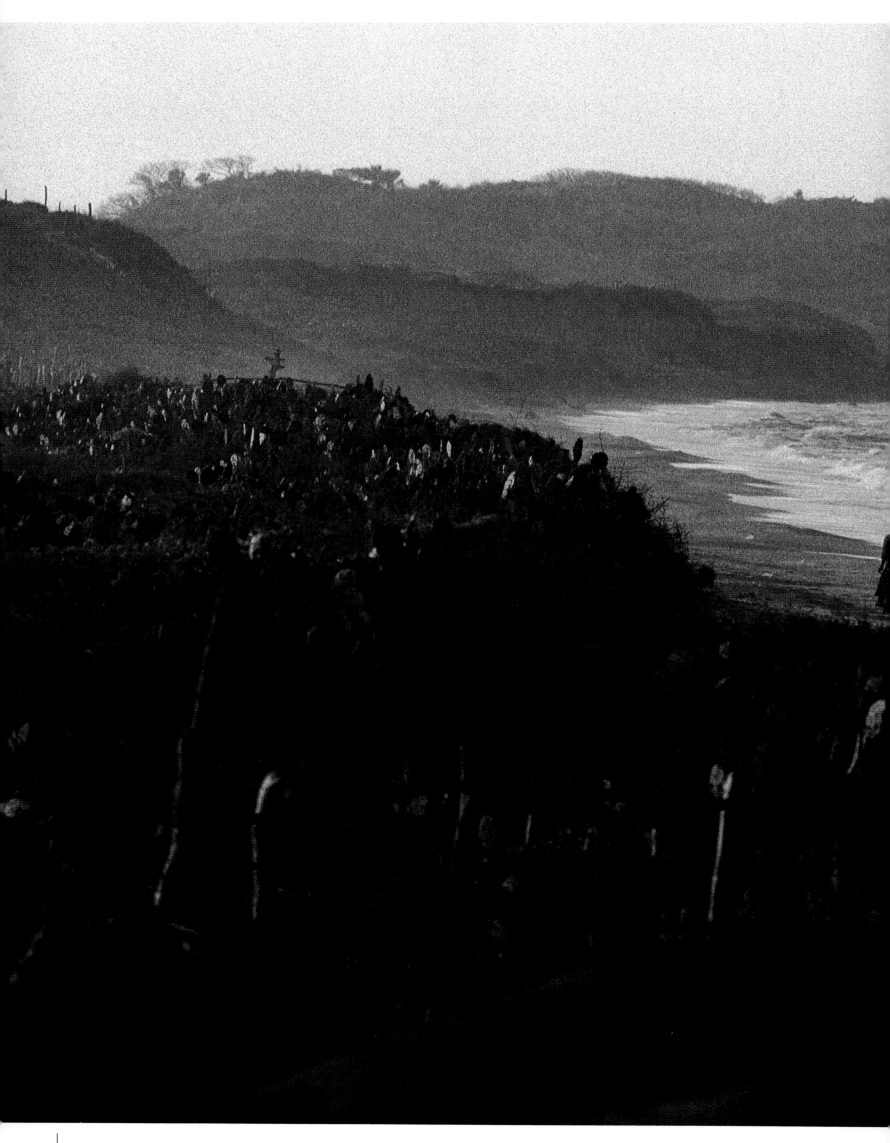

Massive cactus-clad dunes rise from the shore below Veracruz.

CONTENTS

THE GULF

A SKETCH

WITH SOME

SOMBER TINTS

by John Graves

IF THERE WERE MUCH LOGIC in maritime nomenclature the Gulf of Mexico would be called not a gulf but a sea, the category of saltwater expanses just below that of the oceans. Of the world's dozens of seas that are known as such, only four have more surface area than the Gulf's 582,000 square miles, and only one of those four outplumbs its average depth of just over a mile. That is of course a lot of water, and fairly restless water it is. A huge flow enters the basin from the Caribbean via the Yucatán Channel, then spreads out in a confusion of seasonally varying currents and countercurrents that ultimately reconverge to exit strongly through the Straits of Florida, forming the initial component of the mighty Gulf Stream.

A rough roller-measure check of a nautical chart shows a "smoothed" Gulf perimeter (that is, not counting the shores of bays or barrier islands and spits) of about 3,000 miles from Cabo Catoche

The morning sun winks offshore from Texas' 135-mile-long Padre Island. A fishing boat cuts a wake through the maze of southwest Florida's Ten Thousand Islands.

at the northern tip of Yucatán to Cape Sable in Everglades National Park, of which more than half belongs to the United States and the rest to Mexico. The physical character of any given part of that long coast is tied in with things like land contours, rainfall, plant growth, and where the stretch lies in relation to the Tropic of Cancer, which cuts across the Gulf just below its centerline and gives it a range of climates from temperate to fully tropical, together with a special susceptibility to hurricanes.

There are only a few places around the Gulf that derive drama from rough land meeting the waves, as for instance much of the California coast does, or New England's. In part of northern Florida rolling hills dip to the sea, and at some points elsewhere there are rocky sections of the kind that biologists call "hard shore," such as the tropical reef coral of the Florida Keys and Yucatán, Campeche's limited zone of limestone cliffs, and a couple of mountain spurs near Veracruz, greened-over lava flows with juttings of gray craggy stone ashore and in the breakers. It was in one of these latter scenic neighborhoods that Hernando Cortés found affable Totonac Indians in their fine stone towns, and built his own short-lived first settlement, destroying his ships in the anchorage to stop defection among his troops.

In sight of much of the Mexican shoreline also, inland mountains loom unforgettably beyond the level seaside lands, among them huge protrusions like Orizaba and the Cofre de Perote, dramatic enough. But the rule around the Gulf is low-lying shore, whether it be the lush flatness of the better-watered parts of the Mexican *tierra caliente*, the Louisiana marshes and swamps and bayous, and the channeled mangrove tangles of Tabasco and south Florida, or the more windswept sort of low sandy shore found on the coast's plentiful barrier islands and spits. These elongated interpositions between bay waters and open sea were all shaped by similar forces of current and wind, but vary considerably in their looks, according to what sort of vegetation their climate allows them as cover. Some have palms and tropical undergrowth beyond their handsome beaches and mangroves on the mainland side. Along the northern coast many barriers have low wind-sculptured forests of oak and pine down their centers, while others to the west are nearly barren.

It is usual to define "virginity" on this continent as the state of the lands and waters before white people showed up. In general that seems fair, though questions do arise about such matters as whether ancient spearmen helped wipe out animals like mammoths and giant bison away back in Pleistocene times. As for the Gulf, it is pretty well accepted that before the Spanish ever hove into view,

Delicate seagrass anchors windswept dunes of Padre Island on the Texas coast. Basalt mountains greet blue waves along the Costa del Oro near San Andreas Tuxtla in Veracruz.

Barnacled mangrove swamps, vast marshlands, and stately palm groves characterize far flung places on the 3,000-mile Gulf Coast.

an old Mayan system of clearing rain forest for corn-fields had played much hell with the face of nature on the Yucatán peninsula, and may even have been a factor in that civilization's collapse. It does seem, however, that natives around the rest of the coast had created no disasters. In most places the seaside lands and the inshore waters accessible to dugout canoes held a wealth of forms of life, some edible or otherwise useful and some not, some large and many small, all part of the shape of things on their particular stretch. Certain creatures, or variations of them, flourished along the whole coast from Yucatán through Florida—most of the kinds of fish, porpoises in rollicking herds, deer, great and small cats whether spotted or tawny, wild canines including lobo wolves near the Rio Grande and red ones up from there, an assortment of doves and pigeons and quail and turkeys, ducks and geese in their array of species, and other water and shore birds. Other fauna were found only in the tropical Mexican rain forests- -pacas, agoutis, big tapirs, howler and spider monkeys, curassows and guans and other land birds—or in some nearby niche, like the flamingos of certain hypersaline lagoons. Long, slim-snouted crocodiles inhabited salt bays and mangroved inlets on that same tropical shore and across the way in the Keys and south Florida, while their relatives the alligators thrived in fresher wet places from Texas to the Everglades. Huge, slow, vegetarian manatees or sea cows were confined to frost-free zones in winter but swam northward along both the Florida and western coasts in summer, as did the monk seals found thickly in the lowermost Keys and on coral islets of the southern Gulf, and multitudinous big sea turtles of several species to six or eight hundred pounds.

Black bears on wooded temperate coasts from Texas east, even bison in some places. Shellfish of hundreds of kinds from the big tropical marine snails called conchs, to oysters in reefs miles long, in brackish waters from the middle Texas coast on around through northern Florida. Spiny lobsters in coral crannies or sometimes marching in queer single file across flat bottoms, shrimp in almost solidly massed schools, redfish in shoals that turned acres of bay water rusty bronze. Cranes, both whoopers and sandhills in tens of thousands, wintering from Louisiana southwestward . . .

The list could go on and on. And all these beasts and birds and fish and other beings were just the ones to be found in the narrow belt that was the rim of the land at the sea and the rim of the sea at the land.

By now many people know that estuaries are a main key to the richness of seacoasts, which in general are much richer than the deeps offshore.

These are the fecund places where fresh water flows into salt water, mixes with it, and brings in sediment and dissolved nutrients from the land it drains. In temperate climates most estuaries are grassy, channel-laced marshes at the tidal mouths of rivers or alongside brackish bays. In the tropics and subtropics they are usually mangrove swamps in the same kinds of places. I seem to have slipped into the present tense, but with wry knowledge that there have been some changes since virgin times . . . The estuaries, full of fertility and detritus and crannies, support and shelter a pullulation of living things. They are nurseries for the fry of many species of fish, and for larval and infant shrimp and crabs and snails and their kin, everybody eating somebody else. Here too, in the temperate brackish waters, are the reefs and bars of oysters, dependent on moderated salinities and on the tide-borne flow of plankton. With such an assortment of edibles laid out, larger fauna like fish and birds and beasts, including men, gather to share in the plenty.

Mangroves deserve a short digression. Most people see them as hostile trees, forming thickets with prop roots and low branches that trip you up, harboring hordes of little avid mosquitoes. In terms of their function, though, they are fascinating. Of the four species of trees on the Gulf called mangroves only one, the black, can take any cold at all. The essential mangrove is the red, the prop-rooted one, which can stand in shallow water on its own, backed usually by the others—the black, the white, the buttonwood—in their zones of increasing dryness. Throughout the southern Gulf wherever surf doesn't pound, whether in brackish or purely salt water, mangrove thickets are biological factories, building peaty soil out of trapped sediment and their own shed leaves and thus pushing land outward, concentrating fertility, giving refuge to millions of small creatures and attracting larger ones. Their outer edges are fine places to cast a lure or fly for predators lurking among the prop roots—snook and young tarpon and the like in brackish places, gray snapper and barracuda elsewhere.

Estuaries and mangroves . . . Most sections of the primeval Gulf Coast had plenty of one or the other and often of both, and currents of life rippled out from them. If an area had neither, things tended to get a bit tough, as things did around the two long saline bays of southern Texas and northern Tamaulipas, both called Laguna Madre. That region's only real river, the Rio Grande, fed no big bay and formed no rich delta but hurried its fertility past smidgens of marsh directly to the Gulf, as it does today. Backed by thorny dry hinterlands, not tropical

Mossy bald cypress arise from the brackish backwaters of southeast Texas' Trinity and Galveston bays.

Vibrant with wildlife, the Texas coast attracts millions of migratory water-fowl in winter. Year-round denizens like the American alligator and her-mit crab bask in the temperate climate.

enough for mangroves to work their magic, short of rainfall, those shores lay within the domain of wandering bands of little-known natives—Coahuiltec and/or Tamaulipec, it is said—who evidently had pretty slim pickings. The lagoons held plenty of fish in season, but the bands appear to have taken little advantage of this, spending most of their time scrounging inland among their native mesquites and cacti.

None of the rest of the Gulf's Indians were that hard up. Physically and culturally they seem to have been a rather varied lot, representing probably different waves of old Asian invaders, different minglings and migrations, and different adaptations to seaboard surroundings. Our clearest view is of those tribes of tropical Mexico with whom the early Spanish had many dealings, always to the Indians' sorrow. That the Maya of the Yucatán peninsula, for instance, were living in a state of decadence atop the remains of a splendid civilization and quarreling with their brethren, is a known thing, as is much else about them. That the imperial hold of the gory, new-rich Aztec on their Gulf Coast vassals such as the Totonac was recent and tenuous, is another, and a happy circumstance that turned out to be for the Spanish invaders, providing them with allies. But clockwise around the Gulf from those more sophisticated tribes the record is spottier, in terms of how people lived and what they were like.

Most had certain things in common tied in with seaside life: dugout canoes, long bows with reed or cane arrows, varying kinds of fishing gear, a knowledge of local channels and tides and weather signs. But there were also big differences, often but not always traceable to climate and the fertility of waters and soils. A fair example of environmental affliction, I think, is those thirsty, cactus-eating (anything-eating, for that matter), migratory bands just north and south of the Rio Grande. A fair example of the opposite extreme is the natives of the Mexican tropics, where a damp eternal summertime meant that neither food nor clothing nor shelter was much of a problem either inland or on the shore. Living was fat, and it doesn't seem accidental that the continent's first real civilization developed in that neighborhood. Upshore, the less advanced but competent Huastec had a good life in the region around present Tampico. In a similar zone across the Gulf in south Florida and the Keys, where winter might waft an occasional breath but not with frost, an aggressive tribe called Calusa, skillful on the water, took nearly all their sustenance from the sea, and the sea was so generous that these people could live in fixed villages without farming and feasted all year long, according to a Spanish captive of theirs, on seafood ranging from conch to whale meat and manatee.

Where there was winter, village-dwelling required the storage of food for the cool months when land and sea went more or less dormant. On the northern coast from the bayou country east, all the groups seem to have done some farming of corn and other crops and to have lived comfortably enough in their hamlets in years without drouths or hurricanes or extra-bitter winters. Some of them were tribes, and others subtribes with inland connections to Southern Farmers like the Creek and Choctaw. Their names still ring strong, though most are only place-names now, when that: the Houma and Chitimacha of the bayous, the Biloxi and Pascagoula, the Mobile, the Pensacola, Chisca, Apalachicola, and Apalache, and around the Florida coast to below Tampa Bay the large nation known as Timucua, south of whom on mangroved shores dwelt the warlike Calusa.

West of the bayou lands a pair of unrelated tribes, the Atakapa and the Karankawa, led far less easy lives for reasons that apparently had less to do with environment than with culture, or maybe genes. We know more about the Karankawa, thanks to old Cabeza de Vaca, who was their involuntary guest for a time, and they are worth a passing glance. A tall and well-built people, they controlled the barrier islands and bays and a thin strip of mainland from the Corpus Christi area to Galveston Bay, defending their territory stoutly and ritually devouring slain trespassers. With reasonable rainfall most years and good estuarial bays, that section is productive even now, and in Indian times it must have been immeasurably richer, its waters thick with turtles and fish in season and reefed with millions of oysters, its coves dark with waterfowl in winter. Good alluvial soil lay near the bays.

Yet the Kronks, as they were called by early Anglos who clashed with the ones not eliminated by Spanish weapons or disease, planted no crops, had no villages, gluttonized in the fat warm months, then went very hungry during the mild coastal Texas winters. Except for powerful bows which they used expertly their equipment was mainly make-do stuff. They had no fishhooks but took fish with arrows and crude traps as best they could. The canoes which were vital to them were hacked-out, clumsy affairs with the bark left on. Valiant and unyielding, they seem to have been stuck in a sort of obstinate cultural primitivism, tough and so proud of it that they subjected themselves to hardship.

There was a fair amount of warfare among adjacent bands around the coast, and just about all were described by whites at one time or another as fierce. Some do seem to have despised all outsiders from the start: both the Karankawa and the Calusa may have been so. Others developed ferocity fast after initial contact with Spaniards, most of whom were not any more humanitarian toward native pagans than Anglo-Saxons would prove to be later. The hardy Iberians confiscated Indians' stored food, shot them down when opposed, drafted them as bearers of expeditionary baggage, and often shipped them off as slaves to the Caribbean or Mexico, where hard labor in mines and fields, rough treatment, malnutrition, and—most particularly—European diseases had wiped out the original work forces incredibly soon and kept on wiping out replacements. New Spain, present Mexico, lost about three-fourths of its natives in the 1500s.

In fairness, Spanish missionaries had gentler aims, but north and east of the subjugated Mexican coast they found few converts for many decades, sometimes attaining martyrdom. And afterward, when the good fathers did manage to establish missions in north Florida and later in Texas these seem usually, for however long they lasted, to have disseminated about as much disease and decimation as enlightenment. The Florida tribes that accepted a full dose of Christianity, the Timucua and Apalache, were among the first to dwindle to nothing.

Most of the varied native coast-dwellers kept on fighting back when they had to, and made their truculent contribution to the fact that for about a century and three-quarters after Cortés defeated the Aztec no permanent European towns managed to take hold anywhere on the Gulf Coast beyond Tampico, the northernmost of the string of Spanish port settlements established just after that conquest. There were other reasons as well. In Mexico and in Central and South America, the conquerors had bitten off a very large chew, and much remained to be done—subduing interior tribes, fortifying wild borderlands and pushing them outward, locating and working mines, setting up ranches and plantations and learning about new crops, and trying desperately always to bolster the dwindling work force with slaves from anywhere and everywhere.

With all that energy being channeled into consolidation, efforts during the 1500s to extend the Spanish hold to parts of the Gulf Coast north and east of Tampico were botched affairs. They tended to fall into the hands of treasure-hungry gentlemen-adventurers, among whom there was no Hernando Cortés with his gift for tempering a love of gold to the demands of wise procedure. Most expeditions were launched from Spanish Cuba, began with landings on the Gulf side of the Florida peninsula, and ended in disaster. Among the leaders were

A delicate web spun in the Florida
Everglades symbolizes the fragile
ecosystem. A butterfly feasts on flea-
bane. Ibis cross the full moon in
search of night roosts.

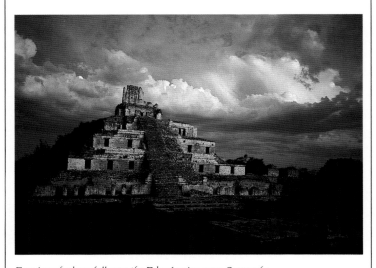

Evening shadows fall over the Edzná ruins near Campeche.

some familiar to us from history books: Juan Ponce de León, seeker of the Fountain of Youth, who died of Calusa-inflicted wounds in 1521; Pánfilo de Narváez, who vanished in the Gulf in a makeshift boat in 1528, though his treasurer Alvar Nuñez Cabeza de Vaca, with a scant three other survivors of a very rough trip, turned up in western Mexico eight years later; Hernando De Soto, who succumbed to a fever on the Mississippi in 1539; and others later, all losers. These probers and roamers did add to geographical knowledge—especially De Soto, whose frantic search for precious metals took him through north Florida and parts of what are now Georgia, Alabama, Mississippi, and Arkansas, abusing and killing natives all over the place and enraging them into reprisal. But they didn't add to much else, and certainly not to settlement. One levelheaded leader of those times, Pedro Menéndez, did get a few things done. In terms of the Gulf, his main contribution was the establishment in 1565 of durable San Agustín, our St. Augustine. It was on the Atlantic side of Florida, but provided a base from which in following decades military and religious advances, slowed by periodic Indian revolts, moved across to the Apalache country on the Gulf and installed a Spanish presence there.

It is interesting if a bit futile, records being scarce, to speculate about the effect the Spanish may have exerted on the balance between man and the natural world that had existed before they came. The gold-mad expeditions would have made no dent in all that richness, but along the settled coast from Tampico south the balance must have teetered and dipped after whites moved in, more commercial in their view of nature and more prodigal in their notion of how to use its bounty. Bigger living things with more raw material in them undoubtedly suffered first. It is known that the seals of the coral islets off Yucatán were regularly slaughtered by Spaniards for their oil. Big docile manatees yielded lots of oil too, besides delicious meat and skins that

made tough leather. The preferred whips for keeping Indian mine and field slaves diligent in their labors, someone noted, were plaited from manatee hide.

Many things went on in those early Spanish years, whether or not they had lasting effects, though there is little room for them here. Shipwrecks, for instance, were frequent and usually horrendous on wild shores with prickly natives close by. A poignant example is the 1554 death march, down Padre Island and the Tamaulipas coast, of 250 or 300 shipwrecked men, women, and children. Only one person got to Tampico alive, though full of arrow holes. It seems that the vengeful archers involved, some of the cactus-eaters we have mentioned, had been mercilessly slave-raided some years before. There was treasure aboard the wrecked ships also, which could lead to further tales, but won't.

Not having managed to occupy the northern and eastern shores of what Robert Weddle has called the "Spanish Sea" in his indispensable book of that name, the conquistadors' heirs during the late 1500s and afterward were fated to witness an unfriendly influx of other Europeans to the Gulf. During the same era, troubles in Spain itself—plague, feckless rulers, wars—weakened the colonies and made them vulnerable. For a long time the interlopers were not settlers but Dutch, French, and English privateers, licensed and egged on by home governments that were almost steadily at war with Spain for a century and more. The marauders smuggled goods and African slaves into Spanish ports, preyed on the treasure fleets and other shipping, and pillaged coastal towns. Though their main stomping ground was the Caribbean, they swept all Spanish waters. In the Gulf, they and later their successors, the buccaneers and pirates, had a

Morning mists hang in the valley of San Andreas Tuxtla.

In a steamy dawn over Laguna de Tamiahua near Tampico,
a tern and a fisherman's boat wait for the rising tide.

main rendezvous at the broad Laguna de Términos downshore from the port of Campeche, a place with turtles and manatees and Spanish cattle for ships' stores and valuable dyewood for cargo. But they frequented many other spots, raiding the port towns time and again, penetrating all navigable bays and inlets, learning about currents and winds and reefs and bars and Indians, knowledge that would percolate to Europe and help shape campaigns and plans for colonies.

English settlement of Virginia, starting in 1608, brought traders among Indians near Spanish north Florida. Later the seating of English, French, and Dutch colonies at privateer bases in the Caribbean became another Spanish headache, and when South Carolina was colonized in 1670 the hated Protestant Britons were that much closer, with raids and skirmishes and British probes toward the Gulf. In 1682 the Sieur de la Salle floated down the Mississippi from French Illinois and claimed the river and its whole huge drainage for Louis XIV, the Sun King. Three years later when he came back to the Gulf with colonists from France, he bumbled past the big river, landing instead in present Texas on Matagorda Bay with mainly fatal results involving dissension, the leader's murder, and rampaging

Karankawa Indians. Even dead, though, La Salle spooked the Spanish into countermeasures like the permanent settlement of Pensacola in 1696, and later the building of missions and forts in Texas.

But the thin edge of the wedge was in the crack. In 1699 under Iberville, Frenchmen formed a settlement on the Mississippi Sound which after being relocated a time or two became Mobile, and also built a fort forty miles up the Mississippi. In 1717 they founded New Orleans, capital-to-be of the north-spreading vastness La Salle had named Louisiana, and two years later ran Spanish missionaries and soldiers briefly out of east Texas and grabbed Pensacola to hold it for four years.

Etcetera . . . During the rest of the eighteenth century and the early nineteenth, large and rather complex changes derived less from Gulfside squabblings than from wars and treaties and other transactions in Europe and eastern North America. Ownership of various parts of the northern coast shifted back and forth among France, Spain, England, and after 1783 the brand-new United States, with the nationalities of new immigrants varying in accordance. Subsequent events that led to present national and state boundaries in the lands that fringe the Gulf included the mighty Louisiana Purchase of 1803,

A Mexican vegetable farmer nurtures February crops from rich volcanic soils. Lining the highway to Houma and the bayou to the Gulf, the Cajun fishing community of Chauvin blends into Louisiana's immense wetlands.

Texas coastal marsh goes up in smoke as wildlife refuge managers torch sawgrass to encourage new forage and habitat.

the cession of Florida to the United States by Spain in 1819, the Mexican Revolution, the Texas Revolution, and the Mexican War. That is a drastically telescoped account, of course, and leaves out many fine things like the Acadians, Andrew Jackson at the Battle of New Orleans, San Jacinto, and so on. But too much went on in those years to set it all down here.

And all the while new people had been moving in across the northern coast to new farms and plantations, new ranches and towns. The Cotton South now emerged in all its transient glory, based on fertile soil and rain and the sweat of black men. The riches of land and sea were being felt out and exploited, an unpleasant word and idea for many now but not for anyone then. Manifest Destiny was on the march. The old impasse in Gulf Coast settlement was long since gone, and so most definitely was the day of the Indians who had been part of that impasse. Whole tribes had simply evaporated and the rest, what was left of them after all the battles and epidemics, were being harried out of existence, or westward, or driven as remnants to marginal lands where some would blend with the remnants of other tribes, or with whites or blacks. There were many wanderings and mist-shrouded endings. In 1844, it is said, a few last culturally obstinate Karankawa killed themselves a final white settler on the Guadalupe, perhaps for old times' sake, then fled south toward Mexico and oblivion.

For the winners, a Civil War remained to be fought, but we've reached the era that led to now, and I think we'd best leave history.

*S*ince that bustling era the Gulf has received some hard human use, and for a long time it absorbed the use pretty well. Lately, though, the traditional forms of use have been stepped up in pace, new forms have appeared, and wear has started to show. This has all happened quite fast, mainly during the latter half of my own rather extended lifetime.

As a kid in the Depression 1930s I used to fish on the Texas coast with an uncle who lived near it. Most often we would go after speckled trout out of Rockport, then a hurricane-battered village on Aransas Bay, attaching our five-horse outboard to a rented wooden skiff and buying a bucket of live shrimp for bait. Afloat by dawn, we would chug out to where gulls and terns were wheeling and shrieking and diving at frantic baitfish being slashed from below by trout, or to one of my uncle's favored oyster reefs. Some mornings we would take 150 or more trout and a few redfish, keeping them all for freezing or distribution to friends, because everybody back then knew that the yield of the sea was

Encroaching development is common along the Florida Keys.

forever. Often something else would grab our bait. "Damn jack!" my uncle would say as the reel handle rapped his knuckles and a dogged jack crevalle ran in circles around the boat, using up trout-fishing time. "Damn jack!"

On occasion we would go out to Port Aransas on Mustang Island, even smaller and more beat up than Rockport except for the long white Tarpon Inn, where the rich and famous did their resting and eating between bouts with those magnificent fish, then abundant in the bays. Less notable anglers got themselves ferried in groups to the snapper banks far offshore or, as we usually did, hired someone to take them out trolling with big spoons for king mackerel, powerful slim creatures to thirty pounds. Some clambered at no cost out the granite south jetty of the pass, for snook or pompano or whatever else was passing through. Everybody caught fish and kept them, except the tarpon people, whose fish were considered inedible and were brought in for display and photographs, later to be thrown out.

All that was a long while back and I don't remember everything, but the feeling was of water thickly alive with all sorts of active things, and of sparse numbers of locals making a minimal living from the water or from those who came to fish it. There the Gulf and the bays were, still pretty much their old selves despite many years of use, despite small-time shrimpers and haul-seiners and gill-netters, despite us sports who took away all the fish we

could carry. If some things were missing by then, like the big green sea turtles that had been netted there decades before in annual tens of thousands of pounds, we didn't know enough to worry about it. The sea's yield was forever.

The Gulf's present ills exist along almost all of its three thousand miles of coast, and far offshore as well. Their basic cause in both the American and Mexican sections is human mis-use of sea and land, but the flavor of that misuse and some of its effects differ a bit north and south of the border. Among us fortunate gringos, the troubles are linked to prosperity and technology plus the profit motive, some forms of which uncharitable analysts call greed. To the south, though greed survives and technology is rampant in some sections, overpopulation and great poverty are overwhelming considerations.

Mexico, as sentimentalists have long noted, is slow to change, and superficially the Gulf Coast down there looks much as it always has: the old port cities still sleepily and steamily colonial, with arcades and plazas, the shoreline largely free of the garish vacation clutter so common in the United States. The stretch of Tamaulipas toward the Rio Grande is still arid and thorny and rather thinly peopled with dry, tough folk. Southward where the rains and rivers and mangroves commence, things look lusher as they always did, and on down into the tropics they look lusher still until you get close to Veracruz. From that city's environs, however, on around the Gulf's southernmost curve past the old buccaneers' rendezvous at the Laguna de Términos, coastal industrial development is thickly pervasive wherever terrain permits, largely petrochemical and based on the region's oil production.

By report, these industries are often founts of pollution in estuarial lagoons and river mouths, as are sewage from population centers and dire pesticides of kinds no longer legal in the United States, washing off of cropland; in Mexico, with its super-abundance of human problems, environmental concerns tend to be viewed as unaffordable luxuries. Just inland from this industrial strip—and elsewhere on the coast also, for that matter—second-growth vegetation has mainly supplanted the enormous trees of the old rain forests, with their diversity of life. Manatees are gone, as are crocodiles, seals, and God knows what else. The once-multitudinous sea turtles show up but rarely and are said to be grabbed when found. "If you're edible and in Mexico," a friend living there once told me, "you're in trouble."

Clearly enough, life on those shores can no longer be called fat, and the diminishing supply of

Refineries of the La Venta oil field now occupy the vast marshes surrounding the Uspanapa, Coatza-coalcos, and Tonala rivers, once the center of the pre-Columbian Olmec culture. Corpus Christi's Harbor Bridge spans the mouth of the Nueces River, gateway to Texas' largest deep-water port.

fat now has to be shared among many, many appetites, with more appearing all the time. Earth's population overload is very gloomy territory indeed, and Mexico's share of it is considerable. Poor people teem, not only in the old fishing towns and the cities but in clusters of shacks on barrier islands and spits and at the mouths of mainland streams, because the sea and its living bounty, not privately owned, are what they know and what they have. Some harbors have good-sized commercial craft, but mainly what you see everywhere is lots of little boats holding one or two men, hook-and-lining or paying out net astern in a pretty curve of floats. Boatless men wade out from shore with seines or cast-nets, or heave throwlines. Those are the old ways and they work, if not with great efficiency, and it is undoubtedly that lack of efficiency that has kept such a swarm of fishermen from totally wiping out what biologists call "the resource." Despite pollution and everything else, in those still-fertile, winterless waters the resource has kept coming on, after a fashion.

That may be about to end. As was probably inevitable, someone came up with a better way, a rather simple but deadly one. In a period of just about three years, according to a man I know who interests himself in such things and flies up and down that coast often, nearly all river mouths and shallow passes connecting bays with the Gulf have been obstructed with vee-shaped fishtraps, staked shoulder to shoulder. Since hardly anything can come or go without being caught, the effect after initial big harvests has been plainly disastrous. And it's fairly certain that if the breakthrough hadn't been those traps, it would have been something else, such is desperation's pressure.

The sense I have long had of those southern shores, as an alien and infrequent but friendly observer, has been a sense of slow, sad, somewhat romantic decline—my own version, I suppose, of that "timeless Mexico" theme. Now, though, decline is looking faster, and much sadder, and devoid of any romance at all.

*U*p here in gringoland, where things have been booming for forty years or more, the troubles are not so clearly displayed, but anyone who looks can find some large ones. One involves a major loss of inshore nursery habitat. This can and often does come from direct hostile action, as when a developer buys a marsh or a mangrove swamp, dredges parallel cuts that will be canals for pleasure boats, and heaps the spoil between the cuts to make dry land for vacation homes, a lucrative practice known as "fingerfilling." Loss can also derive from pollution; an example is Galveston Bay,

Erosion gouges the marine clays that once supported beach-side housing at Sergeant, Texas. Debris from a century of oystering litters the ramshackle Apalachicola waterfront. Black-necked stilts wade in a secluded cove where their long legs accommodate the varying depths.

subjected to occasional oil spills and serving as a dump basin for the industrialized Houston Ship Channel, once called the most polluted body of water on earth. It can even occur naturally through hurricanes, though as time goes on the chances of a hurricane hitting an estuary instead of a development would seem to be lessening a bit.

Or it can come from monkeying around with nature's hydraulics, as it does in bays whose fresh inflows are shortstopped by upstream dams, and in two of the most productive Gulfside systems of all, the Everglades and the Mississippi River delta. The whole southeastern part of Louisiana is built of sediments laid down by the Mississippi in past ages as its lower course switched about at intervals. Part of the river's flow used to spread out widely into marshes on either side, its fertile silt building up in the grasses and countering geological subsidence—a sort of natural squashing-down—and its water pushing salt water back to create fine nursery conditions in the brackish zone where they mingled. The legendary annual catch of Louisiana shrimpers has depended directly on this complex of things. So have the great beds of oysters there, and the fish, and the furbearers that come to Cajuns' traplines.

Now the lower river is leveed throughout for navigation and flood control, so that the silt and fresh water which used to work out into the marshes, enriching them and making them what they were, are sluiced straight to the Gulf. The land subsides and is no longer built back up. Salt water moves inland, killing marsh vegetation, an influx aided by a maze of canals dug by the Corps of Engineers and by oil companies. The marshes go rotten and melt, caving away in chunks and leaving open salt water. A young marsh biologist I know, inviting me down to fish above Barataria Bay, writes this:

> It is unlikely that much of this area will be around for my grandchildren to fish. See it now—it's going fast, it's a beautiful heartbreaker that is loaded with beautiful edible things and great fighting fish.

The Everglades are similarly loaded with fine things and similarly immersed in trouble, which involves no missing silt but a great deal of missing fresh water. Water used to come steadily and dependably from big Lake Okeechobee in a sheet-flow fifty miles wide, more than a hundred miles long, and only inches deep—a vast wet prairie, a "river of grass," as the Indians called it. That was the Everglades, of which the present national park is only the southernmost fraction. Its long, mangroved, estuarial fringe across the bottom of the Florida peninsula had no counterpart on earth, I am told, and

A Mississippi-berthed Gulf shrimper sorts a haul off the Mississippi Delta.

there was scarcely less richness in the freshwater marshes and swamps and the endless expanses of sawgrass.

Around 1900 farmers began digging drainage canals in the upper 'Glades near the lake in order to use the fertile muck soil, prospered, and were copied by others. Later, hurricane-spawned floods caused problems on the farms and in towns, and in the forties the Corps of Engineers was authorized to build a flood-control system for the whole of south Florida, while at the same time population, development, and new muck-farming were running wild. The end results, insofar as they can be encapsuled here, are a completely diked and managed lake whose "excess" water is squirted directly to the Atlantic and the Gulf; a bewilderment of canals that carry the remainder almost everywhere except where it used to go; shrinkage of the big underground aquifer that was kept full by the sheet-flow; and desiccation of the Everglades during drouths, not only in farming sections but in the national park, with salt intrusion along the estuarial fringe and occasional mass death of fish and alligators in dried-up sloughs. Fires get started, and the muck soil itself, thousands of years in the making and always saturated before, ignites and burns.

Enough grim woes, gentle reader? Just about

enough for a cheerful fellow like me, also, and I'll try to run through the rest fairly fast. What they chiefly stem from is some practices of commercial fishermen and shrimpers, who are by no means all villains, but who are very numerous and efficient. The everlasting yield of the sea that everybody used to believe in, it turns out, was based on harvest of a surplus that the sea could spare, a principle that is being enthusiastically ignored these days.

Shrimpers have been in the public eye of late because of their rebellion against government orders to install turtle excluder devices, called TEDs, on their bottom-sweeping trawls. The turtles, five species of them, did not reach their official endangered status because of shrimpers but through huge overharvest in the past and occupation of their nesting beaches by condos and hotels, among other things. It seems to be a fact, however, that shrimpers of the Gulf and the southeastern U.S. coast—some 18,000 boats in all—are drowning remaining turtles in their nets at a rate of over 11,000 a year. Since endangered creatures get wide sympathy and the shrimpers have among them some reddish-necked types capable of cutting live turtles' throats and issuing death threats against pro-TEDists, their port blockades and such have gained them and the imperiled reptiles a lot of news coverage. Only occasionally noted during the uproar has been the issue of shrimpers' "by-catch"—the enormous numbers of fish, mainly immature, that are hauled in with the shrimp, dumped on deck to die while the shrimp are sorted out and iced, then shoveled overboard. For each pound of shrimp harvested, anywhere from ten to twenty pounds of these "trash fish" are sacrificed, many of commercially valuable species and all a part of the Gulf's food chain. If you like figures, the lowest estimate I've seen for annual Gulf wastage of this kind is 1.6 billion pounds.

Of those pounds a considerable fraction consists of juvenile red snapper, the Gulf's most prized food fish, the adults of which used to be caught in large numbers on the offshore banks by vacation anglers and small-scale commercials using hook and line, without diminishing the next year's catch. Now the population of the species is said to have been reduced by 80 to 90 percent in twenty years, partly through the shrimpers' steady assault on the young and more recently through the ingenuity of "bandit boat" operators. These gentry, aided by video fishfinders, Loran, and other modern blessings, modified a deadly technique called "longlining" to capture the biggest broodstock snappers on deep bottoms, and devastated them in short order—hauling to market, it is said, tractor-trailer-loads at a time for as long as the carnage lasted. So much for the principle of surplus yield.

Standard open-sea longlining is also a bitch, as usually practiced now all around the world. In essence these rigs are like the trotlines familiar to most of us in fresh water, with stagings and hooks arranged at intervals to cover a strip of water. The difference is that a longline, held up by buoys, can be thirty miles long and is attached to a winch at the stern of a boat. The arrangement is baited and laid out during the afternoon, allowed to drift crosswise through a stretch of open sea at night, and reeled in to remove the catch the next day. There are hundreds of such boats, nearly all American, working mainly in the Gulf's wide middle beyond the zones of state and federal control. Their preferred quarry is yellowfin tuna, but they catch great numbers of other large pelagic species, among them bluefin tuna, billfish such as marlin and sailfish, sharks, dolphin-fish, and wahoo. There is much waste. Of the sharks only the fins are usually kept, for the twenty-five-dollars-a-pound Asian soup market. The billfish—prized by sportsmen who generally release them after the fight—are not salable because of legal protection, but reportedly half or more of them are dead when the longline comes in, from struggling so long on the hook. The whole process, according to qualified observers, has cut deeply into populations of all these open-sea fish,

and cuts deeper each passing year. "It's not a good time," one man said wryly, "to be buying a marlin boat."

Other glum examples could be paraded here, other threats examined, but the spectacle's outline is clear. It is quite similar in nature to those trap-plugged Mexican rivers and passes, but Gulfwide and worldwide in scope. If you're edible and in salt water, it seems, you're in trouble.

Shall we turn our eyes toward brighter things? There are some brightish ones, not exactly predominant. Much land typical of different sections of the coast, for instance, has been preserved as wildlife refuges or parkland or whatever. Among these places one of my own favorites is the maze of channels and flats and mangrove islets on the Gulf side of the crowded main Florida Keys, an area called locally "the back country." Federally protected, it is accessible only by boat and you can always find some blue-and-green, unpeopled place to stop in, even if the fishing now is not up to Calusa standards. Another jewel is Horn Island in the barrier chain that outlines the Mississippi Sound, an exultant forested sandy strip full of birds and other life, celebrated in the superb watercolors and sketches of the late Walter Inglis Anderson. Many other patches too, from Padre Island National Seashore to the Dry Tortugas, can make you forget for a time the glitz and clutter elsewhere and let you glimpse what used to be on the coast. People have saved them, people who care.

As for the alleviation of ills, other people who

A Port Arthur fisherman sets his hook on a speckled trout migrating up the Sabine River Ship Channel.

care do try. Rachel Carson's insight and the movement it aroused not only got rid of chlorinated hydrocarbon pesticides in this country, causing the return of brown pelicans, eagles, falcons, and other poisoned species, but also cleared a pathway for private and government action, sometimes effective, against other environmental abuses. Coastal development, a berserk offshoot of the profit motive, gets thwarted here and there, the rights of marshes and mangroves and aquatic life prevailing over those of fingerfillers. Endangered sea turtles have friends as the TED imbroglio attests; so do manatees, of which 1,200 or so still live in Florida waters, though outboard propellers which slice them by accident may eventually spell their doom. Big predators like wolves and bears and panthers are largely gone from Gulfside lands as elsewhere and are likely to remain so, but alligators, which a few years back seemed all to be destined for conversion into purses and belts and cowboy boots, have rebounded under protection. Other success stories could be cited, and even against monumental messes like the one in the Everglades, good people exert themselves hugely.

*I*n terms of "the resource," the Gulf's beleaguered fisheries, some sparkles of hope glint through, at least within the zones of state and federal waters where new regulations as to methods and catch and so on have a chance of enforcement. Market fishermen and shrimpers resist such changes fiercely, proud of their hardworking independence and convinced, for the record at any rate, that the sea's bounty is still eternal. They have much political clout, but opponents, backed by scientific data, have been steadily gaining clout too. In this area the most effective activists are sportfishermen, a quite diverse crowd ranging from fly-rod purists to fish-hogs as bad as my uncle and I used to be. Most fall between the extremes and are capable of unity when they see their sport declining, as it has been. A main rallying point of theirs, the Coastal Conservation Association, has spread in recent years from its Texas origins to branches covering the coast as far as Virginia. It rides herd on shrimpers and other commercials and even on pollutive industry; argues the case for creatures like sharks and mullet and blue crabs; supports such things as game-fish status for certain species, restocking programs, and catch-and-release where they're needed; and in general shines light into dark corners. CCA representatives show up at all governmental hearings concerned with such matters, and officials have come to know that not only do sportfishermen embody a vast lot of cash busi-

ness, but they can make much angry and relevant noise.

None of this appears likely to bring back ruined or damaged estuaries very quickly if at all, nor will it ease Mexico's deathly woes or alter prevalent rapine across the open seas of the planet. It is slowly making some difference, though. The federals appear to be growing pickier about fishing procedures in their seaward realm of sovereignty, and the coastal states are moving by hops and halts and sometimes swoops toward sensible management of inshore waters. In Texas, for instance, nearly all netting is now banned in the bays and along the beaches, and speckled trout and redfish are protected as game species, unmarketable, with even the sporting take strictly governed in terms of size and numbers. Florida has some similar new rules, among them a limit of one killed tarpon per year under a permit costing fifty dollars, which means that very few of those noble, blessedly inedible game fish are now hung up on spikes for display, at least in Florida. Other states are inching in the same direction, and things like "by-catch" are turning into major issues.

It would take more optimism than I can muster, I fear, to believe that Gulf waters will ever again be what they were just forty years ago, and some hungry hard times of the Mexican flavor might wipe out the recent past's gains in a hurry. But inshore at least, decline is being slowed, and you can usually go to the coast with reasonable hope of finding some decent fish, even if you release all or most of them when caught, as a good many anglers are now doing. Their reasons are not often sentimental or tenderhearted but are based on sharp awareness, gained the hard way, of just how fragile and vulnerable the fishery has come to be.

I know a place where a big fingerfill development stands near, with large cruisers tethered in the canals behind large houses, an attached marina, and an airstrip for private planes. But if you go there in a skiff at daybreak and look away from all that, what you see is spartina-grass marsh with spoonbills and shorebirds and herons and skimmers, and an open flat of calm, clear, shallow water showing the swirls of mullet and maybe, if the day is right, the wakes and waving tails of redfish that you can stalk by wading. In the east the new sun is dim and red through mists, and there is no spot on the earth where you'd rather be just now. The fish are only a part of that, but a fine part, and whether the yield is forever or not, you're thankful that at least a little of it has lasted until now.

Mexican shark fishermen ply the offshore waters of Isla de Idolo below Tampico.

PREFACE

THIS COUNTRY'S NEW-FOUND PRE-OCCUPATION with health and fitness has caused some radical changes in our eating habits. Bacon and eggs for breakfast are out; high-fiber cereals are in. Sour cream and butter are out; yogurt and low-saturated-fat margarines are in. Red meat consumption is down, and seafood consumption has spiraled off the charts.

Seafood, especially fish, is a near-perfect food. High in protein, low in fat, and rich in vitamins and minerals, it fills the bill for many health-conscious consumers, who also savor its delicious flavor.

Along the Gulf Coast, we have always enjoyed a seemingly limitless bounty of trout, snapper, redfish, flounder, shrimp, and oysters. But our growing appetite for more and more seafood, combined with ecological imbalances that threaten entire ecosystems, is endangering that supply. It is critical that we move quickly to protect our seafood resources in the Gulf of Mexico.

Coastal marshlands, which nurture young sea life, must be restored and protected. Our bays must be cleaned up. Commercial fishermen must adopt ecologically sound methods of harvesting their catch. Sportfishermen must observe catch-and-release regulations.

One thing each of us can do right now to

The seafood temptations of Tecolutla, a gulfside resort and fishing port in northern Veracruz, include freshly caught snook, drum, river prawn, shrimp, pompano, blue crab, and squid.

slow the demise of the more popular seafood varieties is to try new types of fish. The warm waters of the Gulf are home to dozens of delicious but relatively untried seafood varieties. For example, sportfishermen have known for years that dorado, or dolphin (not to be confused with the mammal of the same name), is a desirable fish for food. But it took the use of the Hawaiian name, mahi-mahi, to popularize it. I have talked to many people who don't know that we have tuna fish swimming in the Gulf and that it is delicious cooked fresh and need not be eaten only from a can. Few of us have tried shark, amberjack, tilefish, sheepshead, and many other savory but less well known fish.

Unfortunately, seafood markets do not always have these varieties because there is little demand for them. And the consumer doesn't know about them because they are not available in the market. It's a "Catch 22" situation that you, the reader, and this book may help to change.

Gulf Coast Cooking: Seafood from the Florida Keys to the Yucatán Peninsula is organized according to five major regions of the Gulf Coast, each with its distinctive culinary traditions: the Florida Keys and West Florida coast, with its Cuban, Caribbean, and Greek influences; the Deep South coast, including the Florida Panhandle, Alabama, and Mississippi; Louisiana, with its Acadian and Creole cuisines; Texas, a melting pot of many ethnic traditions; and the Mexican east coast and Yucatán peninsula, where special chilies and other seasonings characterize the cooking. Of course, some overlap occurs, where one type of cooking blends and melds with the seasonings of another.

The book reflects another important influence—the new wave of young chefs who staff fine restaurants and hotels throughout the Gulf region. They have cross-pollinated the various cuisines, developing new preparation techniques and interesting combinations of ingredients. In addition to recipes from my own files, I have drawn on the expertise of these chefs, other professional cooks, experienced fishermen, seafood aficionados, and some excellent home cooks.

I hope you find in these recipes a delightful mixture of old and new. So cook and savor, substitute and alter, and—above all—enjoy Gulf Coast seafood.

To the friends, old and new, who contributed to this book and whose names are included elsewhere in the text, I extend my great appreciation. It is their book, too. Thanks also to the wonderful people whose contacts and advice helped so much in the background research: Charles Thomas and Thomas Thomas, Florida State Bureau of Seafood Marketing; Steven Otwell, Extension Seafood Specialist, University of Florida; Ann McDuffie, Food Editor, *Tampa Tribune*; Meredith Manning, who organized the Sarasota area; Raymond Huffman, who advised me regarding the Florida Keys; Joyce Clanton, Seafood Marketing, Pensacola; Samantha Scott, WKRG Radio, Mobile; Michael Moody, Specialist, Seafood Technology, Louisiana State University; Michal Durel, Louisiana Restaurant Association; Marcelle Bienvenue, for her advice on things Cajun; Kathy Leonard; the Brennan family at Commander's Palace in New Orleans; Paul McIlhenny of McIlhenny Company, Avery Island; Annette Hegen, Extension Seafood Specialist, Texas A&M University; Tom Bright, Texas Sea Grant College Program; Ann Valentine, Food Editor, *Houston Post*; Ann Criswell, Food Editor, *Houston Chronicle*; G. P. McCreless, whose advice on tilefish and mullet was helpful; Joe Bacon, for his numerous contacts; Tessie Patterson, who was invaluable in her Houston and Louisiana contacts; the Brennan family of Brennan's of Houston; Teresa Byrne-Dodge; George Bolin; Margaret Torregrossa; Ann Griffith; Pat Wallace; Flo Crady Newton; Cassandra Manley; Adele Pieper; Antonio Cosio, President, Camino Real Hotels; Jose Antonio Rivera, General Manager, Camino Real Hotel, Cancun; Kathy Ruiz, who organized the Yucatán area; and Chata DuBose, who researched the Tampico-Veracruz area and translated recipes for me.

Special thanks to recipe testers Meredith Manning, Sarah McMurrey, Lynn Herbert, Andrea Buxton, Nancy Stute, and Margot Armour.

My heartfelt thanks go to the publisher, Bill Shearer, who presented the idea of this book to me and encouraged its completion. And to my editor, Alison Tartt, who made sure not only that the *i*'s were dotted and *t*'s crossed but also that I minded my *p*'s and *q*'s.

And, finally, thanks to my family, who saw me through some tense and preoccupied moments and tasted "shoals" of seafood without complaint.

Virginia Elverson

FLORIDA

*L*AND OF SUNSHINE, citrus, palm trees, and crystal water, Florida has long been a haven for people seeking mild winters and a relaxing lifestyle. It is also a seafood lover's paradise. Shaped on a map like a giant fishing pier extending into the ocean—one side on the Atlantic, the other on the Gulf of Mexico—Florida boasts a variety of marine habitats that can support hundreds of species of fish. The majority of these species are found on the Gulf side, particularly below the Suwannee River, where the shoreline is crenellated by countless bays and inlets with relatively warm, shallow water.

About two hundred years ago, the plentiful finfish attracted Cuban fishermen to the Mullet Keys, Charlotte Harbor, and Tampa Bay. The Cubans salted and dried their catch, then shipped it to Havana and other Spanish colonial settlements for use especially during the lenten season. Today *bacalao*, or dried salted codfish, is still an important part of Spanish and Cuban cuisine in coastal communities.

Dusk falls over a tranquil cove of Marathon Key. A windsurfer heads gulfward from Sanibel Island.

Commercial red snapper and grouper fishery got its start in the area before the Civil War, and not long after, industries developed for harvesting and processing clams, scallops, turtles, oysters, and shrimp. Enormous clam beds in the Ten Thousand Islands area off Florida's southwestern tip were devastated by a red tide in 1945 and have never fully recovered. Most clam harvesting today occurs on the state's eastern coast.

The spiny lobster, known also as the Florida lobster, is harvested from the waters off lower Florida's west coast. This green crustacean, which turns bright red when cooked, is not a lobster at all but a large sea crawfish whose segmented tail section is plump with tender, sweet meat. Spiny lobsters have no claws and weigh about one or two pounds each.

Stone crabs, valued for their claw meat, are another Florida specialty. Fishermen trap them live and remove only one of the two claws, tossing the crabs back into the water. Within two years, a new claw grows to replace the harvested member.

This region has seen other exotic seafood—conch, for example. The conch organism inhabits the spiraled seashell that children hold up to their ears to "listen to the sea." Its sweet, tough meat is chopped up for fritters and slow-simmered chowders or marinated in lime juice for salads.

Green sea turtles once thrived around Cedar Key, in the Indian River district, and among the Keys, particularly Islamorada and Key West. The turtle meat, sliced into steaks or diced for the soup pot, was a prized food. Overfishing has almost wiped out the turtles, which are now recognized worldwide as an endangered species.

Complementing Florida's exceptional seafood is a robust cuisine that reflects diverse ethnic influences. Greek sponge divers settled at Tarpon Springs in 1905, establishing a small sponge-fishing industry that took over the lead in sponge production from the depleted Key West grounds discovered almost a century earlier. The Greeks and other immigrants, including Italians, Chinese, and Cubans, brought their cooking traditions with them.

Florida's agricultural bounty yields an impressive array of fresh vegetables and fruits throughout the year. The state's renowned citrus fruits—oranges, tangerines, grapefruit, lemons, and Key limes—find their way into drinks, salads, marinades, and desserts. (A simple way with grilled fish is to sprinkle fillets with grated orange peel and baste with the fresh juice during the cooking.) Melons, strawberries, coconuts, hearts of palm, pineapples, and more exotic fruits such as guavas, tamarinds, sapodillas, papayas, and carambolas further enhance the regional dishes.

Silhouetted palms dress the manicured St. Petersburg waterfront. Cigar vendor Tony Suarez tends his shop in Tampa's colorful Cuban district, Ybor City. Sailboats, pleasure craft, and floatplanes crowd piers and harbors in the Florida Keys.

A little blue heron explores a
secluded spot in Corkscrew
Swamp.

Highway One's famous Seven-
Mile Bridge spans the distance
between Marathon and the Bahia Honda Keys.

Lobster traps pile up between hauls off the Florida Keys. A salty oysterman sports the Hemingway-style beard so popular along the Florida Gulf Coast.

Stone Crab Claws.

HOT CRABMEAT
AND HEARTS OF PALM
EN COQUILLES

Serves 6

*T*his version of the crab and hearts of palm combination is served hot. It can be extended by adding cooked shrimp (halved lengthwise) or cooked bay scallops.

2½ tablespoons butter, divided
3 or 4 shallots, chopped fine
½ 8-ounce package mushrooms, chopped fine
2 tablespoons flour
½ cup milk
½ cup strong chicken stock
salt and white pepper to taste
1 8-ounce can hearts of palm
1 pound lump crabmeat
6 tablespoons fine dry bread crumbs
3 tablespoons grated Parmesan cheese
chopped parsley

Melt 1 tablespoon butter in a heavy skillet. Sauté shallots and mushrooms, covered, until tender. Remove and set aside.

Melt remaining butter, add flour, and mix well. Add milk and chicken stock and cook until thick and smooth, stirring constantly. Season with salt and pepper. If using canned chicken broth, omit salt.

Drain hearts of palm and cut into quarters. Mix into sauce, then add sautéed shallots and mushrooms. Fold in crabmeat. Divide among six oiled coquille shells and top with a mixture of bread crumbs and cheese.

Preheat oven to 375 degrees and bake until slightly brown. Sprinkle with chopped parsley.

DIJON DEVILED CRAB

Serves 4

4 tablespoons mayonnaise
4 tablespoons Dijon mustard
6 tablespoons Worcestershire sauce or to taste
1 teaspoon Tabasco Pepper Sauce
¼ teaspoon salt
2 tablespoons fine-chopped red bell pepper
2 tablespoons fine-chopped scallion tops
2 tablespoons fine-chopped celery
1 pound lump white or claw crabmeat
2 tablespoons butter
6 tablespoons fine dry bread crumbs

Mix together mayonnaise, mustard, Worcestershire and Tabasco sauces, salt, and chopped vegetables. Fold into crabmeat gently. Divide equally among four buttered ovenproof ramekins.

Melt butter in a small skillet and stir in bread crumbs. Top each ramekin with buttered crumbs.

Broil until crumbs are golden brown and crab is heated through.

STONE CRAB CLAWS

*S*tone crab claws are scrumptious to eat and to behold! The dramatic black-tipped claws filled with sweet, firm-textured meat are a gourmet's delight. The claws are available as a precooked product, either fresh-chilled or frozen. If frozen, they should be thawed in the refrigerator for 12 to 18 hours so that moisture is not lost. Because of their extremely hard shell, stone crab claws are usually served precracked so that the succulent meat is easily removed with a fork. They are frequently served as a cold hors d'oeuvre accompanied by various sauces for spooning or dipping. The following suggestions are equally delicious with blue crab claws or cold boiled shrimp.

MUSTARD SAUCE

2 tablespoons butter, melted
½ cup sour cream
1½ tablespoons Dijon mustard
1 tablespoon chopped parsley
⅛ teaspoon salt

Combine all ingredients. Heat but do not boil.

CURRY SAUCE

½ cup mayonnaise
⅓ cup sour cream
2 tablespoons curry powder
salt to taste

Combine all ingredients and chill.

At Tarpon Springs the foods, wines, language, and customs of Greece meet the Gulf of Mexico.

Oystermen and mullet fishermen dock at a Cedar Key fish house.

CRABMEAT AND HEARTS OF PALM EN COQUILLES

Serves 6

½ cup mayonnaise
⅓ cup prepared chili sauce
1 teaspoon prepared horseradish
2 tablespoons dry sherry
1 8-ounce can hearts of palm
1 pound lump crabmeat
watercress or parsley

Mix mayonnaise, chili sauce, horseradish, and sherry together. Slice hearts of palm into ½-inch rounds and fold into mixture. Fold in crabmeat. Chill.

To serve, divide the mixture among six ramekins and garnish with watercress, parsley, or other fresh herbs.

CRAWFISH TETRAZZINI

Serves 6 to 8

*C*hef Peter Harman at Sanibel Island's Sundial Beach and Tennis Resort suggests this dish as a first course. It's rich, so be sure the serving sizes are not overwhelming. A garnish of chopped scallion tops adds a nice bit of crunch. Crawfish are available in most fish markets, cleaned and frozen—or fresh if in season. If they are unavailable, this dish is also delicious using shrimp or lobster.

4 tablespoons unsalted butter
4 tablespoons Seafood Madness
Seasoning Powder (p. 202)
3 cloves garlic, minced
2 pounds cleaned crawfish tails
2 cups heavy cream
1 pound linguini
½ cup grated Parmesan cheese
chopped scallions (optional)

Melt butter in a heavy saucepan. Add seasoning powder and garlic and heat through. Add crawfish, sauté 1 minute, and add cream. Increase heat and reduce by half to thicken, stirring constantly.

Cook linguini according to directions on package. Combine with crawfish mixture and serve in bowls, topped with Parmesan cheese. Garnish with scallions.

Crabmeat and Hearts of Palm en Coquilles; Shrimp, Scallop, and Mushroom Kabobs; and Gunzmart Family's Kingfish Escabèche (see page 45).

An island of planted palms graces a popular Sarasota beachfront.

SHRIMP, SCALLOP, AND MUSHROOM KABOBS

Serves 8

*M*y ever-imaginative friend Meredith Manning of Sarasota describes this recipe as her latest attempt to solve the hors d'oeuvre dilemma.

2 quarts water
2 tablespoons prepared crab boil
2 pounds shrimp, shelled and deveined
2 pounds sea scallops
2 tablespoons butter
1 pound mushroom caps

MARINADE

2 tablespoons chopped capers
2 tablespoons chopped scallions
10 water-packed or freeze-dried green peppercorns
1 clove garlic, crushed
1 cup prepared Italian salad dressing
2 tablespoons lemon or lime juice

Bring water to a boil, add crab boil, and simmer for about 20 minutes. Add shrimp and scallops and simmer about 2 minutes or until opaque. Drain and set aside.

Melt butter in a skillet and sauté mushroom caps until tender. Remove and combine with seafood in a shallow glass dish.

To prepare marinade, mix capers, scallions, peppercorns, and garlic. Add salad dressing and juice and mix well. Pour over seafood. Refrigerate overnight.

Provide guests with a small plate, a cocktail fork, and a bamboo skewer for making their own kabobs.

SCALLOPS FLORENTINE

Serves 4

callops combine well with spinach and Madeira, as do many other kinds of seafood.

1 10-ounce package frozen
leaf spinach, thawed
6 tablespoons butter, divided
2 scallions, chopped fine
½ cup Sercial Madeira wine
fresh-grated nutmeg to taste
salt and white pepper to taste
1 pound bay scallops
flour seasoned with salt and white pepper
2 tablespoons olive oil
3 tablespoons brandy
1 cup heavy cream
paprika

Drain thawed spinach and squeeze dry. Chop well and set aside.

Melt 3 tablespoons butter in a saucepan. Add scallions and cook until soft. Add Madeira and reduce by half. Add chopped spinach, nutmeg, and salt and pepper, then cook until spinach is heated through. Cover and keep hot.

Toss scallops in seasoned flour, shaking off excess. Heat oil and remaining butter in a skillet. Sauté scallops just until firm and remove from pan. Add brandy and deglaze skillet. Add cream and any liquid that has accumulated in the scallops, then reduce until fairly thick. Add scallops and heat through; taste to correct seasonings.

To serve, make a bed of spinach in center of a plate, top with scallops mixture, and garnish with paprika.

SCALLOPS
WITH KEY LIME SAUCE

Serves 4 to 6

2 pounds bay scallops (or sea scallops, cut in half)
flour seasoned with salt and white pepper
6 tablespoons butter or olive oil, divided
2 tablespoons flour
¾ cup dry white wine
2 cloves garlic, crushed
½ cup heavy cream
¼ cup lime juice
⅓ cup chopped fresh basil
salt and white pepper to taste
4 very thin lime slices

Toss scallops in seasoned flour, shaking off excess. In a skillet melt 4 tablespoons butter and sauté scallops just until done. Remove from pan.

Add remaining butter to pan and stir in flour to make a roux. Add white wine and garlic, stirring to make a smooth sauce. Add cream and stir until smooth. Stir in lime juice, basil, salt, and pepper.

Drain any liquid from scallops and return them to sauce to heat.

Serve in individual shells or ramekins or over hot rice. Garnish with a lime slice.

Scallops Florentine.

LOBSTER SALAD

Serves 4 to 6

*L*obster in any form is always an elegant way to start dinner. The following recipe can be either a first course or a colorful luncheon dish. It can be served on lettuce leaves or mixed with several cups of crisp, torn lettuce pieces. You may want to substitute shrimp or white lump crabmeat for the lobster, or mix them together to make a seafood mélange. Chef Raymond Huffman mixes available shellfish to prepare this salad for lunch at Duck Key Lodge.

yolks of 2 hard-cooked eggs, mashed
2 teaspoons Dijon mustard
1 tablespoon vinegar
2 tablespoons olive oil
2 tablespoons cream
1 or 2 anchovies, washed and mashed (optional)
salt and pepper to taste
½ cup thin-sliced celery
1 cup thin-sliced cucumber
½ cup pickled beets, sliced thin
2 scallions, chopped (including tops)
2½ to 3 cups cooked lobster pieces
lettuce

Mix egg yolks, mustard, vinegar, olive oil, cream, and anchovies together to form a smooth mixture. Add salt and pepper, if needed (taste before adding salt).

Add celery, cucumber, beets, and scallions and mix well. Fold in lobster pieces and serve in individual lettuce cups.

MIXED SHELLFISH SALAD

Serves 6 to 8

*S*eafood and rice combine with a savory dressing to make this light lunch dish. Garnished with slices of avocado and accompanied by crusty bread and a chilled white wine, it makes a summer day seem infinitely cooler.

4 scallions, chopped (including tops)
3 green apples, peeled and chopped
¼ cup vegetable oil
2 to 3 teaspoons curry powder
2 teaspoons celery seeds
2 teaspoons dry mustard
⅓ cup sour cream
1½ cups mayonnaise
juice of 1 lemon
¼ cup chopped parsley, divided
2 cups cooked rice
¾ pound cooked lobster, cut into pieces
½ pound lump crabmeat
1 pound shelled cooked shrimp
salt and white pepper

Sauté scallions and apples in oil until soft but not brown. Add curry powder, celery seeds, and mustard; mix well and cool.

Stir in sour cream, mayonnaise, lemon juice, and half of the parsley. Fold in rice and seafood. Add salt and pepper. Place in serving bowl and garnish with remaining parsley. Refrigerate for several hours before serving.

SHRIMP WITH YELLOW RICE

Serves 4 to 6

*T*his dish, very similar to a classic paella, is popular on the menus at all the Columbia Restaurants. Using local ingredients available in Florida and usually lacking the requisite saffron so essential to paella, the inventive Spaniards recreated a dish as close to the original as possible.

½ cup Spanish olive oil
1 large Spanish onion, chopped
1 large green bell pepper, chopped
¾ cup chopped fresh tomatoes
3 cloves garlic, crushed
2 or 3 threads of saffron (optional)
1 bay leaf
¼ teaspoon yellow food color (optional)
2 teaspoons salt
½ teaspoon Tabasco Pepper Sauce or other hot sauce
2 cups Shrimp Broth
1 cup uncooked rice
1 pound medium shrimp, shelled and deveined
½ cup dry white wine
1 cup fresh or frozen green peas, cooked
4 pimientos, cut into strips

SHRIMP BROTH

shrimp shells
1 small onion, chopped
1 clove garlic, lightly crushed
1 or 2 sprigs of parsley
water

Heat the olive oil in a paella pan or skillet until a slight haze shows. Sauté onion and bell pepper until limp. Add tomatoes, garlic, saffron, bay leaf, food color, salt, and pepper sauce. Cover and cook about 5 minutes.

To make Shrimp Broth, combine all ingredients in a saucepan. Bring to a boil, reduce heat, and simmer for 15 to 20 minutes. Strain.

Add Shrimp Broth and rice to sautéed vegetable mixture and bring to a boil. Reduce heat, cover, and cook about 20 minutes, or until rice is done. Add shrimp and continue to cook a few minutes or until shrimp are opaque. Sprinkle with wine, cover, and let stand for 5 minutes. Serve garnished with peas and pimiento strips.

GRILLED SHRIMP MORUNO

Serves 12

*T*he Gunzmart family in Tampa serves this as a first course, but it makes marvelous cocktail party fare as well. It can also be served as a main course with rice, heating the marinade and spooning it over the cooked shrimp.

1 cup olive oil
1½ teaspoons dried thyme
(or 2 teaspoons fresh thyme, chopped)
2 teaspoons ground cumin
1½ teaspoons paprika
1 teaspoon crushed hot red chilies
3 bay leaves, crumbled
3 tablespoons chopped parsley
3 cloves garlic, crushed
½ cup dry white wine or dry Spanish sherry
juice of 1 lemon
¼ teaspoon ground pepper
1 teaspoon salt
3 pounds medium shrimp, shelled and deveined
(with tail section intact)

Mix all ingredients except shrimp in a blender or food processor. Transfer to a glass or ceramic container. Add shrimp, stirring to coat well. Cover and refrigerate for several hours.

Thread shrimp on skewers and grill over hot coals about 2 to 3 minutes each side, or until browned but still juicy. Serve at once.

BROILED SHRIMP CAYENNE

Serves 6

*R*aymond Huffman is the chef at Duck Key Lodge, a private recreational facility in the Florida Keys. Most of the guests are sportfishermen and are ready for a relaxing dinner at the end of a long day in the sun. One of their favorite shrimp dinners is this spicy broiled dish, which is served with saffron rice.

1 teaspoon salt
1 clove garlic, split
4 tablespoons corn oil
1½ teaspoons lemon or lime juice
1½ to 2 pounds shrimp, shelled and deveined
¼ teaspoon cayenne pepper
6 tablespoons melted butter

Mash salt and garlic together, combine with oil and lemon juice, and pour over shrimp. Sprinkle with cayenne pepper, mix well, and allow to marinate at least 30 minutes. Arrange shrimp in a shallow baking dish, add melted butter, and stir to coat each shrimp.

Broil for 5 to 8 minutes, turning and basting so shrimp cook evenly. Serve with Yellow Rice with Saffron and Peas (p. 54).

SHRIMP AND PASTA SALAD WITH FETA CHEESE À LA GRECQUE

Serves 4

1 pound medium shrimp, cooked,
shelled, and deveined
½ pound feta cheese, rinsed, dried, and crumbled
6 scallions, chopped fine
4 tomatoes, peeled, seeded, and chopped
2 teaspoons chopped fresh oregano
(or 1½ teaspoons dried oregano)
2 tablespoons olive oil
½ cup sliced Calymata olives or ripe olives
¼ teaspoon salt
ground pepper to taste
1 pound pasta, cooked and drained

Combine all ingredients except pasta in a large bowl. Marinate at room temperature for at least 1 hour.

When ready to serve, toss mixture with pasta, coating pasta well. Serve slightly chilled or at room temperature.

COLUMBIA'S SHRIMP SUPREME

Serves 4 as a main course

*T*ampa's famous Columbia Restaurant has served fine food to its loyal patrons since it was founded in 1905. It is now under the management of Cesar Gunzmart and Adela Hernandez Gunzmart, the granddaughter of the founder. They have opened four other Columbias in Florida cities. This popular dish at Tampa's Columbia Restaurant can be served as a first course or as a main course with yellow rice. For a light supper, especially for shrimp lovers, serve it with Columbia's 1905 Salad (p. 55).

16 jumbo shrimp, shelled and deveined
(with tail section intact)
juice of 1 lemon
1 teaspoon garlic powder
1 teaspoon salt
½ teaspoon white pepper
8 strips of bacon
2 eggs, lightly beaten
½ cup milk
flour
vegetable oil

Mix together lemon juice, garlic powder, salt, and pepper and marinate shrimp for about 30 minutes.

Cut bacon strips in half and wrap around shrimp, securing with toothpicks.

Beat eggs and milk together. Dip shrimp in batter, dredge in flour, and deep-fry at 300 degrees about 5 to 8 minutes or until golden brown. Serve at once.

The Florida Everglades meet the Gulf at the mangrove swamps of Ten Thousand Islands near Everglades City.

SHRIMP IN TOMATO AND FETA CHEESE SAUCE À LA GRECQUE

Serves 6

*T*his recipe originated in the Tarpon Springs area, where a small but colorful Greek community carries on the sponge-fishing industry started in the early years of this century. Flavorful Greek ingredients are combined with tomatoes, shrimp, and feta cheese to make a dish that is good for serving a crowd because it is easily multiplied. Chunks of fish can be substituted for the shrimp or mixed with the shrimp for variety.

½ cup olive oil
2 cloves garlic, crushed
1 large onion, sliced thin
⅔ cup dry white wine
4 large tomatoes, peeled and chopped
¼ cup chopped Italian (flat-leaf) parsley
1 teaspoon chopped fresh oregano
(or ½ teaspoon dried oregano)
1 teaspoon salt
½ teaspoon ground pepper
2 pounds shrimp, shelled, deveined, and halved
lengthwise
½ pound feta cheese
sprigs of parsley

In a shallow ovenproof casserole heat oil and sauté garlic and onion until transparent. Add wine, tomatoes, herbs, and seasonings; simmer about 30 minutes or until mixture has thickened. Add shrimp and stir to coat thoroughly.

Crumble feta cheese over top of the casserole. Preheat oven to 450 degrees and bake for about 15 minutes or until shrimp is cooked and cheese has melted. Garnish with parsley sprigs and serve over rice or with crusty bread.

SHRIMP MARINERA

Serves 2

*F*rom Valencia Garden Restaurant in Tampa comes this typical Spanish dish. It is a meal in itself, with the potato, vegetables, and seafood. Although not traditional, the addition of a few chopped canned tomatoes and a dash or two of Tabasco sauce makes a nice variation.

¼ cup olive oil
18 medium shrimp, shelled and deveined
1 small onion, chopped fine
1 small green bell pepper, chopped fine
1 clove garlic, crushed
1 small potato, chopped fine
¼ cup dry sherry
1 teaspoon paprika
⅛ teaspoon chopped fresh oregano
(or large pinch of dried oregano)
salt and pepper to taste
1 cup water
chopped parsley

Heat oil in a skillet and add shrimp. Cook just until pink, remove from skillet, and set aside.

In the same skillet combine onion, bell pepper, and garlic; cook until soft. Add potato, sherry, seasonings, and water; cook until potato is soft and sauce has thickened. Return shrimp to mixture and heat. Garnish with chopped parsley and serve.

JELLIED SHRIMP MOLDS

Serves 6

A cool jellied mold makes a nice start to dinner on a sultry evening. It also works well as a luncheon dish, molded in a ring mold and garnished with artichoke hearts. On Duck Key, Chef Raymond Huffman gives this dish high marks as one of the most popular starters for dinner.

1 envelope unflavored gelatin
¼ cup cold water
1 cup hot water
¼ cup lemon or lime juice
½ teaspoon salt
⅛ teaspoon cayenne pepper
1 tablespoon sugar
2 tablespoons prepared chili sauce
1½ cups cooked shrimp
½ cup sweet pickle relish
lettuce leaves
artichoke hearts (optional)

HORSERADISH SAUCE

½ cup mayonnaise
½ cup sour cream
1 tablespoon prepared horseradish

Soften gelatin in cold water; add hot water and stir until gelatin is completely dissolved. Add lemon juice,

salt, cayenne pepper, sugar, and chili sauce. Cool until slightly thickened but not set. Fold in shrimp and relish; adjust seasonings if necessary. Pour into six ½-cup molds and refrigerate until set.

To make Horseradish Sauce, mix all ingredients well and chill.

Unmold shrimp molds on lettuce leaf cups, garnish with artichoke hearts, and serve with Horseradish Sauce.

MIXED SEAFOOD ENCHILADO VALENCIA

Serves 6

This popular seafood dish is served at the Valencia Garden Restaurant in Tampa. Not to be confused with the Mexican enchilada, this wonderfully homey dish has distinctly Spanish flavors. It can be served with a side dish of rice or linguini or with crusty warm bread to soak up the sauce. David Agliano, the present proprietor and grandson of the original founder, says the recipe has been in the family for years. Valencia's founder, Manuel Beiro, came to Florida from Spain in 1927 and opened the restaurant soon after. It has become a popular gathering place at lunch for the downtown group.

2 pounds mixed seafood (shrimp, scallops, crabmeat, clams, chunks of snapper or grouper fillets, etc.)
½ teaspoon salt
⅛ teaspoon white pepper
½ cup olive oil
1 green bell pepper, chopped
1 large onion, chopped
1 16-ounce can solid-pack tomatoes
3 bay leaves
dash of Tabasco Pepper Sauce
1 tablespoon Worcestershire sauce
1 teaspoon paprika
½ teaspoon ground cumin
2 cloves garlic, crushed
1 cup sherry

Sprinkle seafood with salt and pepper and set aside. Heat oil in a large saucepan. Sauté bell pepper and onion until tender but not brown. Add remaining ingredients and simmer 20 minutes. Add seafood and simmer just until tender. Taste to correct seasonings.

Serve with hot cooked rice.

Sunlovers throng to the clean white sands of Marco Island.
A stately esplanade outlines a stretch of Tampa's bayfront.

MEREDITH'S FLORIDA BOUILLABAISSE

Serves 8 generously

*D*on't be put off because this recipe looks complicated. Most of it can be made a day or two ahead, and then finished about half an hour before serving time. Originally this Mediterranean fisherman's soup was a peasant dish, made from a variety of fish on hand and flavored with the herbs and vegetables of the season. (You can be creative and add anything you might fancy—here's a great opportunity to try some of the Gulf's underutilized species!) Serve the cooked fish on a large heated platter, the broth in a large tureen, and the rouille in a separate sauceboat. Provide guests with a soup plate so that they can choose what they wish. Serve this with garlic-buttered French bread and a light fruity red wine or a dry white one.

3 pounds grouper or other solid white fish, cut into large chunks
2 pounds large shrimp, shelled and deveined
2 pounds sea scallops
4 spiny lobster tails, cooked and quartered (optional)
12 to 16 stone crab claws or blue crab claws, cracked
2 pints oysters, drained (reserve liquid) and sautéed in 6 tablespoons butter

BROTH

2 cups thin-sliced onions
1 cup thin-sliced leeks
2 cloves garlic, crushed
½ cup good-quality olive oil
5 cups water
2 cups dry white wine
1 cup clam juice
2 pounds fish heads and frames
3 pounds chopped ripe tomatoes
½ teaspoon fennel seeds, crushed
1 teaspoon dried thyme (or 2 teaspoons fresh thyme)
2 sprigs of parsley
2 bay leaves
¼ teaspoon saffron
10 water-packed or freeze-dried green peppercorns

ROUILLE

2 green bell peppers, seeded and chopped
1 dried hot chili pepper
1 cup water
2 canned pimientos, drained
4 cloves garlic, crushed
4 tablespoons vegetable oil
4 tablespoons good-quality olive oil
½ cup very fine dry bread crumbs

To make the broth, combine onions, leeks, garlic, and oil in a large pot and cook over low heat until vegetables are translucent. Add remaining broth ingredients, bring to a boil, reduce heat, and simmer for about 30 minutes. Refrigerate overnight.

Reheat broth. Line a heavy colander with three layers of cheesecloth and strain the mixture into a large

Meredith's Florida Bouillabaisse.

pot, pressing well to extract all juices and flavors. Discard residue. Refrigerate until ready to use.

To make the rouille, combine peppers and water and simmer about 10 minutes or until tender. Drain and combine with remaining rouille ingredients except bread crumbs. Blend at low speed until smooth. If the mixture is too thick, add olive oil.

Transfer to a mixing bowl and stir in bread crumbs. Mixture should be thick enough to hold a shape on the spoon. Cover and refrigerate until ready to use.

About 30 minutes before serving time, heat broth. Add chunks of fish and cook for 2 minutes. Add shrimp and scallops; cook for 3 minutes. Add lobster tails and crab claws and heat for about 1 minute. (Observe exact cooking times so that seafood is not overcooked!) Finally add oysters, sauté juices, and oyster liquid and heat through.

With a slotted spoon, remove seafood to a heated platter. Transfer broth to a tureen.

Add enough hot broth to the rouille that it has the consistency of mayonnaise; spoon it into a sauceboat. Serve at once.

INDIAN MIXED SEAFOOD SOUP

Serves 4

*W*hen I met Adela Gunzmart (of Columbia Restaurant fame) in Tampa, I asked her what her family particularly liked that might not be on the menu at the restaurant. This was one of the dishes she mentioned. As a variation, hominy can be substituted for corn, and snapper for scallops. If stone crab claws are not available, substitute blue crab claws (2 or 3 per person), cooked and cracked.

½ pound split peas
1 quart water
2 onions, chopped
1 bay leaf
salt to taste
½ cup olive oil
6 ounces shrimp, shelled and deveined
6 ounces bay scallops
1 cup whole-kernel corn
1 cup sliced okra
salt and white pepper to taste
4 precooked stone crab claws
¼ cup sherry

Combine split peas, water, onions, and bay leaf and simmer for 1 hour. Remove from heat, discard bay leaf, and puree mixture. Add salt and set aside.

In a large skillet heat olive oil. Sauté shrimp and scallops just until opaque. Set aside.

In a 3-quart saucepan combine split pea mixture with corn and okra and simmer 15 minutes. Season with salt and white pepper. Add reserved shrimp and scallops and crab claws; heat through. Spoon 1 tablespoon sherry over each serving.

Smoked Amberjack.

SMOKED AMBERJACK

Serves 6

*T*his wet-smoke method is one of my favorite ways to prepare fish in the summertime. It is a good first course or a light lunch dish. I use a barrel-shaped barbecue smoker with adjustable shelves and a pan for liquid. The fish can be served warm or at room temperature, and any leftovers are delicious used in fish cakes or a salad. Mahi-mahi, snapper, or tilefish can be substituted for amberjack.

2 quarts water
¾ cup salt
½ cup brown sugar
sprig of fresh thyme
2 bay leaves
2 to 3 pounds amberjack fillets
1 onion, sliced

CAPER SAUCE

4 tablespoons butter (not margarine)
2 tablespoons capers

PEPPERCORN SAUCE

1 8-ounce carton sour cream
2 tablespoons water-packed green peppercorns, crushed
salt to taste

Mix together water, salt, brown sugar, thyme, and 1 bay leaf and stir until salt and sugar are dissolved. Pour over fillets and refrigerate overnight.

When ready to smoke, build fire with charcoal briquettes. When the briquettes are covered with gray ash (about 20 to 30 minutes), add twigs of water-soaked pecan, walnut, or apple wood to flavor smoke. Fill the water pan with water, adding the sliced onion and remaining bay leaf. Allow water to come to a simmer.

Remove fish from brine, pat dry, and place on oiled grill over the pan of water. Cover smoker and proceed according to manufacturer's directions. Fish will be done in 30 minutes to 1 hour, depending on thickness of fillets. Serve with either Caper Sauce or Peppercorn Sauce.

To make Caper Sauce, brown butter, cool slightly, and add capers. Serve warm. To make Peppercorn Sauce, mix ingredients, refrigerate for 1 hour, and taste for salt; serve chilled.

GUNZMART FAMILY'S KINGFISH ESCABÈCHE

Serves 6

*E*scabèche is a marvelously flavored cold dish in which the fish is first cooked, then layered with vegetables, spices, and herbs, and finally marinated to allow the flavors to permeate the fish. The longer it marinates, the firmer the fish becomes—overnight is just about the right amount of time for my family. Ling or tuna also makes an excellent escabèche. The fish should be a firm, dense-textured type. In any of the stronger fish, be sure to discard the bloodline, or dark flesh, after cooking and before proceeding with the recipe.

2 pounds kingfish, cut into ¾-inch steaks
salt to taste
½ cup olive oil
4 onions, sliced in rounds and halved
4 green bell peppers, cut into thin strips
4 garlic cloves, minced
3 bay leaves
½ teaspoon paprika
1 cup pitted green olives
¼ cup white vinegar
½ cup olive oil
salt and pepper to taste

Sprinkle fish steaks with salt and sauté in olive oil over medium heat just until done. Drain on paper towels.

In the same oil over low heat, sauté onions and bell peppers until onions are translucent but still firm. Add remaining ingredients and mix well. Remove from heat.

In a glass dish alternate layers of fish and vegetable mixture, ending with a layer of vegetables. Cover and refrigerate several hours or overnight. Allow to come to room temperature before serving.

SMOKED MULLET SPREAD

Makes 4 cups

*I*n Florida smoked mullet is readily available, especially along the upper coast and Panhandle. Called "cracker food," it has a distinctive nutty flavor. My friend Meredith Manning in Sarasota utilizes it as the basis of this hors d'oeuvre. If mullet is unavailable, try smoked amberjack, tuna, or mackerel.

3 cups smoked mullet, skinned, boned, and flaked
1 cup mayonnaise
½ cup fine-chopped celery
½ cup fine-chopped onion
¼ cup fine-chopped red bell pepper
¼ cup chopped green bell pepper
1 small clove garlic, crushed
4 tablespoons Worcestershire sauce
1 tablespoon capers
1 tablespoon water-packed green peppercorns
salt and fresh-ground black pepper to taste

Combine all ingredients. Chill several hours or overnight. Serve with water biscuits or melba toast.

POMPANO FILLETS IN FOIL

Serves 1

*T*he versatility of fish in foil is a remarkable boon for the cook. It can be prepared for any number, assembled early in the day, refrigerated, and cooked in the oven or outside on the charcoal grill. The seasonings can be altered by adding or subtracting items to suit the cook's taste, always keeping in mind that the combination of flavors must be harmonious as well as compatible with the fish. Flounder, snapper, trout, and other varieties are delicious in this dish, too.

1 6- to 8-ounce fish fillet
salt and pepper to taste
1 teaspoon softened butter, margarine, or oil
1 tablespoon condensed
cream of celery soup, undiluted
1 tablespoon white wine
2 basil leaves, chopped (or pinch of dried basil)
1 mushroom, sliced
1 thin slice of onion
1 tablespoon sliced almonds
1 teaspoon parsley

Place fish on a square of buttered aluminum foil. Sprinkle with salt and pepper and rub with butter or oil.

Mix soup, wine, basil, and mushroom slices. Spread on top of fish and cover with onion slice, almonds, and parsley. Fold the edges of the foil together.

Preheat oven to 425 degrees and bake for 15 minutes, or grill over hot charcoal for 15 to 20 minutes. (If the packet has been refrigerated, increase the cooking time.)

Two seasoned Florida fishermen inspect their nets.

BROILED SNAPPER, GREEK STYLE

Serves 4

There are several good restaurants around the Tarpon Springs—Clearwater area, all having dishes typical of Greek cuisine. One of the most delicious—and simplest—of the fish dishes is baked whole snapper seasoned simply with oil, lemon, and oregano. The recipe works best using one small fish per person, but it is equally good with a four- or five-pound fish (which should serve six people). It is also possible to use fish fillets, but remember to decrease the cooking time accordingly; it is not necessary to turn fillets.

4 small whole snappers, cleaned and scaled
salt
3 tablespoons dried oregano
1 cup olive oil, divided
juice of 2 lemons, divided
lemon slices
chopped parsley

Dry fish and sprinkle with salt and oregano inside and out. Refrigerate for about 1 hour.

Arrange fish on an oiled broiler pan and brush with half the oil and half the lemon juice.

Broil under a hot broiler for about 10 minutes. Turn fish and brush with remaining oil and lemon juice. Broil another 10 minutes, or until the fish flakes. Serve on hot plates, garnished with lemon slices and sprinkled with chopped parsley.

CUBAN-STYLE YELLOWTAIL SNAPPER

Serves 1

In Marathon, down in the Florida Keys, Pedro Gonzales is the chef and owner of Don Pedro Restaurant. While his wife acts as hostess to see to the comfort of the guests, Pedro prepares authentic Cuban cuisine, often using the yellowtail snapper found in the Keys. The whole snapper is seasoned and deep-fried very quickly, using no batter to coat the fish. It is crisp and clean.

juice of 1 lime
1½ teaspoons garlic powder
1½ teaspoons ground black pepper
¾ teaspoon salt
1 1½-pound whole snapper, cleaned and scaled
oil

Mix together lime juice and seasonings. Rub mixture over fish, coating the inside as well as the outside. Marinate for at least 30 minutes.

Heat oil to 350 degrees. Deep-fry fish for 5 minutes. Remove and drain on paper towels.

Serve with Yellow Rice with Saffron and Peas (p. 54).

YELLOWTAIL SNAPPER, PORT OF SPAIN

Serves 4

*Y*ellowtail snapper is the most popular fish in the Florida Keys, moist and delicately flavored. It lends itself to a variety of preparations. Marker 88 Restaurant in Islamorada has the reputation of being one of the finest in the state, and Chef Wesley Brage uses an interesting combination of fruits for saucing this dish.

4 tablespoons Worcestershire sauce
juice of 2 lemons, divided
salt and white pepper
2 pounds snapper fillets
flour
2 eggs, beaten with a little milk
clarified butter
½ cup each chopped bananas, apples, and pimientos
½ cup tomatoes, peeled, seeded, and chopped
1 tablespoon butter
1 tablespoon chopped parsley

Mix together the Worcestershire sauce, juice of 1 lemon, salt, and pepper. Brush mixture on fish. Dredge fish in flour, then in egg.

Heat clarified butter in a skillet and sauté fish on one side. Place fish, sautéed side down, in a buttered baking dish and add pan juices. Preheat oven to 450 degrees and bake 8 to 10 minutes.

Meanwhile mix together fruit, pimientos, tomatoes, juice of remaining lemon, butter, and parsley; simmer until heated through. The apples should remain crisp.

Pour fruit mixture over baked fish and serve.

FRIED SQUID, GREEK STYLE

*F*or the past twenty years Mama Maria's Greek Cuisine Restaurant in Tarpon Springs has been preparing real Greek dishes—no frills, no tourist trappings, just good Greek food. The business is family-owned and the recipes are simple—more method than measurements. One of Greece's typical coastal dishes, fried baby squid, can be found here at Mama Maria's. Serve it with a good Greek salad and a loaf of bread.

For this dish you must purchase whole baby squid, cleaned, with the hard spine and ink sac removed. Retain the tentacles. Mama's dredges them in flour and fries them in very hot olive oil until golden brown. Drain them on paper towels and arrange on the plate. Sprinkle a bit of dried oregano over them, with a little salt, and serve with lemon wedges.

The mixed catch at a Key Largo fish house includes snapper, pompano, amberjack, grouper, lobster, and stone crab.

Dry-docked sloops get their hulls scrubbed at Fort Walton Beach, one of Florida's fastest growing recreational areas.

POACHED SWORDFISH STEAKS WITH THREE SAUCES

Serves 8

*R*aymond Huffman, chef at the lodge on Duck Key, prepares cold dishes such as this to serve to hungry fishermen at lunchtime out on the boat. When combined with a green salad, bread, and cheese (plus the requisite libations), it is satisfying without being too heavy. Cookies or cake and coffee complete the meal.

2 cups dry vermouth
2 cups water
4 whole scallions or 4 slices of onion
12 peppercorns
4 allspice berries
1 bay leaf
1 teaspoon salt
2 pounds swordfish steaks (about 1 inch thick)

FRESH PEPPER SAUCE

½ medium onion, chopped fine
1 medium red bell pepper, chopped fine
2 ribs celery, chopped fine
1½ tablespoons fresh lime juice
4 tablespoons olive oil
1 teaspoon cumin seeds, toasted
dash of cayenne pepper
⅛ teaspoon salt

FRESH TOMATO SAUCE

6 small tomatoes, peeled and chopped
½ onion, chopped fine
3 tablespoons capers, drained
1 2¼-ounce can sliced ripe olives, drained
¼ teaspoon chopped fresh thyme
½ teaspoon chopped fresh oregano
½ small clove garlic, crushed
2 teaspoons chopped parsley
¼ teaspoon salt

MUSTARD WITH MINT MARIGOLD DRESSING

2 tablespoons Dijon mustard
½ cup mayonnaise
1½ teaspoons Mexican mint marigold or tarragon, chopped
1 to 2 tablespoons Pernod or ouzo
½ cup heavy cream

Combine vermouth, water, scallions, and seasonings in a large flat pan and bring to a boil. Reduce heat and simmer, covered, about 20 minutes. Strain, return liquid to pan, and bring to a boil. Remove from heat.

Place fish steaks in pan in a single layer, spooning hot liquid over them. Cover pan and let stand for 10 minutes. Remove cover, turn fish steaks, and cover again. Let stand for another 10 minutes. The fish is done at this point but should be left to cool in the liquid with the cover removed.

When cool, drain fish and refrigerate until ready to serve.

To make sauces, mix all ingredients well and refrigerate several hours. Serve fish chilled and accompanied by one or all of the sauces.

GRILLED SWORDFISH STEAKS IN PACKETS, À LA GRECQUE

Serves 1

*T*his could be called a Florida Greek barbecue. Each packet contains one serving of wonderfully seasoned fish, crispy onions and red bell peppers, and some great juices that you'll want to soak up with crusty bread or pour over hot buttered rice. Any firm fish can be used—try shark, tuna, redfish, ling, pompano, mullet . . . you name it. Serve the steaks in their packets so that the aroma can be savored as the foil is opened.

1 8-ounce swordfish steak
salt and ground black pepper
paprika
fresh oregano leaves (or crumbled dried oregano)
or fine-chopped fresh rosemary
(or powdered dried rosemary)
thin slices of onion
thin slices of red bell pepper
1 teaspoon lemon juice
2 tablespoons olive oil or melted butter

Place steak on a square of buttered or oiled aluminum foil and season with salt and pepper and a liberal sprinkling of paprika. Add oregano or rosemary and top with onion and red bell pepper slices. Sprinkle with lemon juice and olive oil.

Fold over corners of foil securely to make a packet. Grill about 12 inches above hot coals for about 20 minutes. (Cooking time will vary with type and thickness of fish.)

Grilled Swordfish Steaks in Packets, à la Grecque.

Violet's Baked Mahi-Mahi, Island Style.

VIOLET'S BAKED MAHI-MAHI, ISLAND STYLE

Serves 6

*V*iolet Allen, who grew up in Nevis-St. Kitts in the Virgin Islands, has lived in South Florida for over ten years and knows the local seafood well since the two areas share so many of the same species. The Gulf fish called dolphin (not to be confused with the mammal dolphin), also known as dorado and mahi-mahi, is becoming one of the most popular finfish around the Gulf Coast.

3 cloves garlic
3 teaspoons salt
1 tablespoon water-packed green
peppercorns, drained
1 teaspoon cracked black pepper
2 pounds mahi-mahi, grouper, or snapper fillets
1 onion, sliced thin
2 stalks celery, sliced thin
1 red bell pepper, sliced thin
12 stuffed olives, sliced
1 teaspoon fresh thyme
(or large pinch of dried thyme)
2 tablespoons chopped parsley
2 tablespoons capers
6 tablespoons olive oil
juice of 4 limes

With a mortar and pestle mash the garlic, salt, and green and black pepper to make a paste. Rub into fish fillets and place them in a buttered baking dish. Marinate for 30 minutes or longer.

Cover fish with remaining ingredients; cover dish with foil. Preheat oven to 350 degrees and bake for 20 minutes, or until fish flakes easily.

Serve directly from the baking dish with rice or crusty French bread to soak up the juices.

Marco Island beachlovers forsake lounge chairs for sunwarmed sands.

FILLETS OF TROUT
IN TOMATO SHELLS

Serves 8

*F*illets from fine-textured fish such as trout, sheepshead, flounder, and sea bass can all be used in this recipe. The fillets should be trimmed to a size that can be rolled up and fit inside a tomato shell. If desired, a cooked shrimp could be placed in the center of the roll to add a little interest.

8 unpeeled tomato shells
8 fish fillets
salt
onion salt
paprika
ground white pepper
lemon juice
vegetable oil
sprigs of parsley

SAUCE VELOUTÉ

10 tablespoons butter
10 tablespoons flour
1½ cups veal, chicken, or fish stock
½ teaspoon chopped fresh oregano
(or ⅛ teaspoon dried oregano)
⅛ teaspoon grated nutmeg
grated zest of 1 lemon
salt to taste

Remove seeds and pulp from tomatoes and drain well. Season fillets with remaining ingredients except parsley and set aside.

To make Sauce Velouté, melt butter in a heavy saucepan, stir in flour, and cook for 2 to 3 minutes.

Add stock, whisking constantly, and cook until thick. Add remaining ingredients and stir well.

Salt tomato shells and place 1 tablespoon Sauce Velouté in the bottom of each. Spread seasoned fillets with Sauce Velouté and roll up to fit into shell. Spoon equal portions of any leftover sauce into the rolled fillets.

Place each tomato shell in an individual ramekin just large enough to hold it. Preheat oven to 350 degrees and bake for 20 to 30 minutes or until fish flakes easily.

Garnish with parsley sprigs and serve.

Tarpon Springs sponges are trimmed by Gilbert Graham for worldwide marketing. Greek divers still harvest sponge varieties from the clear Gulf waters.

FILLET OF TROUT
WITH RUSSIAN SAUCE

Serves 6

*V*alencia Garden Restaurant always features on its menu a Spanish fish dish which is garnished "à la Russe." In this recipe a paste is made of butter and chopped eggs. When dotted over the hot fish fillets, it melts right into them. Flounder, catfish, or any other mild, fine-textured fish can be substituted for the trout in this recipe.

2 pounds trout fillets
½ teaspoon salt
¼ teaspoon white pepper
2 eggs, beaten well
¼ cup milk
1½ cups fine dry bread crumbs
2 to 3 tablespoons vegetable oil
½ cup butter, softened
3 eggs, hard-cooked and chopped fine
⅓ cup minced parsley
2 tablespoons minced pimiento
2 lemons, sliced

Sprinkle fillets with salt and pepper. Beat eggs and milk together, dip fillets in egg mixture, and roll in bread crumbs.

Brush grill or skillet with only enough oil to keep fish from sticking. Heat grill and cook fillets about 5 minutes on each side or until golden. Remove from heat and keep warm.

Mix butter, chopped eggs, parsley, and pimiento. Dot over hot fillets and garnish with sliced lemons. Serve at once.

Pine-topped dunes of powdery white sand accent the Gulf Islands National Seashore between Pensacola and Fort Walton Beach.

GRILLED TUNA KABOBS

Serves 6

*T*una, because it is a "fat," dense-textured fish, is a natural for grilling, but the leaner varieties such as swordfish, shark, or wahoo can be substituted in this recipe since an oil marinade is used. The trick here is not to over-cook the fish but to keep the center slightly pink. At that point it will be completely done and even continue to cook a little before you eat it. For a great taste, try putting fresh or dried bay leaves between the skewered cubes of fish.

2 pounds fish fillets, cut into 1-inch cubes
1 pound fresh mushrooms, cleaned
1 cup olive oil
½ onion, chopped
½ bay leaf, crushed
½ teaspoon salt
¼ teaspoon cayenne pepper

SAUCE

4 tablespoons lime juice
¾ cup olive oil
2 tablespoons chopped parsley
2 teaspoons chopped fresh oregano
¼ teaspoon salt

Place fish cubes and mushrooms in glass or ceramic bowl. Mix together olive oil, onion, bay leaf, salt, and cayenne pepper and pour over fish and mushrooms, tossing to coat each piece. Cover and refrigerate for at least 4 hours.

To make sauce, mix all ingredients well and let stand for 1 to 2 hours. (This sauce keeps well in the refrigerator for several weeks.)

Thread fish and mushrooms on skewers and grill over very hot coals, or under broiler, for about 8 minutes, turning to sear all sides and brushing with marinade. Do not overcook.

TUNA FILLETS AU POIVRE

Serves 4

*F*resh tuna is a popular fish in the southern part of Florida. To the delight of the guests at Sanibel Island's Sundial Beach and Tennis Resort, Chef Peter Harman prepares it often using this recipe. Other kinds of firm-textured varieties, like swordfish and shark, are also delicious prepared this way.

4 6-ounce tuna fillets (approximately 1 inch thick)
4 tablespoons Pommery mustard
1 tablespoon cracked black pepper
4 tablespoons olive oil
1 cup shiitake mushrooms, sliced
½ cup scallions, sliced thin
¼ cup fine-chopped red bell pepper
2 tablespoons water-packed
green peppercorns, drained
2 ounces brandy
⅔ cup heavy cream

Place fillets on a plate and rub the top side of each with 1 tablespoon of the mustard. Divide black pepper equally and press into fish.

Heat oil in a heavy skillet and place fillets, mustard side down, in oil. Sear 1 minute and turn. Immediately add mushrooms, scallions, red bell pepper, and peppercorns. Cook 1 minute and flame the pan with brandy. Add cream, increase heat, and cook for another 2 minutes to reduce liquid. (It is important to observe cooking times so fish will not be overcooked!)

Serve fillets topped with sauce.

RAYMOND AND RONNIE'S TUNA "PREPARATION"

*W*hen fishermen and cooks get together to exchange ideas (and swap tall stories), I've heard some pretty interesting techniques discussed. One evening down on Duck Key, Raymond Huffman, superchef, and Ronnie Trobis, fishing boat captain, were talking about tuna, having just caught a big one that day. Some of the tuna steaks would be frozen for future use and then later prepared using the following method, which keeps the tuna's white color and delicate flavor.

Thaw the fish, put it in a saucepan, and cover it with water. Bring to a boil and drain off water immediately. Cover fish with a mixture of half water and half milk. Bring to a boil and remove from heat immediately. Let stand a few minutes, then rinse. It is then ready to be made into salad, a casserole, or any dish requiring cooked tuna.

Bound for offshore reef fishing, a powerboat slices the blue waters out from Naples.

YELLOW RICE WITH SAFFRON AND PEAS

Serves 6 to 8

*I*n many of the recipes from the Florida coast, especially those of Spanish origin, yellow rice or saffron rice is suggested as an accompaniment. Some recipes from the Yucatán also suggest this dish. For variation, omit the peas and dill seed, if desired, or add toasted slivered almonds for texture.

1½ cups long-grain converted rice
3 tablespoons butter
3 cups water
1 teaspoon salt
2 tablespoons chopped chives
2 tablespoons chopped parsley
1 tablespoon dill seed
large pinch of saffron
1 10-ounce package frozen peas, thawed

Sauté rice in butter until transparent. Add water and bring to a boil. Cover with buttered paper and a layer of paper towels, then cover with lid.

Preheat oven to 325 degrees and bake for 18 to 20 minutes, or cook over low heat for 20 minutes.

Fluff with fork and add remaining ingredients. Taste to correct seasonings.

Press into a buttered mold, cover loosely with foil, and keep warm in a hot-water bath or a 175-degree oven until ready to serve.

CHILLED AVOCADO SOUP

Serves 6

*T*he subtle flavor of an avocado can be overwhelmed by a strongly flavored stock and completely ruined by overcooking. This version of avocado soup is uncooked and thinned with a delicately flavored vegetable stock that enhances the flavors of the combined ingredients to produce a refreshingly cool first course. Lump crabmeat or cooked shrimp can be added just before serving.

3 cups water
½ carrot, chopped
½ onion, chopped
1 small tomato, chopped
1 sprig of parsley
½ bay leaf
3 peppercorns
2 ripe avocados, peeled, seeded, and chopped
1 small clove garlic, crushed
2 scallions, chopped (including tops)
3 to 4 tablespoons white wine vinegar or lime juice
10 drops Tabasco Pepper Sauce or to taste
1½ teaspoons salt
white pepper to taste
pinch of sugar
4 tablespoons fine-chopped cilantro
1 tablespoon fruity olive oil (optional)

In a saucepan mix water, carrot, onion, tomato, parsley, bay leaf, and peppercorns and bring to a boil. Reduce heat and simmer, uncovered, for about 20 minutes. Strain and set aside.

Combine avocados, garlic, scallions, vinegar, and Tabasco sauce. Puree in blender or food processor. Thin with a little of the reserved stock as necessary to blend.

Transfer avocado puree to large bowl and add about 2½ cups of the reserved stock. Season with salt and pepper; add sugar, cilantro, and olive oil. Mix well and chill several hours before serving.

COLUMBIA'S 1905 SALAD

Serves 4

*W*hen Columbia Restaurant was founded in 1905 by Casimiro Hernandez, Sr., it was a corner cafe located in Ybor City, the center of the Florida cigar industry and the gathering place for the Spanish and Cuban population of Tampa. Always filled with patrons drinking steamy cups of Cuban coffee and enjoying delicious Spanish food, it soon became a favorite establishment of the local gentry. Columbia's 1905 Salad is a delicious reminder of those early days.

½ head iceberg lettuce, cut into chunks
2 ripe tomatoes, cut into eighths
3 ounces Swiss cheese, cut into julienne strips
12 large shrimp, shelled, deveined, cooked, and
cut in half lengthwise
½ cup pitted Spanish olives
2 teaspoons grated Romano cheese

DRESSING

4 cloves garlic, minced
1 teaspoon dried oregano
(or 2 teaspoons chopped fresh oregano)
1 teaspoon Worcestershire sauce
1 egg yolk
½ cup Spanish olive oil
⅛ cup white wine vinegar
juice of 1 lemon (optional)
salt and pepper to taste

Toss together all salad ingredients except Romano cheese.

To make dressing, combine garlic, oregano, Worcestershire sauce, and egg yolk. Beat until smooth with a wire whisk. Add oil gradually, beating to form an emulsion. Stir in vinegar and lemon juice and season with salt and pepper.

Add dressing to salad and toss well. Garnish with Romano cheese.

Garish facades along Panama City's beachfront beckon the tourist trade. A Cedar Key oysterman shucks oysters on deck, discarding shells that will rebuild reefs. An Ybor City pedestrian takes a break to bask in the winter sun.

MANGO COBBLER

Serves 6 to 8

Anyone who has lived in the southern part of the United States knows fruit cobblers, the most popular ones being those made from wild blackberries, dewberries, or peaches. A warm cobbler served with cold heavy cream is summer's most delectable dessert. Along most of the Gulf Coast, mangoes are plentiful in the markets during the season, so for a change, try making the following cobbler from this delicious fruit.

6 cups sliced ripe mangoes
(about 5, depending on size)
½ cup sugar
½ teaspoon cardamom seeds, crushed
2 tablespoons flour
4 tablespoons lime juice
Basic Pastry (p. 208)

In a deep pie dish or other 2-quart baking dish, toss together mangoes, sugar, cardamom seeds, flour, and lime juice.

Roll out Basic Pastry dough to cover top of baking dish, crimping edges to seal. Cut slits for steam to escape.

Preheat oven to 425 degrees and bake for 45 to 50 minutes, or until crust is brown and crisp. If necessary, cover edges of crust with strips of foil to prevent burning.

FROZEN KEY LIME PIE

Serves 8

Artist, art dealer, and raconteur Loring Hayden of Sarasota has a deft hand in the kitchen when it comes to preparing his favorite desserts. He learned to cook when he lived in Paris in a sixth-floor walk-up apartment and declares that the climb up the stairs necessarily simplified his cooking ideas. His version of this traditional Florida dessert is easy but delicious.

½ cup lime juice
grated zest of 1 lime
1 14-ounce can sweetened condensed milk
1 8-ounce container frozen nondairy whipped topping, thawed
2 tablespoons Grand Marnier
1 prepared chocolate cookie crust

Mix lime juice, zest, and condensed milk. Fold in whipped topping. Add Grand Marnier, mix, and spoon into crust. Freeze overnight.

To serve, remove from freezer and let stand before slicing.

Brown pelicans perch atop Alligator Point pilings.

KEY LIME TART

Makes 2 tarts

PASTRY SHELLS

3 cups flour (or 2 cups all-purpose flour and 1 cup whole wheat flour)
4 tablespoons sugar
2 teaspoons salt
1½ sticks butter
¼ cup shortening
1 whole egg
2 to 3 tablespoons cold water
(depending on egg size)

FILLING

6 whole eggs
5 egg yolks
2½ cups sugar
1 cup lime juice
grated zest of 3 limes
¼ teaspoon salt
1 cup plus 3 tablespoons butter

To make pastry shells, sift together flour, sugar, and salt. Cut butter and shortening into small pieces and mix with flour until the pieces are the size of small peas. Work in egg and water.

Turn the dough out onto a board and with the heel of one hand slide small portions of the mixture in a "smearing" motion to layer the fat into the flour.

Divide dough into two balls. Wrap each in plastic wrap and refrigerate for 1 hour. Roll out to fit pie tin. Prick the bottom well (it may be necessary to prick again during baking). Preheat oven to 425 degrees and bake until lightly browned. Cool.

To make filling, beat eggs, yolks, and sugar until pale and thick. Add lime juice, zest, and salt, mixing well. Stirring constantly, cook over low heat for about 15 minutes, or until filling is thick and slightly translucent. Do not overcook or egg will curdle. Remove from heat.

Whisk in butter a little at a time, letting each bit melt before adding the next. Divide filling between the two baked and cooled pastry shells.

Place pies on oven rack about 6 inches from broiler. Broil about 2 minutes or until filling is brown on top. Watch carefully to see that tops do not burn. Remove from oven and cool until filling is set.

PINEAPPLE–KEY LIME CAKE

*T*his recipe makes a densely textured, moist cake because the whole wheat flour does not have the gluten content of all-purpose flour and therefore doesn't rise as easily. For a lighter cake, substitute all-purpose flour or a combination of whole wheat and all-purpose.

3 cups whole wheat flour (or all-purpose flour or
2 cups whole wheat and 1 cup all-purpose)
1 teaspoon salt
1 teaspoon soda
1 teaspoon ground allspice
2 cups sugar
1½ cups vegetable oil
3 eggs, beaten
1 8-ounce can crushed pineapple, undrained
1 cup chopped pecans
grated zest of 3 limes
¼ cup lime juice

Butter and sugar the sides of a Bundt pan. Set aside.

Sift together flour, salt, soda, allspice, and sugar. Mix oil and eggs and add to flour mixture. Stir in pineapple, pecans, zest, and juice, mixing well. Pour into Bundt pan.

Preheat oven to 350 degrees and bake for 65 to 70 minutes, or until toothpick inserted in middle comes out clean.

Cover loosely with foil and cool in pan before removing.

CITRUS CRISPS

¾ cup butter
½ cup powdered sugar
4 teaspoons grated orange zest
(or 3 teaspoons lime or lemon zest)
¼ teaspoon orange extract (or lemon)
1 cup flour
½ cup cornstarch
½ teaspoon salt
1 cup walnuts or pecans, toasted and chopped

Cream together butter, sugar, zest, and extract. Work in flour, cornstarch, and salt. Add nuts and roll in waxed paper to form logs. Chill until firm or freeze. Slice into ¼-inch slices and place 2 inches apart on an ungreased baking sheet. Preheat oven to 375 degrees and bake about 10 to 15 minutes or until brown on edges. Cool.

A gill netter on the Suwannee River checks the water's depth and current.

PUDÍN DE ARROZ CUBANO

Serves 10 to 12

*R*ice puddings have a niche in every cuisine. They are always popular desserts, from nursery fare to this elegantly molded version. The sweetened coconut cream, guava marmalade, and guava shells are available in specialty stores and Cuban markets.

2 cups short-grain rice
3 cups water
3 cups light cream or half-and-half
⅔ cup sugar
⅛ teaspoon salt
1 large strip of lime zest
3 envelopes unflavored gelatin
1 cup cold water
1 9½-ounce can sweetened coconut cream
1 teaspoon vanilla extract
2 cups heavy cream
guava shells

GUAVA SAUCE

1 15-ounce can guava marmalade
1 tablespoon dark rum

Soak rice in water overnight. Drain rice and add light cream, sugar, salt, and zest. Cook over low heat for 20 to 30 minutes or until very tender.

Meanwhile soften gelatin in cold water. Add to hot cooked rice, stirring to dissolve gelatin. Stir in coconut cream and vanilla extract. Cool.

Whip cream to soft peaks and fold into rice mixture. Pour into 4-quart ring mold, cover, and chill overnight to set.

To make Guava Sauce, heat marmalade in a heavy saucepan. Stirring constantly, cook over medium heat until reduced by one-fourth. Stir in rum and chill.

To serve, unmold pudding on platter, fill center with Guava Sauce, and garnish with guava shells.

DEEP SOUTH

*A*LONG THE GULF SHORES of Mississippi, Alabama, and the upper Florida coast, the pace of life is leisurely. This is Deep South territory, with its heritage of hospitality, good humor, and relaxed conversations over iced tea laced with lemon and fresh mint.

Coastal cities such as Biloxi, Mobile, and Pensacola reflect their colorful past as old seaport towns. Historic Pensacola, one of the most Spanish of Florida cities, can trace its origins to 1559—even before the settlement of St. Augustine—when Don Tristan de Luna and his 1,500 followers arrived at a site on what they called Santa Maria Bay (now Pensacola Bay). But within two years, a hurricane wiped out their settlement, and it was not until 1698 that Pensacola resumed its story. Biloxi and Mobile were established soon afterward, but by French settlers.

A mullet seiner searches for fish schools near Mobile Bay.
Trimmed to catch the eye as well as the Gulf breezes, a restored
Victorian cottage presides at Biloxi.

When it comes to fish, large red snapper and pompano are particular favorites in this region. Pompano is a thin, deep-bodied fish with a firm flesh. Its sweet, delicate flavor is best enjoyed within an hour or two after the fish is pulled from the water. Pompano *en papillote*—sealed in a paper bag or in cooking parchment and seasoned with herbs, spices, or sauces—is a classic dish here.

Shrimp, blue crab, and Apalachicola Bay oysters are the favored shellfish; flounder, redfish, and black drum are some of the most prized catches of finfish. Mullet, grilled or smoked, is very popular.

Here, as in many places on the coast, frying is the time-honored method for preparing almost any kind of seafood. Depending on local customs, it is often perked up by catsup, pepper, sherry, or dill pickles and accompanied by french fries or hush puppies and coleslaw. More complex are creamy concoctions of seafoods bound together by richly flavored sauces and served over toast points, piled into pastry shells, or rolled into crepes.

Despite the strength of tradition in this region, new young chefs are adding to the culinary options in coastal restaurants. Grilling has become a popular way to present seafoods, accompanied by wine- or liqueur-based sauces. And long-neglected species of fish, such as tilefish and grouper, are beginning to appear on menus in hotels and restaurants. Which all goes to show that good eating is the strongest Southern tradition of all.

The Dog River winds past pulp mills on the east shore of Mobile Bay. Spanish moss entangles rusty ironwork in Mobile's historic Fort Conde district.

The colorful and elaborate new paint job on this Biloxi shrimp boat reflects Southern pride in the local seafood industry.

Modern Mobile skyscrapers overlook the modest, preserved structures of another era. In another part of the city's downtown area, rows of storefronts await restoration.

Crab Soufflé with Curry Sauce.

Gulfport shrimp boats bob at dockside.

CRAB SOUFFLÉ
WITH CURRY SAUCE

Serves 4 to 6

A *soufflé is always an elegant little lunch or supper dish.
This one, made with the rich body meat of blue crabs,
is further enhanced with a creamy curry sauce. Not a
recipe for weight-watchers but as an occasional treat, it will garner
rave notices. It may be made with lump crabmeat, but since the
lumps will be broken up while mixing the soufflé, I recommend
using special-grade, the white crabmeat from the body. It has a
lot of texture but not enough to break down the soufflé.*

3 tablespoons butter or margarine
¼ cup flour
1¾ cups cold milk
1½ teaspoons Tabasco Pepper Sauce or to taste
1 teaspoon salt
1 tablespoon Creole mustard or other coarse-grained
mustard
1 tablespoon grated onion
6 eggs, separated
1 pound special-grade crabmeat

CURRY SAUCE

2 tablespoons butter or margarine
2 tablespoons flour
1 teaspoon curry powder or to taste
1 cup cold half-and-half
salt to taste

In a large saucepan melt butter, add flour, and cook for
1 minute. Add milk and stir constantly until mixture
has thickened and is smooth. Add Tabasco sauce, salt,
mustard, and onion. Mix well and remove from heat.
Beat egg yolks slightly and add to mixture. Fold in
crabmeat.

Whip the egg whites until they hold soft peaks.
Stir about 2 tablespoons of the beaten whites into the
crab mixture, then carefully fold in the remaining whites.
Spoon mixture into an 8-cup soufflé dish and set in a
pan of water (about 1 inch deep). Preheat oven to 300
degrees and bake for 1 hour and 15 minutes, or until a
silver knife inserted in center of soufflé comes out almost clean. Check after baking 1 hour.

To make Curry Sauce, melt butter in a small
saucepan. Add flour and curry powder and cook 1 to
2 minutes. Add half-and-half and cook, stirring constantly until thick and creamy. Add salt and taste to
correct seasonings. Spoon over individual servings of
soufflé.

*Dominich Ditchare weighs in the
shrimp catch for counter sales.*

CHEF HENRY'S CRAB CAKES

Makes 12 to 18

C *hef Henry Douglas of Mobile's Radisson Admiral
Semmes Hotel has worked with chefs from New Orleans, Washington, and Alabama, and some of his recipes incorporate various food ideas from each area. Here he combines the traditional Southern crab cake with a touch of Creole
seasoning for additional interest. Chef Henry's Dill-Dijon Mustard Sauce (p. 77) or his Creole-Style Mustard Sauce (p. 206)
makes a delicious accompaniment to these crab cakes.*

4 tablespoons butter
¾ cup fine-chopped onion
¼ cup fine-chopped green bell pepper
¼ cup fine-chopped red bell pepper
¼ cup fine-chopped celery
3 egg yolks
1 whole egg
¼ cup mayonnaise
2 teaspoons cider vinegar
2 teaspoons lemon juice
1 teaspoon salt
½ teaspoon ground white pepper
¾ teaspoon dry mustard
3 or 4 drops Tabasco Pepper Sauce or to taste
2 teaspoons Worcestershire sauce
2 teaspoons Creole seasoning powder
2 tablespoons chopped parsley
1 cup fresh bread crumbs
1 pound special-grade crabmeat
flour
vegetable oil or butter

Melt butter in a skillet and sauté onion, bell peppers,
and celery just until tender. Transfer to a mixing bowl.

Combine egg yolks, whole egg, and mayonnaise
and beat well. Beat in vinegar, lemon juice, seasonings, and parsley. Mix in bread crumbs and fold in
crabmeat.

Divide into equal portions and shape into cakes.
Dust with flour and sauté in hot oil or butter, turning
to brown both sides. (For a first course, make small
crab cakes and allow two per serving.)

In Bayou La Batre, Alabama, Sean Johnson handles bushels of freshly steamed blue crabs for regional sales.

DEVILED CRAB WITH AVOCADOS

Serves 6

My good friend Helyn Tucker has lived in various parts of the United States from coast to coast and from border to border. A dyed-in-the-wool gourmet, she has garnered food ideas from each area of the country. From the Gulfport-Mobile area she developed the following dish, which combines elements of Louisiana, the Deep South, and Florida.

2 ripe avocados, peeled and sliced
½ cup white wine vinegar
1 small garlic clove, cut into pieces
6 tablespoons butter
5 tablespoons flour
3 cups milk
1 teaspoon Creole-style mustard
2 teaspoons salt
3 tablespoons lemon juice
2 teaspoons Worcestershire sauce
2 tablespoons chopped parsley
⅓ cup dry sherry
3 cups crabmeat
1 cup shredded sharp cheddar cheese

Place avocado slices in shallow dish and sprinkle with vinegar and garlic. Marinate for about 30 minutes, turning occasionally.

In a saucepan, melt butter, add flour, and stir over medium heat, blending well. Add milk gradually, stirring until mixture thickens.

Remove from heat and stir in remaining ingredients except crab and cheese; mix well. Fold in crabmeat.

Remove avocados from marinade and arrange in shallow baking dish. Spoon hot crab mixture over avocados and sprinkle cheese on top. Preheat oven to 325 degrees and bake about 10 minutes, or until avocados are just heated through and cheese is melted. Do not overbake.

FLORIDA LOBSTER CHARDONNAY

Serves 4

Spiny lobsters, also known as rock lobsters, make just about as scrumptious a seafood dish as anything from the Gulf waters. Unlike Atlantic lobsters, these creatures do not have edible claws, but the tails are filled with delicious and easily prepared meat. Sometimes they are available fresh, but more frequently they will be found packaged and frozen in the shells and can be thawed in the refrigerator overnight. At the Pensacola Hilton, Executive Chef Ken Dyer prepares them with a wonderfully silky Chardonnay sauce and garnishes the finished dish with a colorful julienne of vegetables.

4 6- to 7-ounce spiny lobster tails
1 cup butter or margarine, melted
½ cup bottled clam juice
1 pint heavy cream
½ cup Chardonnay wine
6 ounces bay scallops, halved
6 ounces small bay shrimp, shelled and deveined
1 small red bell pepper
1 small carrot
1 small zucchini squash

Make a lengthwise cut down the top center of each lobster tail, pry open, and peel the meat out of the shell. Close empty shell and place the lobster meat directly on top. Pour melted butter over the tails. Preheat oven to 350 degrees and bake 10 to 12 minutes, or until the meat loses its transparency. Keep warm.

In a saucepan heat clam juice over medium heat and reduce by one-half. Add cream and wine and reduce again by one-half. Add scallops and shrimp. Cook for 2 to 3 minutes. Keep warm.

Cut the red bell pepper, carrot, and zucchini into very fine julienne strips. Blanch in boiling water for 30 seconds. Remove, refresh under cold water. Drain well.

To assemble, place lobsters on individual serving plates, top with Chardonnay sauce, and garnish with vegetables.

CHILLED LOBSTER
AND SHRIMP SALAD

Serves 6

1 rock lobster tail, cooked (about 1 cup meat)
2 pounds medium shrimp, shelled,
deveined, and cooked
1 cup peeled, seeded, and chopped cucumber
¼ cup chopped green bell pepper
1 stalk celery, including leaves, chopped fine
⅔ cup peeled and seeded tomato
¼ cup sliced pimiento-stuffed olives
½ cup chopped scallions
3 tablespoons drained capers
½ cup olive oil
⅓ cup white wine vinegar
½ teaspoon salt or to taste
ground white pepper to taste

Cut the lobster meat into bite-size pieces and halve the shrimp. Combine the seafood with remaining ingredients except the oil, vinegar, and seasonings.

In a small bowl combine oil, vinegar, salt, and pepper, whisking to mix well. Pour over salad ingredients and mix. Cover bowl with plastic wrap and chill several hours or overnight. Serve in lettuce-leaf cups.

OYSTER STEW

Serves 6

*E*very cook in the South has a personal method of preparing oyster stew. In most cases the simpler the recipe, the better. Savor the delicate taste of oysters in this seductively creamy soup.

½ cup butter
1 quart oysters, drained
2 quarts half-and-half
2 teaspoons salt (less if using salted butter)
1 teaspoon ground white pepper
½ teaspoon paprika
6 tablespoons chopped celery leaves

Melt butter in a large saucepan. Add oysters and sauté about 3 or 4 minutes, or until the edges begin to curl. Add half-and-half, salt, and pepper. Heat to boiling, but do not allow to boil.

To serve, pour into individual soup plates or a heated tureen, sprinkle with paprika, and garnish with celery leaves.

Florida Lobster Chardonnay.

DILL-FRIED OYSTERS

Serves 6

*T*he oyster beds around Apalachicola in Florida's Pan-handle have been famous for generations. All along the upper coast and into Alabama and Mississippi these tasty mollusks are prepared in multitudinous ways. Here is a new twist on fried oysters, as enjoyed on the Deep South coast of the Gulf.

2 eggs, beaten
½ cup dill pickle juice
½ cup fine-chopped dill pickle
2 teaspoons salt
½ teaspoon pepper
2 pints oysters, drained
¼ teaspoon dried dill weed
2 cups flour

DILL SAUCE

⅔ cup chopped dill pickle
½ cup sour cream
¾ cup mayonnaise

Combine eggs, pickle juice, chopped pickle, salt, and pepper. Add oysters and marinate for 1 hour.

Combine dill weed and flour. Drain oysters and dredge in flour. Fry at 375 degrees in 2 to 3 inches of oil for 3 to 5 minutes, or until golden brown. Serve with Dill Sauce.

To make Dill Sauce, combine ingredients and mix thoroughly.

OYSTERS ROASTED IN THE SHELL

*A*s a boy growing up in Pensacola, seafood connoisseur Herb Barranger fished miles of coast along the Florida Panhandle and in Alabama. On his way home from school, and later from work, he stopped to net mullet that were then grilled for dinner the same night. But one of his favorite occasions was the oyster roast. These are his instructions for this traditional feast.

The main requirements for an oyster roast are sacks of oysters and a hot charcoal fire. It helps to have as many grills as there are couples to share the bounty, along with several sauces for "dipping and sopping."

Place the oysters on grill racks over hot fires and cover them with wet burlap sacks; steam for about 20 minutes. This opens the shells slightly and makes it easier to insert an oyster knife or beer-can opener to pry open the shell. Wear heavy gloves for this! The oysters can be eaten immediately with lemon or red sauce, but Herb makes a garlic butter using ½ cup melted and slightly browned butter for each clove of garlic. He spoons the garlic butter over the opened halves and puts them back on the grill until the "skirts ruffle." With bread to sop up the juices, a good salad, and ice-cold beer, it's a great and satisfying meal.

Dill-Fried Oysters.

CURRIED SCALLOPS

Serves 4

4 tablespoons butter
½ teaspoon curry powder
1 pound bay scallops
½ cup dry white wine
1 cup heavy cream, divided
salt and white pepper to taste
2 egg yolks
2 cups hot cooked rice
2 scallions, chopped, including tops
chutney

Melt butter in heavy saucepan; add curry powder and mix well. Add scallops and sauté for 1 to 2 minutes. Remove from pan.

Deglaze pan with wine and reduce by half. Add ¾ cup cream, salt, and white pepper. Boil for about 2 minutes; reduce heat.

Beat yolks with remaining ¼ cup cream and add a little of the hot sauce, mixing well. Pour yolk mixture into sauce and stir to thicken. Be sure that the sauce does not boil or egg yolk will curdle. Stir in scallops and heat well but do not boil.

Serve in individual shells over cooked rice, topped with chopped scallions and chutney.

CREAMED SCALLOPS FLAMBÉES

Serves 6

1 cup dry white wine
2 pounds scallops
6 tablespoons butter
1 8-ounce package mushrooms, sliced
⅓ cup diced red bell pepper
½ cup fine-chopped scallion tops
2 tablespoons brandy
⅔ cup heavy cream
1 tablespoon Pernod or other anise-flavored liqueur
salt and pepper to taste
2 teaspoons cornstarch dissolved in
1 tablespoon water (optional)

In a saucepan bring wine to a simmer. Add scallops and poach for 1 minute. Remove and drain. Discard wine.

Melt butter in a heavy skillet and sauté mushrooms, bell pepper, and scallions for about 2 minutes. Add reserved scallops. Pour brandy over the dish and flame. Add cream, Pernod, and seasonings; bring to a boil for about 1 minute to reduce cream to a sauce consistency.

For a thicker sauce, dissolve cornstarch in water and stir into mixture.

Serve over pasta or rice.

CURRIED SHELLFISH STEW

Serves 8

*T*his marvelous stew is from the files of gourmet and professional cook Carol Maupin. It would be a good choice to serve in place of oyster stew and could become a holiday tradition in your house.

¼ cup butter
1 tablespoon fine-chopped onion
2 teaspoons curry powder
½ pound raw shrimp, shelled, deveined, and sliced
¼ pound sea scallops, sliced
½ pound lump crabmeat
3 cups milk
2 cups half-and-half
2 tablespoons sherry
salt and white pepper to taste
6 or 8 saltine crackers
chopped parsley

Melt butter in a heavy saucepan and sauté onion until soft. Add curry powder and cook 1 minute. Mix in shrimp and scallops and cook 2 minutes. Add the crabmeat, milk, and half-and-half; bring to a boil and immediately remove from heat.

Add sherry and salt and pepper. Let stand over hot water until ready to serve.

Just before serving, crush crackers and add to the soup. Serve garnished with chopped parsley.

SHELLFISH SALAD

Serves 6 to 8

*C*hilled shellfish salad is always a popular lunch dish. This one is based on a creamed cottage cheese sauce and is excellent served over thick slices of juicy red tomatoes.

1 cup creamed cottage cheese
¼ cup mayonnaise
1 teaspoon lemon juice
¼ teaspoon ground white pepper
¼ teaspoon salt
1 tablespoon dill weed
2 tablespoons chopped onion
¼ cup fine-chopped red bell pepper
1 tablespoon drained capers
1 pound lump crabmeat
1 pound small cooked shrimp (51 to 60 count)
¼ cup blanched slivered almonds (optional)

Combine cottage cheese, mayonnaise, lemon juice, pepper, salt, dill weed, and onion in a blender or food processor and mix until smooth. Fold in remaining ingredients and taste to correct seasonings.

Chill well and serve on tomato slices or in lettuce cups.

Oysters Roasted in the Shell (see page 67).

"Topless" oysters are a seafood specialty of the Florida Panhandle.

SHELLFISH AMANDINE EN COQUILLES

Serves 8

*T*he unusual combination of a cottage cheese–based sauce with seafood is surprisingly good. Vary the proportions of shellfish to suit your tastes, or substitute or add scallops if you like.

2 cups creamed cottage cheese
1 tablespoon Worcestershire sauce
1 teaspoon lemon juice
½ teaspoon ground white pepper
3 tablespoons Sercial Madeira wine
2 tablespoons chopped onion
2 tablespoons pink peppercorns, softened in hot water and drained
2 tablespoons oil-packed sun-dried tomatoes, chopped
2 tablespoons oil from tomatoes
2 pounds lump crabmeat
2 pounds cooked small shrimp (51 to 60 count)
½ teaspoon salt or to taste
2 tablespoons butter
½ cup dry bread crumbs
2 tablespoons grated Parmesan cheese
½ teaspoon paprika
½ cup sliced almonds

In a blender or food processor combine the cottage cheese, Worcestershire sauce, lemon juice, pepper, Madeira, and onion. Mix until smooth but not liquified. Fold in peppercorns, tomatoes, oil, seafood, and salt. Divide the mixture among eight ramekins or shells.

In a skillet melt butter and add bread crumbs, tossing to cover. Mix in Parmesan cheese, paprika, and almonds. Divide the mixture and sprinkle over each ramekin. Preheat oven to 350 degrees and bake about 20 minutes, or until hot and bubbly and lightly brown on top.

A Mobile mansion stands proud.

SHELLFISH AND RICE CASSEROLE

Serves 8 to 10

This takes me back to the first dinner parties we gave as brides—and very nervous hostesses. How we did mine the casserole ideas, canned-soup sauces, and any other sure-fire dishes we could find. Then we discovered "cuisine" as opposed to "food." Becoming a little more self-assured, we ventured into the world of "haut cuisine" with its sauces and reductions, terrines and quenelles. Having done that stint, we've come full circle back to the casserole-salad-dessert dinner theme. And high time, too.

1 cup bottled clam juice
1 cup dry white wine
½ cup water
1 cup uncooked rice
8 tablespoons butter, divided
⅓ cup flour
2 cups milk
½ cup Amontillado sherry
1½ teaspoons salt
1 8-ounce package mushrooms, sliced
1 small red bell pepper, chopped fine
¼ cup chopped parsley
½ cup chopped scallion tops
2 cups cooked shrimp
1 cup lump crabmeat
1 cup cooked bay scallops
2 cooked rock lobster tails, sliced
⅔ cup sliced almonds
½ teaspoon paprika

In a large saucepan mix clam juice, wine, and water. Add rice and cook until liquid is absorbed.

In a separate pan, melt half the butter. Add flour and stir for 2 minutes. Add milk and stir until mixture thickens. Add sherry and salt.

In a skillet, melt remaining butter; add mushrooms, bell pepper, parsley, and scallion tops and sauté for several minutes. Do not brown.

Combine rice, sauce, and sautéed vegetables, mixing well. Fold in seafood. Taste to correct seasonings. Turn mixture into a buttered casserole and sprinkle with almonds and paprika. Preheat oven to 375 degrees and bake about 25 minutes, or until heated through and slightly brown on top.

SOUTHERN SOUSED SHRIMP

Serves 12 to 18

Each section of the country has its own way of pickling shrimp. This one is typical of the southern Gulf Coast and is excellent cocktail party fare.

1 cup olive oil, divided
4 cloves garlic, chopped fine
2 medium onions, sliced thin
4 pounds shrimp, shelled and deveined
¼ cup white wine vinegar
¼ cup lemon juice
¼ cup dry vermouth
2 lemons, sliced very thin
10 scallions, including tops, chopped fine
2 teaspoons salt
2 teaspoons dry mustard
¼ teaspoon cayenne pepper or to taste
½ teaspoon mustard seed
1-inch piece of fresh ginger root, sliced very thin

Heat ½ cup olive oil in a heavy skillet. Sauté garlic and onions until transparent but not brown. Add shrimp and cook, stirring constantly, just until opaque. Remove from heat and cool.

In a glass or noncorrosive bowl, make a marinade from the remaining oil and remaining ingredients. Add cooled shrimp and onion mixture; mix thoroughly. Chill 6 hours or more, stirring occasionally. Serve cold, but not cold enough to congeal the oil.

SHRIMP COCKTAIL

Serves 8

Unlike many shrimp cocktail recipes, this one contains no tomatoes and should be made early in the day so that it can marinate several hours before serving.

1 cup olive oil
½ cup white wine vinegar
2 tablespoons chopped parsley
⅔ cup chopped scallions, including green tops
1 rib of celery, chopped fine
2 tablespoons coarse-grained mustard
1 teaspoon salt
¼ teaspoon paprika
⅛ teaspoon cayenne pepper
ground white pepper to taste
2½ pounds shelled, deveined, and cooked shrimp
1 bunch of fresh spinach leaves, washed and dried

Whisk together all ingredients except shrimp and spinach. Fold dressing into shrimp, cover, and refrigerate several hours before serving. Serve on a bed of shredded spinach leaves.

Deviled Crab with Avocados (see page 64); Shellfish and Rice Casserole; and Southern Soused Shrimp.

Moored sailboats float sleepily at a Pensacola Bay dock during the off-season.

SHRIMP FETTUCCINE

Serves 6 to 8

*F*rom Mobile, Chef Henry Douglas of the Radisson Admiral Semmes Hotel shares this recipe for a fettuccine dish that is rich and silky, familiar and comforting all at the same time. The brandy adds an elusive flavor that gives the dish a nice snap. This kind of attention to detail has won Chef Henry the "Taste of Mobile" award three times.

3 quarts water
1½ pounds spinach fettuccine
¾ cup vegetable or olive oil, divided
1 pound medium shrimp, shelled and deveined
4 cloves garlic, crushed
½ cup brandy
1½ cups heavy cream
salt and ground white pepper to taste
1 cup freshly grated Parmesan cheese

In a large pot bring water to a boil. Add fettuccine and return to a boil for 3 minutes, or until the pasta is cooked but still firm—*al dente*. Drain, rinse with cold water, and drain again. Transfer to a large warm bowl, add ¼ cup oil, and toss gently. Cover and set aside.

Pour remaining oil in a large skillet and place over medium heat. When hot, add shrimp and sauté 1 minute. Add garlic and brandy and sauté for 2 minutes. Add cream, cooked fettuccine, salt, and pepper. Simmer 5 minutes. Remove from heat and sprinkle with cheese, tossing well. Serve at once.

STUFFED SHRIMP HORS D'OEUVRES

Serves 4

*S*hrimp prepared in this manner is neither a salad nor a cocktail but something of both. Highly seasoned cream cheese stuffs the shrimp. It is served on a bed of dark green spinach leaves, fine-shredded red cabbage, and creamy spears of Belgian endive and, finally, dressed with a garlicky vinaigrette. Buy the largest shrimp you can find. Since they will be cleaned and butterflied before cooking, you'll find that as soon as they are put in hot water, they will fan out and curl into neat little "cups" that can be filled with the cheese mixture.

12 jumbo shrimp, shelled (with tail intact) and deveined
water seasoned with a slice of onion, ½ lemon, ½ teaspoon salt, and dash of cayenne pepper
1 3-ounce package cream cheese
1 tablespoon cream
3 teaspoons dill pickle relish
1 tablespoon fine-chopped parsley
1 tablespoon fine-chopped scallion tops
liberal dash of Tabasco Pepper Sauce
1 bunch of fresh spinach, washed and stemmed
1 cup shredded red cabbage
12 Belgian endive leaves
Basic Vinaigrette Dressing (p. 207)

Make a cut lengthwise in the vein side of each shrimp, slicing only about halfway through so that the flesh will hold together. Cook in seasoned water until barely done. Drain and cool.

Combine cream cheese, cream, relish, parsley, scallion tops, and Tabasco sauce; mix well. Place a spoonful of filling on each shrimp. Cover and chill in refrigerator until ready to use.

To serve, make a bed of whole spinach leaves and shredded cabbage on each plate. Place three shrimp in the center and arrange three endive leaves decoratively around the shrimp. Drizzle with vinaigrette.

A shrimp boat shares its territory with an offshore oil rig.

SHRIMP, CHICKEN, AND SAUSAGE JAMBALAYA, MOBILE STYLE

Serves 4 to 6

*T*he increased travel and commerce along the Alabama-Mississippi-Louisiana coast over the past one hundred years has inspired some interesting cuisine that combines elements of Southern cooking with similar Creole and Cajun traditions. This jambalaya, served by Chef Henry Douglas, is a good example of adaptive cooking techniques. It remains a Southern dish nicely flavored with Acadian inspiration.

½ cup vegetable oil
½ pound smoked sausage, sliced
1 pound medium shrimp, shelled and deveined
½ pound breast of chicken, boned,
skinned, and cubed
1 cup chopped onion
½ cup chopped green bell pepper
1 cup chopped celery
1 cup chopped scallions, including tops
1 clove garlic, chopped fine
1 16-ounce can tomatoes, drained (reserve liquid)
1 teaspoon ground black pepper
¼ teaspoon cayenne pepper
1 teaspoon salt (or less if using salted stock)
1 cup converted rice
1½ cups chicken stock
1½ tablespoons Worcestershire sauce
chopped parsley

In a large heavy pot heat oil. Sauté sausage, shrimp, and chicken until lightly browned. Remove with a slotted spoon and set aside.

In the same oil sauté onion, pepper, celery, scallions, and garlic until the onion is translucent. Add drained tomatoes, black pepper, cayenne pepper, and salt. Cook 5 minutes. Stir in rice. Mix together reserved liquid from the tomatoes, stock, and Worcestershire sauce to equal 2½ cups and add to rice mixture. Bring to a boil, then reduce heat to a simmer. Add sausage, shrimp, and chicken and cook, uncovered, for about 30 minutes or until rice is done. Stir occasionally during cooking.

When ready to serve, spoon into a serving dish and sprinkle with parsley.

*An early-morning beachcomber
disturbs gulls feeding along a beach.*

PENSACOLA SEAFOOD KABOBS WITH CARDINALE SAUCE

Serves 4

*C*hef Ken Dyer at the Pensacola Hilton dresses up this mixed seafood grill with a wonderfully rich sauce that can be served separately for purists and weight-watchers.

1 large yellow bell pepper, cut into 8 pieces
1 large red bell pepper, cut into 8 pieces
1 small green bell pepper, cut into 8 pieces
1 pound swordfish fillets, cut into 8 pieces
12 large shrimp, shelled and deveined
16 large scallops
4 cherry tomatoes
8 medium mushroom caps
1 red onion, cut into 8 pieces
vegetable oil
salt to taste

CARDINALE SAUCE

½ cup clam juice
1 pint heavy cream
2 tablespoons ground thyme
1 tablespoon fine-chopped shallots or onion
4 ounces lump crabmeat

Blanch the peppers in boiling water for 1 minute. Refresh in cold water and drain thoroughly.

Thread peppers, seafoods, tomatoes, mushrooms, and onion onto four 12-inch skewers in a uniform and colorful manner. Grill over a charcoal fire or broil under the broiler for 8 to 10 minutes, brushing with oil and turning several times. Sprinkle lightly with salt.

To make Cardinale Sauce, heat clam juice in a heavy saucepan and reduce by half. Add cream, thyme, and shallots and reduce again by half. Stir in crabmeat and taste to correct seasonings.

To serve, remove kabobs from skewers and pour sauce over each serving as desired.

SEAFOOD SAUCE OVER OMELETTE SHORTCAKE

Serves 8

*W*hat to serve for lunch, brunch, or that pre-theater supper is sometimes a puzzle. Carol Maupin, whose traditional style of cooking has its roots in the Deep South, has a good solution. Carol is a protégé of the late Helen Corbitt and worked with her over a number of years at the Junior League Tearoom and Neiman-Marcus in Houston. Carol puts her own stamp of individuality on each dish she prepares, giving Helen Corbitt credit for the original inspiration. Any seafood will be satisfactory in the sauce, which also lends itself to additional seasonings such as dill weed, curry powder, lemon or lime zests, and so on.

SEAFOOD SAUCE

3 tablespoons butter
3 tablespoons flour
1 cup half-and-half
1 cup chicken broth
½ cup dry white wine
2 cups cooked seafood, chopped (shrimp, crab, lobster, or any white fish)
salt and white pepper to taste

OMELETTE SHORTCAKE

4 tablespoons butter, divided
1 8-ounce package mushrooms, sliced
8 large eggs, separated
1 teaspoon salt
⅛ teaspoon ground white pepper
4 tablespoons flour
1 shallot, chopped fine
chopped parsley

To make Seafood Sauce, melt butter in a heavy saucepan. Add flour and cook until bubbly. Stir in half-and-half, chicken broth, and wine. Stirring constantly, cook until sauce has thickened.

Fold in seafood, salt and pepper, and optional herbs or spices. Simmer about 5 minutes over low heat. Keep hot in a double boiler until ready to serve.

To make Omelette Shortcake, melt 2 tablespoons butter in a skillet and sauté mushrooms until golden. Set aside.

Beat egg yolks until lemon-colored and smooth. Beat in salt, pepper, and flour. Set aside.

Melt remaining butter and add shallot. Sauté 1 minute. Pour into two 9-inch round cake pans and spread to cover the bottoms and sides. Set aside.

Beat egg whites until stiff and fold into reserved yolk mixture. Divide between the two cake pans and spread evenly in pans. Preheat oven to 350 degrees and bake about 15 minutes, or until a cake tester comes out clean.

To serve, invert one pan onto the serving dish to release the omelette. Cover with half the Seafood Sauce. Stack with second omelette and cover with remaining sauce. Spoon reserved mushrooms over the top and garnish with parsley.

AMBERJACK MOUSSE LOAF

Serves 8 to 10

*T*his fish loaf stirs up memories of ladies' summer lunches in the South. My grandmother served this and similar dishes accompanied by cold asparagus (canned, in those days) and usually a pickled peach. There was always iced tea with fresh mint from the garden and fresh fruit and cookies for dessert. It's a nostalgic culinary memory.

4 egg yolks
2 tablespoons dry mustard
¼ teaspoon cayenne pepper
1 teaspoon salt
½ teaspoon ground white pepper
2 cups milk
2 envelopes unflavored gelatin
1 cup cold water
4 tablespoons white wine vinegar
½ cup mayonnaise
2 tablespoons chopped fresh dill
(or 1 tablespoon dried dill)
½ cup chopped scallions
½ cup fine-chopped red bell pepper
2½ cups cooked amberjack fillets, flaked
(about 1½ pounds)

CUCUMBER SAUCE

1 small cucumber, unpeeled, grated, and
squeezed dry (about ⅔ cup)
1 cup sour cream
4 tablespoons mayonnaise
salt to taste

Beat together egg yolks, dry mustard, cayenne pepper, salt, and white pepper. Add milk and cook over hot water, stirring constantly until mixture has a thin custard consistency. Remove from heat.

Soften gelatin in cold water. Add vinegar and mix with hot custard. Cool.

Fold remaining ingredients into cooled custard and pour into an oiled 6-cup mold. Cover with foil or plastic wrap and refrigerate overnight.

To make Cucumber Sauce, mix ingredients and refrigerate until ready to use.

To serve mousse, unmold on a serving dish and garnish with thin slices of cucumber and sprigs of fresh dill or parsley. Serve with Cucumber Sauce.

As a variation, the egg whites from the eggs used in this recipe can be whipped and folded into the cooled custard mixture just before it is poured into the mold and refrigerated. This makes a dish with a somewhat lighter texture and greater volume, so an 8-cup mold is needed.

The crowded harbor at Bayou La Batre is Alabama's busiest seafood port.

An old-timer checks his crab traps at Bay St. Louis, Mississippi.

AMBERJACK CHOWDER

Serves 6 to 8

*T*his recipe is also good with other fish varieties that are more assertive in flavor. The fennel seasoning is a good match for a stronger-flavored fish.

½ pound bacon, cut into 1-inch pieces
1 small onion, halved and sliced thin
4 medium potatoes, peeled and cubed (about 3 cups)
1 small green bell pepper, seeded and sliced thin
1½ teaspoons salt
¼ teaspoon ground black pepper
½ tablespoon fennel seeds, crushed
2 cups water
4 cups milk or half-and-half
1 pound amberjack fillets, cut into 1-inch pieces
4 tablespoons chopped parsley
1 tablespoon fresh chopped fennel leaves (optional)

Brown bacon pieces in a heavy pot. Remove and drain on paper towels.

Add onion to the bacon fat and cook 5 minutes but do not brown. Add potatoes, bell pepper, salt, black pepper, fennel seeds, and water. Cover and cook until potatoes are tender.

Add milk and fish. Cook about 5 to 8 minutes or until fish is done. Add parsley and fennel leaves; taste to correct seasonings.

Apalachicola's annual Oyster Festival attracts a smorgasbord of seafood concessionaires.

GULF SNAPPER FRANGELICO

Serves 4

*C*hef Ken Dyer of the Pensacola Hilton developed this dish using the liqueur that is everyone's favorite these days. Frangelico, cream, and pecans combine to make a terrific sauce for the fish. The alcohol evaporates during cooking, leaving a delicately flavored cream sauce accented with crisp pecans.

½ pound unsalted butter or margarine, melted
4 8-ounce red snapper fillets
½ cup dry white wine
¼ cup fresh lemon juice
1 pint heavy cream
¼ cup Frangelico liqueur
1 cup chopped pecans
chopped parsley

Butter a baking dish with part of the melted butter. Place fillets on the dish. Combine wine and lemon juice and pour over fish. Preheat oven to 350 degrees and bake for 10 to 12 minutes, or until fish flakes easily.

Meanwhile, combine cream, liqueur, and pecans in a saucepan and cook over medium heat until reduced by half. Divide evenly over fillets and garnish with parsley.

CHEF HENRY'S YELLOWFIN GROUPER WITH DILL-DIJON MUSTARD SAUCE

Serves 6

*C*hef Henry Douglas combines dill with Dijon mustard for a tangy sauce that complements the sweet flavor of grouper or other similar fish.

6 6-ounce yellowfin grouper fillets
flour seasoned with salt and pepper
¼ cup vegetable oil
6 tablespoons butter
watercress or parsley

DILL-DIJON MUSTARD SAUCE

¾ cup chicken stock
⅓ cup dry white wine
1 cup heavy cream
2 teaspoons dried dill weed
3 tablespoons Dijon mustard
juice of 1 lemon

Dredge fish in seasoned flour, shaking off excess.

Heat oil and butter in a skillet and sauté fillets for 2 to 3 minutes on each side, or until golden. Drain on paper towels.

To make Dill-Dijon Mustard Sauce, combine stock, wine, and cream in a small saucepan. Reduce by one-half, stirring constantly. Add remaining ingredients and season to taste. (If using canned stock, omit salt.) Keep warm until ready to use.

To serve fillets, arrange on a serving platter and spoon about 3 tablespoons of Dill-Dijon Mustard Sauce over each piece. Garnish with watercress or parsley.

FRIED GRITS

*W*hen I was growing up, both my grandmothers served fried grits as a breakfast dish, along with bacon and eggs. It is also a very good dish with fried fish, making an interesting change from fried potatoes. Try it with a very spicy fish dish. The combination works well.

Prepare grits according to the directions on the package, then season well with salt and butter. Pour into a loaf pan and refrigerate overnight to set.

When ready to serve, cut the grits loaf into slices or squares; dredge in seasoned flour and fry in butter or margarine until crisp and brown.

For spicier grits to accompany a mild fish dish, add grated cheese and chopped jalapeño or bell peppers to grits during cooking.

Long weathered piers jut out over the shallow waters of Mobile Bay.

LIMPING SUSAN

Serves 8

*N*o one seems to know how this dish got its name, but the recipe comes from the files of Carol Maupin. It's a wonderful Southern dish to serve with a fish stew and a green salad, followed by a great dessert.

¼ cup fine-chopped salt pork
1 cup uncooked rice
1 onion, chopped fine
3 cups chicken broth
2 cups mashed canned tomatoes
2 tablespoons chopped parsley
salt and pepper to taste
1 cup cooked whole okra
1 cup slivered cooked chicken (or shrimp)

In a heavy saucepan fry salt pork until crisp. Add rice and stir until golden brown. Add onion and cook until soft, then add broth. Reduce heat, cover, and cook about 1 hour or until rice is done.

Add tomatoes, parsley, and seasonings, stirring with a fork. Preheat oven to 325 degrees and bake, uncovered, for 30 minutes.

Just before serving add okra and chicken, mixing well.

CORN CRISPS

Makes 2 dozen

*T*hese crunchy little tidbits from the Deep South go well with seafood cocktails and salads. Carol Maupin, who shared this recipe, suggests making up a large batch so you won't run out.

1 cup water
⅞ cup cornmeal
½ teaspoon salt
1½ tablespoons melted butter
⅛ teaspoon cayenne pepper
melted butter
poppy seeds

Bring water to boil and pour over cornmeal, stirring well. Add salt, butter, and cayenne pepper and mix well.

Drop by teaspoons onto a well-buttered cookie sheet. Flatten to about ¼ inch thick with a spatula (or use your fingers after dipping them in water). Brush with melted butter and sprinkle with poppyseeds. Preheat oven to 350 degrees and bake 18 to 20 minutes or until brown around the edges. Cool on a rack.

GRITS SOUFFLÉ

Serves 6

*G*rits is a chief item in Southern cuisine. It is served as a starch at dinner, replacing the potato, and is ubiquitous on breakfast plates in Florida and parts of the eastern shores of the Gulf Coast. In this recipe Carol Maupin has adapted the late Helen Corbitt's inspiration for a soufflé made with grits. It's a fine dish indeed.

2 cups milk
½ cup grits
1 teaspoon salt
½ teaspoon baking powder
½ teaspoon sugar
2 tablespoons melted butter
3 eggs, separated

Scald the milk and add grits. Cook until thick. Add salt, baking powder, sugar, and butter.

Beat the egg yolks and add to grits mixture. Beat the egg whites until they form soft peaks and fold into grits. Pour into a well-buttered 1½-quart casserole.

Preheat oven to 325 degrees and bake, uncovered, for 25 to 30 minutes, or until puffed and brown on top.

A solitary walker explores a deserted stretch of beachfront near Gulf Shores, Alabama.

CHOCOLATE CHUNK COOKIES

Makes about 4 dozen

A little sweet something adds a nice finish to any meal. These cookies hit the spot when a big dessert is just too much, although the quantity of chocolate can be increased a bit for confirmed "chocoholics." Chef Henry Douglas counts this among his most popular buffet desserts.

1⅛ cups flour
1¼ teaspoons baking soda
½ teaspoon salt
½ cup vegetable shortening
¼ cup brown sugar
½ cup granulated sugar
1 tablespoon honey
1 teaspoon Grand Marnier
1 egg, beaten
1 teaspoon vanilla extract
½ pound semisweet chocolate, cut into chunks

Sift together flour, soda, and salt.

In a separate bowl, cream together shortening and sugars. Add honey, Grand Marnier, egg, and vanilla extract, beating thoroughly. Add the dry ingredients and fold in chocolate.

Drop from a teaspoon onto a buttered cookie sheet. Preheat oven to 350 degrees and bake for about 10 minutes. Remove from cookie sheet and cool on a rack.

A fresh coat of paint protects this charming cottage from the salt air.

This Mississippi roadside tavern is a favorite gathering place on a damp coastal night.

SPICED PECAN PIE

Serves 6 to 8

3 eggs, separated
1½ cups packed dark brown sugar
1 teaspoon ground cinnamon
1 teaspoon ground allspice
½ teaspoon ground cloves
½ teaspoon salt
2 tablespoons flour
¼ cup butter, browned
1 cup pecans, toasted
1 unbaked Basic Pastry shell (p. 208)

Mix all ingredients except pecans and egg whites, blending well. Stir in pecans.

Whip egg whites to form soft peaks. Add one-fourth of the whites to mixture and stir; then fold in remaining whites and pour into pie shell.

Preheat oven to 400 degrees and bake for 35 to 40 minutes, or just until set. Cool.

PECAN SHORTBREAD COOKIES

½ pound butter
⅔ cup powdered sugar
½ teaspoon vanilla extract
1½ cups flour
⅛ teaspoon salt
1 cup toasted and chopped pecans

Cream together butter, sugar, and vanilla extract. Work in flour and salt. Add pecans and roll into logs in waxed paper. Chill (or freeze) until firm.

Cut into ¼-inch slices and place about 2 inches apart on an ungreased baking sheet. Preheat oven to 375 degrees and bake approximately 15 minutes, or until edges are brown. Cool.

CHOCOLATE VELVET CAKE

Serves a crowd—it's rich!

*I*n *the South we do like it rich! This recipe is a favorite with guests at the Pensacola Hilton, and Chef Ken Dyer suggests serving small portions, even to a confirmed "chocoholic."*

¾ cup unsalted butter
2½ pounds semisweet chocolate
5 eggs, separated
1⅓ tablespoons instant coffee
6 tablespoons Kirschwasser liqueur or cherry brandy
6 tablespoons dark crème de cacao
½ cup creamy peanut butter
3 cups heavy cream
½ cup powdered sugar
⅛ teaspoon salt

FROSTING

8 ounces semisweet chocolate
1 tablespoon powdered sugar
3 tablespoons milk
coffee

Melt butter and chocolate together in the top of a double boiler over simmering water. Do not let the water boil or exceed a temperature of 115 degrees. Set aside.

In a large bowl mix together egg yolks, instant coffee, Kirschwasser, crème de cacao, and peanut butter. Set aside.

Whip cream to stiff peaks and set aside in the refrigerator.

Whip the egg whites to form soft peaks. Add sugar and salt and continue whipping to form stiff peaks. Set aside.

Add chocolate mixture to egg yolk mixture, stirring constantly and mixing well. Fold in beaten egg whites. Finally, fold in whipped cream. Pour into a 10-inch springform pan, cover with plastic wrap, and refrigerate overnight.

To prepare frosting, melt chocolate, sugar, and milk together in the top of a double boiler over simmering water. Thin with coffee as needed until frosting has the right consistency for spreading.

Remove cake from pan and spread frosting on top and sides. Refrigerate to set frosting. Serve in very small portions.

PINEAPPLE UPSIDE-DOWN CAKE

Serves 6 to 8

*S*outherners *like their desserts sweet and rich and their coffee strong. We used to have pineapple upside-down cake about once a month when I was growing up, but lately it seems to have disappeared from the culinary scene. At its best, it is a wonderful conglomeration of a simple cake covered with a sugary, buttery brown topping with the tangy taste of pineapple. To achieve the real thing, it must be baked in a heavy iron skillet. My friend Helyn Tucker has an easy formula for cleaning these old-fashioned utensils: set the thing in the fireplace on the hot embers just before going to bed. The next morning all the accumulated grease will be burned off, and it only needs to be wiped with a damp sponge and oiled with vegetable oil.*

1¼ cups sifted cake flour
¼ teaspoon salt
1 teaspoon baking powder
½ cup granulated sugar
½ cup milk
1 egg
1 teaspoon vanilla extract
⅓ cup shortening or butter, melted
4 tablespoons butter
½ cup brown sugar
6 pineapple slices
12 maraschino cherries
1 cup heavy cream, whipped

Sift together flour, salt, baking powder, and sugar. In a separate bowl, beat together milk, egg, and vanilla extract. Gradually add to flour mixture. Add melted shortening and beat well until batter is creamy and smooth. Set aside.

Melt butter in a heavy skillet. Add brown sugar and stir until dissolved. Spread evenly over the bottom of the skillet.

Arrange pineapple and cherries in skillet to make a decorative pattern. Top with batter.

Preheat oven to 350 degrees and bake for about 50 minutes, or until a toothpick comes out clean. Cool for about 10 minutes and turn out onto a cake plate. The topping should come out clean, but if the worst has happened, rearrange the fruit on top of the cake, spooning the sugar in between as needed.

Serve warm, topped with whipped cream.

LOUISIANA

OUISIANA'S SHORES and marshes, and bays and bayous yield a variety of seafood. Crabs and oysters are prepared in many delicious ways; shrimp of various sizes appear in soups, sauces, and stuffings; redfish, trout, flounder, and pompano are stuffed, baked, or broiled in traditional recipes. And the crawfish—which is not really a saltwater creature—is the uncrowned king of Louisiana seafood.

In Louisiana, as in France, food is taken quite seriously. Indeed, the cuisine that has developed here had its origins in France, but it has been layered many times over with Indian, Spanish, African, and West Indian influences.

Two strong traditions have shaped Louisiana's culinary history—Acadian and Creole. Acadian, or "Cajun," cuisine is country cooking. In its beginnings, necessity was the foremost ingredient. Louisiana Cajuns from southern France emigrated to Nova Scotia in the early 1600s, establishing a colony they called Acadia. The British drove the Acadians out of Canada in the mid-1700s, and many of them migrated to Louisiana, where they settled in the bayou country and resumed their life of farming, trapping, and fishing. They learned to cook anything that swam or flew, seasoning it liberally with local herbs and vegetables—okra, ground

A forest of shrimpboat masts jut over Delcambre Harbor near Vermilion Bay. A slant-drilling rig probes the substrate of southwestern Louisiana's deep marsh country.

sassafras leaves (filet gumbo), bay leaf, cayenne peppers, native bird's-eye peppers, scallions (green onions), tomatoes, garlic, bell pepper, eggplant. The Cajun dishes that are culinary landmarks today—jambalaya, gumbo, crawfish étouffée, dirty rice, and crawfish pie, among others—developed over a long period of time, with local cooks adding and subtracting ingredients as they were available. Indeed, lists of ingredients for such dishes vary greatly from one cook to another even today.

In contrast, Creole cuisine has been described as city fare—the cooking of plantation owners, fine restaurant kitchens, and affluent New Orleanians. Its rich meunière and hollandaise sauces, soufflés, casseroles, mousses, and mousselines are reminiscent of the grand cuisine of France—in dishes like crabmeat au gratin, shrimp Creole, and oysters Bienville. But despite its upper-class origins, Creole cooking has incorporated many Cajun ingredients, such as rice, scallions, okra, Tabasco sauce, and roux—that mixture of skillet-browned oil and flour used to flavor gumbo and countless other Louisiana dishes.

Today the distinction between these two cooking styles has blurred, and all Louisianans can enjoy the exceptional food that is their heritage.

A Chauvin shipbuilder eyes his work. Oyster boats sit idle at their moorings alongside weathered Grand Isle piers.

Gas and oil rigs dot the tide-lands of the Mississippi Delta.

In Cajun country, music and dancing, food and fellowship are the ingredients of almost any weekend.

A Cajun trio sets up toe-tapping rhythms down by the Bayou Teche. An Acadian beauty browses in the open-air French Market. Gloomy crypts of an ancient cemetery in New Orleans' Garden District rise above soggy ground. Twenty-eight live oak trees, now more than two centuries old, form a canopy at the entrance to the historic Oak Alley Plantation.

On Bourbon Street a red-veiled
Mardi Gras celebrant pauses to
make a phone call.

French Quarter architecture features delicate
ironwork, graceful balconies, and shuttered
windows dating back to the eighteenth
century.

Ralph and Kacoo's Crab Finger Hors D'Oeuvre.

HOT CRABMEAT DIP

Serves 6 to 8

*M*organ City's Janet Robinson is around seafood a lot—her son-in-law's Bay Ice and Seafood Company distributes seafood all over Louisiana. Janet is a natural cook who loves to entertain. At cocktail parties she often serves this crabmeat dish with corn chips to dip in it. When spooned into small pastry shells, it makes an elegant entrée.

½ cup butter, divided
1 rib celery, chopped fine
1 small onion, chopped fine
½ cup sliced fresh mushrooms
2 tablespoons chopped parsley
1 8-ounce package cream cheese
1 pound crabmeat
½ teaspoon Tabasco Pepper Sauce
⅛ teaspoon cayenne pepper

In a skillet melt half of the butter and sauté celery, onion, mushrooms, and parsley until soft. Set aside.

Melt remaining butter with cream cheese in the top of a double boiler or in a microwave, mixing well.

Combine the two mixtures, then fold in crabmeat and seasoning.

Keep hot in a chafing dish and serve with corn chips or spoon into patty shells and serve at once.

RALPH AND KACOO'S CRAB FINGER HORS D'OEUVRE

*O*ne of the favorite "Heart Healthy" dishes at all the Ralph and Kacoo's restaurants in Louisiana is this crab finger hors d'oeuvre. The sauce should marinate for an hour or so to develop the flavors, which makes it a marvelously easy party dish to prepare ahead of time. Try the sauce with shrimp or lobster tails. In fact, it is also good for binding cold seafood salads.

32 cooked crab claws
½ cup red wine vinegar
¼ cup lemon juice
1 teaspoon chopped tarragon leaves
10 cloves garlic, chopped fine
1 cup chopped scallions
1 cup chopped parsley
1 cup chopped celery
¾ teaspoon salt
¾ teaspoon sugar
¾ teaspoon ground black pepper
1 cup olive oil

Crack the crab claws and remove half the shell. Refrigerate until ready to use.

Mix remaining ingredients except the olive oil, making sure that the salt and sugar have dissolved. Mix in the olive oil and refrigerate.

When ready to serve, arrange crab claws on a serving platter and cover with sauce.

SAUTÉED SOFTSHELL CRAB
WITH ROASTED PECANS
AND LEMON MEUNIÈRE

Serves 1

*B*rigtsen's Restaurant in New Orleans became an acclaimed landmark of Louisiana cooking just four months after it opened. Chef and owner Frank Brigtsen received his most important training at K-Paul's under the tutelage of the famed Paul Prudhomme and claims his "Modern Louisiana" style derives from a blend of Paul's Cajun cooking, the Creole food of New Orleans, and the new American cuisine which has developed during the past ten years. Critics agree that he is one of the most innovative interpreters of Louisiana cuisine. The following recipe showcases his originality.

¾ cup flour
1 tablespoon Creole seasoning powder, divided
1 jumbo softshell crab, cleaned
¼ cup clarified butter
1 tablespoon plus 1 teaspoon
unsalted butter, divided
¼ cup roasted pecans
1 tablespoon thin-sliced scallions
⅛ teaspoon minced garlic
2 drops Worcestershire sauce
¼ cup fish stock
3 drops fresh lemon juice

Combine flour with 1 teaspoon seasoning powder and set aside. Season crab with about 1 teaspoon seasoning powder.

Heat a heavy skillet over medium-high heat and add clarified butter. Dredge crab in seasoned flour, shake off excess, and sauté about 1½ to 2 minutes or until golden brown. Turn and cook about 1 to 1½ minutes on second side, or until done. (Frank notes that softshell crabs "pop" while they cook, so be careful.) Drain crab on paper towels.

Discard half of the clarified butter and return skillet to heat. Add 1 teaspoon softened unsalted butter and cook about 10 to 15 seconds or until dark brown, shaking skillet constantly. Add pecans, scallions, garlic, and ⅛ teaspoon of the seasoning powder; cook for 10 seconds. Add Worcestershire sauce, stock, and lemon juice. Bring to a boil. Add remaining tablespoon of unsalted butter and shake skillet until butter has been completely incorporated. Remove from heat.

To serve, remove pecans and scallions with a slotted spoon and pour sauce onto plate. Add crab and top with pecan mixture.

A diner enjoys the elegant ambience of a typical French Quarter restaurant.

GALATOIRE'S
CRABMEAT MAISON

Serves 6

*W*ith its antique ceiling fans and rows of large mirrors, Galatoire's in New Orleans is unmistakably a turn-of-the-century Creole restaurant. The waiters serve their many regular customers with old-style friendliness. A longtime favorite is this crabmeat appetizer.

½ cup mayonnaise (preferably homemade)
3 tablespoons French Dressing
3 scallions, chopped fine
1 teaspoon small capers, drained
½ teaspoon chopped parsley
1 pound lump crabmeat
6 lettuce cups
12 slices of tomato
lemon juice

FRENCH DRESSING

½ cup white wine vinegar
2 tablespoons Creole mustard or other coarse-grained mustard
1½ cups olive oil
½ teaspoon salt
⅛ teaspoon ground white pepper

To make French Dressing, mix together vinegar and mustard. Slowly whisk in olive oil, a little at a time, to form an emulsion. Season with salt and pepper.

To assemble salad, mix together mayonnaise, dressing, scallions, capers, and parsley. Fold in crabmeat carefully to preserve the lumps. Divide in six equal portions and serve each in a lettuce cup with two slices of tomato on the side. Squeeze lemon juice over the salad just before serving.

GALATOIRE'S CRABMEAT YVONNE

Serves 6

6 artichokes
1 pound mushrooms, sliced
½ cup clarified butter
2 pounds backfin lump crabmeat
salt to taste
ground white pepper to taste
¼ cup fine-chopped parsley
6 lemon wedges

Bring a large pot of water to a boil. Cut stem from artichokes flush with the base and boil artichokes for 45 minutes, or until a leaf pulls off easily. Remove from pot, drain, and cool. Pull off leaves and reserve for another purpose. Remove choke and slice the bottoms. Set aside.

In a large skillet sauté mushrooms in clarified butter. Add reserved artichoke bottoms and crabmeat. Heat through, stirring gently. Season with salt and pepper and sprinkle with parsley. Serve on toast points with a lemon wedge on the side.

CRAB IMPERIAL

Serves 8

Supercook Kathy Leonard of Lafayette developed this recipe, which incorporates her mother's famous mayonnaise recipe. The dish could be served as a main course or, in smaller portions, as a delectable first course for a larger party.

2 eggs
1 green bell pepper, chopped fine
1 4-ounce jar chopped pimientos
1 tablespoon dry mustard
1 teaspoon salt
½ teaspoon ground white pepper
⅛ teaspoon cayenne pepper or to taste
1 cup Helen Burdin's Mayonnaise
3 pounds lump crabmeat
paprika

HELEN BURDIN'S MAYONNAISE

3 eggs
3 teaspoons salt
3 teaspoons dry mustard
3 teaspoons sugar
dash of Tabasco Pepper Sauce
¼ teaspoon cayenne pepper
4¾ cups vegetable oil, divided
juice of ½ lemon

In a large mixing bowl beat eggs well. Add bell pepper, pimientos, dry mustard, salt, white pepper, cayenne pepper, and mayonnaise. Mix well. Fold in the crabmeat carefully. Do not break up the lumps.

Divide the mixture among eight ramekins or spoon into a 13-by-9-inch ovenproof dish. Top with a thin layer of mayonnaise and sprinkle with paprika. Preheat oven to 350 degrees and bake for 10 to 15 minutes or until heated through.

To make Helen Burdin's Mayonnaise, mix the eggs, salt, dry mustard, sugar, Tabasco sauce, and cayenne pepper in a mixer or food processor. Add half the oil in a slow but steady stream. Add lemon juice, then the remaining oil. Mix only until all the oil is incorporated in a smooth emulsion.

HAZEL WHITITH'S CRAWFISH ETOUFFÉE

Serves 4

*F*rom the files of the test kitchens of McIlhenny Company, which makes Tabasco Pepper Sauce, comes this easy version of a classic Acadian dish.

¼ cup vegetable oil
1 cup fine-chopped onion
½ cup fine-chopped celery
½ cup fine-chopped green bell pepper
2 cloves garlic, crushed
1 tablespoon tomato paste
1 teaspoon cornstarch
¾ cup fish stock
1 pound shelled crawfish tails (or shrimp)
1 cup thin-sliced scallions
¼ cup chopped parsley
½ teaspoon Tabasco Pepper Sauce
¼ teaspoon salt or to taste
hot cooked rice

In a large skillet heat oil over medium-high heat. Add onion, celery, bell pepper, and garlic. Cook 8 to 10 minutes or until tender, stirring frequently. Stir in tomato paste and cook 1 minute.

In a small bowl combine cornstarch and fish stock, stirring until smooth. Add to vegetables in skillet and bring to a boil, stirring constantly. Add crawfish, scallions, parsley, Tabasco sauce, and salt. Cook 5 minutes or until crawfish are tender, stirring frequently. Serve over hot rice.

Hazel Whitith's Crawfish Etouffée.

A vendor arranges his fruits and vegetables before a busy market day.

Deep in the Atchafalaya River country, the Sidney Horton family shares a Saturday afternoon crab and shrimp boil.

Mr. B's Crawfish and Fettuccine.

MR. B'S CRAWFISH AND FETTUCCINE

Serves 4

*H*ere is one of the signature dishes of Mr. B's restaurant in New Orleans.

1 cup cold unsalted butter, cut into
tablespoon-size pieces
⅔ cup chopped mixed red and green bell peppers
⅔ cup chopped onions
2 cups cooked and shelled crawfish tails
½ teaspoon Brennan's Creole Seasoning
for Fish (p. 202) or to taste
⅛ teaspoon crushed red chilies or to taste
⅔ cup chopped peeled tomatoes
4 tablespoons sliced scallions
1 pound fettuccine, cooked
4 whole boiled crawfish (optional)

Melt 2 tablespoons butter in a large sauté pan. When hot, sauté bell peppers and onions for 1 minute. Add crawfish tails, seasoning powder, and red chilies. Sauté 2 to 3 minutes. Add tomatoes and scallions and sauté 1 minute. Add remaining pieces of cold butter two at a time, swirling the pan and stirring with a fork. When butter has been incorporated, taste to correct seasonings.

Divide cooked fettuccine into four portions and place each in the center of a warm plate. Spoon crawfish mixture around pasta and garnish with a whole boiled crawfish.

CRAWFISH VERSAILLES

Serves 6

*F*rom the talented hands of Gunter Preuss, chef and owner of the Versailles Restaurant in New Orleans, comes this wonderfully delicate crawfish dish. Chef Preuss apprenticed in the great kitchens of Europe, and his menu reflects the classic French tradition with an emphasis on Louisiana's seafood.

2 tablespoons butter
1 tablespoon sliced scallions
1 tablespoon fine-chopped shallots
2 tablespoons fine-chopped garlic
½ cup white wine
juice of ¼ lemon
1¾ cups medium Béchamel Sauce (p. 204)
1½ tablespoons fresh dill weed
(or 1 tablespoon dried dill weed)
1½ pounds boiled and shelled crawfish tails
salt to taste
pinch of cayenne pepper
⅓ cup grated Parmesan cheese
6 boiled crawfish tails

Melt butter in a saucepan and sauté scallions, shallots, and garlic for 2 minutes without browning. Add wine and lemon juice; cook until reduced by half. Add Béchamel Sauce and dill and reduce by a third. Add crawfish and simmer 10 minutes. Add salt and cayenne pepper.

To serve, spoon into individual ramekins or small seashells and sprinkle with Parmesan cheese. Preheat oven to 350 degrees and bake until cheese is golden brown. Garnish each portion with a boiled crawfish tail.

OYSTER AND ARTICHOKE SOUP

Makes 5 cups

3 tablespoons butter
1 small garlic clove, crushed
1 medium onion, chopped
¼ cup water
3 tablespoons flour
1 10¾-ounce can concentrated chicken broth
(or 3 cups strong homemade stock)
1 can water (omit if using homemade stock)
⅛ teaspoon cayenne pepper
1 14-ounce can artichoke hearts
2 16-ounce jars oysters, divided
½ teaspoon fresh marjoram, chopped fine
(or ¼ teaspoon dried marjoram)
1 tablespoon chopped parsley

In a heavy saucepan melt butter. Add garlic, onion, and water; cover and "sweat" over medium heat until soft. Stir in flour, mix well, and cook for 1 to 2 minutes. Add stock and water (or homemade stock) and cayenne pepper, stirring until mixture has thickened.

Drain artichoke hearts and blanch for 2 minutes in boiling water. Refresh in cold water and drain. Remove leaves from bottoms. Chop bottoms in medium-size pieces and set aside; add leaves to stock.

Chop half of the oysters and add to stock. Slice remaining oysters in large pieces and set aside.

Cook soup about 2 minutes, remove from heat, and puree in blender or food processor. Return to heat. Add reserved oyster and artichoke pieces, marjoram, and parsley. Heat oysters about 2 minutes or just until done. Taste to correct seasonings. (If using canned chicken broth, the soup should need no salt.)

PATOUT'S OYSTER ALEXANDER

Serves 12 as first course, 6 as main course

*P*atout's Restaurant in New Orleans is pure Cajun. Owners Liz and Ronnie Alting *(she is the daughter of the original Patout restaurateur, he is the chef)* are affable and gracious hosts, making sure that guests understand what Cajun cuisine means. Ronnie has a simple definition: "Cajun" is just three peppers—black, red, and white; the secret is in knowing just how much of each to use. The following recipe illustrates this philosophy. The Altings guarantee that Oysters Alexander will make Oysters Bienville and Rockefeller obsolete. The recipe really requires the full amount of oyster liquor, so it's worth shucking them yourself if you can't buy it. If you end up with more liquor that you need, don't throw it away! The extra can be worked in to give the dish an even more intense oyster flavor.

1 cup margarine or butter
3 medium onions, chopped fine
1 medium green bell pepper, chopped fine
1 rib celery, chopped fine
2 cloves garlic, crushed
½ loaf French bread (day-old is fine)
3 cups oyster liquor
3 pints unwashed shucked oysters
1 pound medium shrimp, shelled and deveined
1 teaspoon dried thyme
(or 1 tablespoon fresh thyme)
1 teaspoon dried basil (or 1 tablespoon fresh basil)
6 drops Tabasco Pepper Sauce
1 tablespoon salt
2 teaspoons cayenne pepper
1 teaspoon white pepper
1 teaspoon black pepper
1 cup sliced scallions, including green tops
1 cup chopped parsley
24 cleaned oyster shells
(or 6 4-ounce ramekins for main course)
grated Parmesan cheese

Melt margarine in a heavy 4- to 6-quart pot over medium-high heat. Add onions, bell pepper, celery, and garlic; cook 45 minutes to 1 hour or until vegetables are very soft, stirring occasionally. (If oyster liquor amounts to more than 3 cups, add the extra at this time and cook until liquid has evaporated.) Set aside.

Preheat oven to 200 degrees. Slice bread thin and place on cookie sheet and bake about 30 minutes or until dried thoroughly but not brown. Place dried bread in bowl, add oyster liquor, and set aside to soak.

Cut all except 24 oysters in half and set aside. Cut shrimp in thirds.

Add shrimp, herbs, and Tabasco sauce to vegetable mixture. Mix salt and peppers together and add all but 1 teaspoon to mixture, cooking about 4 to 5 minutes or until shrimp turn pink. Add oyster halves and cook until they begin to curl around the edges. Mash bread and oyster liquor together and add to mixture. Reduce heat to low and cook, stirring constantly, until mixture has a smooth consistency. Remove from heat and add scallions and parsley. Refrigerate the mixture

Avery Island pickers gather the capsicum peppers that are then rendered into the McIlhenny Company's patented hot sauce.

for at least 2 hours. (The time can be reduced by spreading dressing in a shallow pan before refrigerating it.)

Arrange shells (or ramekins) on a cookie sheet. Place a whole oyster in each shell and sprinkle with reserved salt and pepper mixture. Divide oyster dressing among the shells, mounding over the oyster. Preheat oven to 375 degrees and bake for 25 to 30 minutes. Sprinkle generously with Parmesan cheese and place under broiler to brown for a minute or two before serving.

OYSTER-ARTICHOKE APPETIZER

Serves 8

*O*ysters and artichokes have a natural affinity, each complementing the delicate taste of the other while providing texture contrast. The following dish can be prepared ahead of time and run under the broiler to heat through and brown just before serving; it is also delicious at room temperature. It's a good idea to prepare it no more than an hour or so before serving so that refrigeration is not necessary. (This dish can be served as a main course, too.)

2 tablespoons butter
8 to 10 scallions, including tops, chopped
1 clove garlic, crushed
2 8-ounce cartons fresh mushrooms, sliced
1 cup Sauternes or other fruity white wine
1 bay leaf
2 16-ounce jars oysters, drained
2 tablespoons flour
1 cup light cream
6 to 8 drops Tabasco Pepper Sauce
salt and pepper to taste
2 10-ounce packages frozen artichoke hearts, cooked
¼ cup buttered dry bread crumbs

In a heavy skillet melt butter and add scallions, garlic, and mushrooms. Cover and cook until tender but not brown. Remove vegetables with slotted spoon and set aside.

Add wine and bay leaf and bring to a boil. Reduce heat, add oysters, and cook about 2 minutes or until the edges curl. Remove oysters with a slotted spoon and set aside with vegetables.

Reduce liquid to ¾ cup. Mix flour with a little of the cream to make a smooth paste, then mix in remaining cream. Stir into wine mixture and cook until thick, stirring constantly. Season with Tabasco sauce, salt, and pepper. Add cooked artichoke hearts and reserved oysters and vegetables, mixing lightly.

Turn into a shallow 7" x 12" casserole and arrange oysters and artichokes in a single layer. Sprinkle with bread crumbs and broil until brown on top. Serve at once.

GALATOIRE'S OYSTERS EN BROCHETTE

Serves 4

*S*ince Galatoire's takes no reservations, the lines get long early; but the restaurant is open all day, so go in the afternoon for a late lunch. Chef Gouch's Oysters en Brochette make an admirable beginning to a memorable dinner at one of the oldest establishments in the Crescent City's French Quarter.

12 strips of bacon, cut in half
24 raw oysters
1 egg
¾ cup milk
¼ teaspoon salt
⅛ teaspoon pepper
flour
oil

Fry bacon until not quite crisp. Divide bacon pieces and oysters among four 8-inch skewers; fold bacon over and thread onto skewer, alternating with oysters.

Combine egg, milk, salt, and pepper, beating well to mix. Dip each skewer into the batter, roll in flour, and fry in 3 inches of hot oil at 350 degrees until golden. Serve on toast points with lemon wedges.

CHRISTIAN'S OYSTER CHOWDER

Serves 6

*C*hris Ansel, proprietor of Christian's Restaurant in New Orleans, suggests this chowder with oysters. It makes a nice change from the familiar fish soups, and one with a real Creole taste. The folks from Louisiana seem to have "oyster water" on hand all the time, but that isn't the case at our house. So I doubled the amount of oysters called for in the original recipe and used the oyster liquor from the jars, adding enough water to make up the difference.

1 small green bell pepper, chopped fine
1 small onion, chopped fine
2 ribs celery, chopped fine
1 clove garlic, chopped fine
6 cups oyster water, divided
2 tablespoons butter
2 tablespoons flour
¼ teaspoon dried thyme
1 bay leaf
1 cup chopped potatoes
2 cups oysters, blanched for 1 minute, drained, and chopped
½ cup heavy cream
salt and pepper to taste

Combine bell pepper, onion, celery, and garlic in 1 cup oyster water and cook until vegetables are tender and liquid has almost evaporated. Set aside.

In a saucepan melt butter and stir in flour to make a roux. Add remaining oyster water, thyme, and bay leaf and cook until thick, stirring frequently. Add potatoes and cook until tender.

Add reserved cooked vegetables, oysters, and cream, mixing thoroughly. Season with salt and pepper.

CREOLE OYSTER CHOWDER

Serves 4

*R*andy Cheramie, chef and owner of Randolph's Restaurant in Golden Meadow, shares this unusual recipe for oyster chowder, which is prepared in three parts. Each bowl is assembled individually to hold the rich, creamy soup. Be sure to serve oyster crackers on the side.

32 medium oysters
1⅓ cups oyster liquor or water
1 teaspoon salt
⅛ teaspoon cayenne pepper or to taste
2 cloves garlic, crushed
1 tablespoon olive oil
4 cups heavy cream, simmered and reduced to 2 cups
1 tablespoon cornstarch
⅓ cup water
2 scallions (including tops), chopped
4 tablespoons unsalted butter
cracked black pepper
paprika

In a small saucepan combine oysters, oyster liquor or water, salt, cayenne pepper, garlic, and olive oil. Stir gently over high heat until oysters curl and liquid just begins to boil. Remove from heat and keep warm.

In a separate pan heat reduced cream to boiling. Mix cornstarch and water and pour slowly into cream, stirring constantly until thick and creamy. Keep warm.

In a small skillet mix scallions and butter and sauté for 1 minute.

Strain the oyster mixture, saving the oysters, and divide the liquid equally among four chowder bowls. Whisk ½ cup cream mixture into each bowl. Add 8 oysters to each bowl and stir to mix. Float 1 tablespoon of the scallion mixture on each bowl and sprinkle with cracked black pepper and paprika.

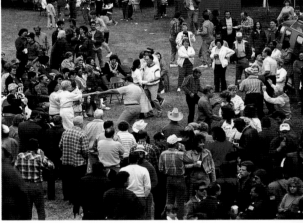

Shirley Kay of Empire totes half-shelled oysters for a festival crowd at historic Fort Jackson in the Mississippi Delta. Behind festival concession tents, jambalaya pots steam under the seasoned eyes of local chefs.

A French Quarter street musician blasts his trumpet in hope of tourists' tips.

OYSTERS BROUSSARD

Serves 6 to 8

Robert Wall is a New Orleanian who loves to cook. This is his adaptation of an old recipe for oyster appetizers in the shell. If you prefer to buy oysters in the jar instead of unshucked, go to a fish market and request deep oyster shell halves. Scrub them thoroughly in cold water before using.

3 cloves garlic, chopped
1 cup canned tomatoes, drained and pureed
½ cup dry bread crumbs
2 8½-ounce cans artichoke hearts,
drained and pureed
1 cup heavy cream
¼ cup fine-chopped celery
1 teaspoon salt
dash of cayenne pepper
3 tablespoons butter
1 8-ounce package fresh mushrooms, chopped fine
½ cup scallions, chopped fine
¼ cup chopped parsley
½ pound lean ham, chopped fine
¼ cup sherry
½ pound crabmeat
36 large oysters (about 3 jars or 3½ pints), drained
(reserve liquor)
36 oyster shells
1 cup grated Parmesan cheese
lemon wedges

In a large saucepan combine garlic, tomatoes, bread crumbs, artichoke hearts, cream, celery, salt, and cayenne pepper. Mix well and bring to a boil; reduce heat, cover, and simmer for 15 minutes, stirring occasionally.

In a separate pan melt butter and sauté the mushrooms about 5 minutes. Add scallions, parsley, ham, sherry, and crabmeat. Combine with artichoke mixture and simmer about 5 minutes. Remove from heat, cover, and chill 1 to 2 hours.

Place one oyster in each shell, moistening with reserved oyster liquor. Spoon chilled crab mixture over the top, dividing it equally among the 36 shells. Place filled shells on a bed of rock salt on a baking sheet; preheat oven to 450 degrees and bake for 8 minutes. Remove from oven, sprinkle with Parmesan cheese, and return to oven for about 5 minutes, or until cheese melts and browns slightly. Serve with lemon wedges.

OYSTER, EGGPLANT, AND MUSHROOM CASSEROLE

Serves 6

On Avery Island in the southern part of Louisiana, where Tabasco Pepper Sauce is made, the climate is conducive to exotic plants and wildlife. The Jungle Gardens and bird sanctuary on the island attract thousands of visitors each year. Camellias, azaleas, bamboo, and other semitropical vegetation provide a lush background for the many varieties of water birds that come each spring and summer to nest there. Easily grown vegetables, such as eggplant, combine well with local oysters, and the resulting dish has become a Louisiana tradition.

2 medium eggplants
36 oysters (about 2 10-ounce jars) and their liquor
¾ cup butter or margarine, divided
1 8-ounce package fresh mushrooms, sliced
¼ cup chopped shallots, divided
1 cup seasoned bread crumbs, divided
¼ to ½ teaspoon Tabasco Pepper Sauce
¼ cup chopped parsley
3 cloves garlic, chopped fine
1 teaspoon dried basil leaves
½ teaspoon ground thyme
salt to taste
1 cup grated mild cheddar cheese
½ cup evaporated milk

Pierce eggplants several times with a fork and place on a baking sheet. Preheat oven to 350 degrees and bake 30 minutes or until very tender. Test with a skewer to see if the center is done. Remove from oven and cool.

Meanwhile, in a saucepan heat oysters in their liquor until the edges begin to curl. Remove oysters with a slotted spoon and set aside.

To the oyster liquor add ¼ cup butter, mushrooms, and 2 tablespoons shallots. Simmer 10 minutes or until liquid is reduced to ½ cup.

Chop reserved oysters and add to saucepan. Add ½ cup bread crumbs and Tabasco sauce, mixing well. Set aside.

In a small skillet melt ¼ cup butter and sauté remaining shallots over low heat for 5 minutes. Add parsley, garlic, remaining bread crumbs, basil, thyme, and salt. Mix well.

Peel eggplants and slice into ¼-inch slices. Arrange half the slices in the bottom of a 10" x 6" shallow casserole dish.

Cover with half the bread crumb mixture and half the oyster mixture. Repeat with the remaining eggplant slices, bread crumb mixture, and oyster mixture.

Sprinkle cheese over the top and drizzle the milk over the cheese. Sprinkle additional bread crumbs over the cheese, if desired, and dot with the remaining ¼ cup butter.

Preheat oven to 350 degrees and bake for 20 to 30 minutes, or until the cheese has melted and the top has browned.

MIXED SHELLFISH
AND RICE CASSEROLE

Serves 10 to 12

*T*his time-tested dish from the files of New Orleanian Violet Jackson has great versatility. One friend is so enamored of it that she serves it as a side dish at Thanksgiving, omitting the shrimp but retaining the crabmeat.

1 cup uncooked long-grain rice
1 cup uncooked wild rice
3 tablespoons butter
2 large onions, chopped
2 cups chopped celery
½ bell pepper, chopped
1 pound medium shrimp, shelled and deveined
1 pound crabmeat
1 4-ounce jar chopped pimientos
2 4-ounce cans sliced mushrooms
2 10 ¾-ounce cans condensed cream of
mushroom soup
¼ cup sliced almonds

Cook rice according to directions on packages. Mix together and set aside.

Melt butter in a heavy skillet and sauté onions, celery, and bell pepper just until soft. Add reserved rice. Add shrimp, crabmeat, pimientos, and mushrooms, mixing well. Spoon into a buttered 6-quart casserole and pour mushroom soup over the top. Preheat oven to 350 degrees and bake for 35 minutes. Uncover, sprinkle with almonds, and bake an additional 10 minutes.

PATOUT'S SHELLFISH AND
EGGPLANT DRESSING

Serves 8 to 12

2 pounds medium shrimp, shelled and deveined
shells from shrimp
4 cups water
1 cup margarine or butter
3 large onions, chopped fine
2 medium green bell peppers, chopped fine
2 ribs celery, chopped fine
4 medium eggplants
1½ teaspoons cayenne pepper
1½ teaspoons ground white pepper
1½ teaspoons ground black pepper
1½ tablespoons salt
4 to 6 dashes Tabasco Pepper Sauce
1 teaspoon dried thyme
(or 1 tablespoon fresh thyme)
1 teaspoon dried basil (or 1 tablespoon fresh basil)
1 pound cooked crabmeat (claw or white)
1 cup chopped scallions
1 cup chopped parsley
grated Parmesan cheese
bread crumbs

Place shrimp shells and water in saucepan, bring to a boil, reduce heat to medium high, and cook until liquid is reduced to about 2 cups. Strain and set aside.

Melt margarine in a large heavy pot; add onions, bell peppers, and celery and cook about 35 to 40 minutes or until very soft, stirring occasionally.

Meanwhile, peel eggplants, cut into 1-inch cubes, place in a saucepan, cover with water, and cook just until tender. Drain and puree until smooth, using a blender, food processor, or sieve. Mix eggplant, shrimp stock, vegetables, seasonings, and herbs and simmer for about 10 minutes, stirring occasionally. Add shrimp and cook about 5 to 7 minutes or until pink. Add crabmeat, heat through, remove from heat, and add scallions and parsley. (The dressing can be prepared in advance to this point.)

Spoon hot dressing into a casserole or individual ramekins. Sprinkle generously with Parmesan cheese and bread crumbs and run under broiler to brown. (If you have made the dressing ahead, place casserole in a 350-degree oven for 45 minutes or until heated through, then brown. Ramekins will take 15 to 20 minutes.)

A New Orleans oyster bar highlights its cuisine with a window display.

MIXED SHELLFISH CREPES

Serves 4

*T*abasco Pepper Sauce, named for the river and town in Mexico where the peppers originated, has been made by the McIlhenny family since the mid-nineteenth century. The peppers are grown on family-owned Avery Island, located in the bayou country of southern Louisiana. The sauce is made from peppers and locally mined salt, then aged in wooden barrels, with vinegar added to sharpen the fiery taste even more! The sauce enhances the flavor of most seafood dishes, and the following recipe, from the company's files, is a toothsome example.

1 pound shrimp, shelled and deveined
shells from shrimp
2 tablespoons olive oil
1 small carrot, chopped fine
1 rib celery, chopped fine
1 onion, chopped fine
2 tablespoons dry sherry
½ cup tomato puree
1 quart heavy cream
salt to taste
½ teaspoon Tabasco Pepper Sauce
¼ teaspoon ground white pepper
2 tablespoons butter or margarine
1 pound shelled crawfish tails (optional)
1 pound fresh mushrooms, cleaned and quartered
1 bunch of scallions, sliced thin (including tops)
8 ounces lump crabmeat
8 crepes, about 8 inches in diameter (see Crepes for Savory Dishes, p. 208)

Refrigerate shrimp. Clean and chop shells.

Heat oil in a saucepan. Add shells and cook over high heat until red. Lower heat and add carrot, celery, and onion. Cook 5 minutes.

Stir in sherry, tomato puree, and cream. Simmer, stirring often, until reduced by half. Add salt, Tabasco sauce, and pepper. Strain and set aside.

In a separate saucepan melt butter. Add reserved shrimp and cook over medium heat until slightly opaque. Add crawfish, mushrooms, and scallions. Cook over low heat for 5 minutes. Fold in crabmeat and half the sauce mixture to make the filling.

To serve, pour a thin layer of sauce into a shallow baking dish. Spoon equal portions of the seafood filling onto the unbrowned side of each crepe, using about half of the mixture. Roll and place, seam side down, in baking dish. Spoon remaining filling mixture over crepes. If desired, moisten with remaining cream sauce.

Preheat oven to 325 degrees and bake, covered, 20 to 25 minutes or until heated through.

JACKSON FAMILY CRAB AND SHRIMP GUMBO

Serves 8 to 12

*V*iolet Jackson is a long-time New Orleanian. She is one of those cooks who use the time-honored method of "a pinch of this, a dash of that." The family has pinched and dashed a few things together to come up with this crab and shrimp gumbo. Note that it differs from more traditional recipes in that it is not based on a roux.

1¼ cups vegetable oil
1 large white onion, chopped fine
2 stalks celery, chopped fine
6 cloves garlic, chopped fine
½ green bell pepper, chopped fine
4 sprigs parsley, chopped
2 8-ounce cans tomato sauce
1 8-ounce can whole tomatoes, crushed
2 cups water
1½ pounds fresh okra, cut into pieces
(or 2 10 ½-ounce packages frozen cut okra)
2 bay leaves
1½ teaspoons salt
1 teaspoon ground black pepper
4 pounds shrimp, shelled and deveined
4 cooked hard-shell crabs, broken in half
½ pound lump crabmeat
cooked rice

Heat oil in a large heavy saucepan. Add onion, celery, garlic, bell pepper, and parsley and simmer until soft. Add tomato sauce and whole tomatoes. Simmer 5 minutes. Add water, okra, bay leaves, salt, and pepper, stirring to mix well. Add shrimp and hard-shell crabs, cover, and cook over low heat until shrimp and okra are tender. Remove from heat and keep covered.

When ready to serve, add lump crabmeat and heat over low heat just until warmed through. Serve over boiled rice.

JANET ROBINSON'S PEPPER SHRIMP

*J*anet Robinson of Morgan City guarantees that this is the fastest and best idea yet, especially if you are in a hurry and have a crowd to feed.

Dehead the shrimp, leaving the shells on, and lay them side by side in a flat dish. Completely cover with ground black pepper. Don't be afraid of using too much—the flavor has to penetrate the shells. Cover with melted butter or margarine and broil 6 to 8 minutes or until the shells separate from the shrimp.

Now for a little lagniappe, have some corn on the cob ready, roll it in the pepper-butter juice, and enjoy the flavors! Dip French bread in the butter-pepper mix as well. (No salt is necessary if salted butter is used.)

Jackson Family Crab and Shrimp Gumbo.

SESAME-BATTERED SHRIMP WITH BUTTERNUT SAUCE AND CINNAMON BASIL SAUCE

Serves 4

*T*his sesame-battered shrimp with two sauces is the creation of Frank Brigtsen, chef and owner of Brigtsen's Restaurant in New Orleans. In 1987, only a year after the restaurant opened, Chef Brigtsen was named one of sixteen innovative young chefs in the Third Annual American Chefs' Tribute to James Beard, and in 1988 Food and Wine magazine chose him as one of America's Ten Best New Chefs.

16 large shrimp
½ cup Creole seasoning powder, divided
2 cups flour
1½ cups fine bread crumbs (unseasoned)
¾ cup raw sesame seeds
3 eggs
3 cups milk
oil

BUTTERNUT SAUCE

½ cup unsalted butter
2½ cups peeled and chopped butternut squash
½ cup fine-chopped yellow onion
heads and shells of 16 large shrimp
2 teaspoons salt
½ teaspoon cayenne pepper
½ teaspoon ground white pepper
pinch of nutmeg
1½ cups Seafood Stock (p. 203), Stock Using
Clam Juice (p. 203), or water
1 cup heavy cream

CINNAMON BASIL SAUCE

2 tablespoons unsalted butter
¼ cup Seafood Stock (p. 203) or Stock Using
Clam Juice (p. 203)
½ cup plus 2 tablespoons heavy cream
2 teaspoons fine-chopped fresh cinnamon basil leaves
(or 1½ teaspoons dried basil and
⅛ teaspoon ground cinnamon)
small pinch of cayenne pepper

To prepare shrimp, remove heads and shells, leaving tails intact. Reserve heads and tails. Devein shrimp and set aside. Mix 2 tablespoons seasoning powder with flour and set aside.

In a separate bowl mix bread crumbs, sesame seeds, and 2 tablespoons seasoning powder.

In another bowl whisk eggs with 1 tablespoon seasoning powder, gradually adding milk.

Sprinkle shrimp lightly with seasoning powder, dredge in seasoned flour, and place in batter.

Heat oil in a deep fryer to 375 degrees. Remove shrimp from batter and dredge in seasoned bread crumbs. Fry immediately in small batches so as not to overcrowd the fryer. Cook about 4 minutes or until golden brown. Drain on paper towels.

To make Butternut Sauce, in a heavy saucepan melt butter over medium heat. Add squash and onion and cook until soft. Add reserved shrimp heads and shells, salt, peppers, and nutmeg and cook about 5 minutes. Add stock or water and cream. Bring to a boil. Reduce heat and simmer the mixture for 20 minutes. Puree in a food mill, pressing firmly on the solids to extract flavors. Strain. Thin the sauce if necessary with warm cream. Adjust seasonings and keep warm.

To make Cinnamon Basil Sauce, heat a heavy skillet over medium heat. Add butter, stock, and cream. When the mixture boils, add cinnamon basil and cayenne pepper. Cook until reduced by one-fourth. Remove from heat and keep warm.

To serve, spoon about 2 tablespoons of each sauce on a plate, side by side. Place 4 shrimp in the center of the plate and garnish with a sprig of fresh cinnamon basil or an edible flower.

SHRIMP WITH PERNOD

Serves 6 to 8

*T*he distinctive flavor of licorice, frequently associated with New Orleans and Creole cuisine, probably dates back to absinthe and the famous old Absinthe House, a popular gathering place in the French Quarter around the turn of the century. Absinthe, a liqueur which contains oil of wormwood and anise, was later banned because its continued use causes delirium and hallucinations. However, the anise flavor is found in such liqueurs as Pernod, anisette, ouzo, and Herbsaint, to name a few. All of these may be used—with restraint—to impart a delicate flavor to this dish. Any firm-textured fish fillets can be substituted for the shrimp, if desired.

4 tablespoons butter
4 whole scallions, chopped (with tops)
3 pounds shrimp, shelled and deveined
1 cup dry white wine, divided
1 tablespoon flour
1½ cups heavy cream
salt and white pepper to taste
4 tablespoons Pernod or other anise-flavored liqueur
2 tablespoons chopped fresh Mexican mint marigold
or 1 tablespoon chopped fresh tarragon
(or ½ teaspoon dried tarragon)

Melt butter in a heavy saucepan, add scallions and a little water, then cover and "sweat" until scallions are limp but not brown. Add shrimp and half the wine, cover, and simmer for 2 to 3 minutes, or until shrimp are just done. Remove shrimp and set aside.

Add remaining wine, increase heat, and cook until reduced by one-fourth. Reduce heat.

Mix flour with a little cream to make a smooth paste. Add remaining cream to flour paste and pour into wine mixture, stirring constantly over medium heat until smooth. Add salt and pepper and cook until slightly thick. Add Pernod and Mexican mint marigold or tarragon. Stir in reserved shrimp and heat through. Serve over hot cooked rice.

MR. B'S SHRIMP CHIPPEWA

Serves 4

*T*his is a signature dish of the popular New Orleans bistro and can become addictive. Try it for lunch with a crisp salad and fruity white wine.

8 tablespoons unsalted butter
1 pound medium shrimp, shelled and deveined
4 medium shallots, chopped fine
1 clove garlic, chopped fine
1 cup thin-sliced mushrooms
2 tablespoons chicken broth
½ cup heavy cream
⅛ teaspoon ground white pepper
salt to taste
French bread

In a large skillet melt butter over medium heat. Add shrimp, shallots, garlic, and mushrooms and sauté for 4 minutes. Add chicken broth and cream; stir and simmer for 2 minutes or until thick. Add pepper and salt. Serve at once with French bread for dipping.

SHRIMP AND CHICKEN SUPREME

Serves 6

*T*his long-time favorite is from the files of Shirley Wall, who grew up in a New Orleans family of good cooks. The dish harks back to the good old days when we weren't watching calories or cholesterol, so treat yourself and your friends to a really delicious dinner when you feel like kicking over the traces.

¼ cup butter
1 8-ounce package fresh mushrooms, sliced
2 tablespoons sliced scallions
2 10 ¾-ounce cans condensed cream of chicken soup
½ cup sherry
½ cup light cream or half-and-half
1 cup shredded cheddar cheese (about 4 ounces)
2 cups cooked chicken pieces
2 cups shelled, deveined, and cooked shrimp
2 tablespoons chopped parsley
hot buttered rice

In a large saucepan melt butter, add mushrooms and scallions, and sauté 5 minutes.

Add soup and stir in sherry and cream, mixing thoroughly. Add cheese and stir over low heat until cheese has melted.

Add chicken and shrimp and heat but do not boil. Just before serving stir in parsley. Serve over rice.

Terrebonne Bay shrimp are weighed in at the Cocodrie docks.

COMMANDER'S SHRIMP AND ANDOUILLE SAUSAGE WITH CREOLE MUSTARD SAUCE

Serves 4

*C*hef Emeril Lagasse mixes the elements of Creole and Cajun cooking together with his own ideas of good food to create some marvelous dishes. This combination of sausage with seafood, wine, cream, mushrooms, and onions illustrates his inventiveness in using today's concepts of American cuisine. Andouille sausage is a Cajun smoked pork sausage available in specialty stores, but any other good smoked pork sausage, such as Kielbasa, can be substituted. Try this dish over angel hair pasta and with a chilled light red wine.

6 to 8 ounces Andouille sausage, cut into half moons
10 ounces medium shrimp, shelled and deveined
4 tablespoons thin-sliced scallions
½ cup sliced mushrooms
1 teaspoon fine-chopped garlic
¼ cup white wine
2 cups heavy cream
1½ tablespoons Creole mustard or other coarse-grained mustard
1 teaspoon Worcestershire sauce
salt and pepper to taste

Heat a heavy skillet and sauté sausage. Drain off fat and discard.

Add shrimp, scallions, mushrooms, and garlic and sauté 1 minute. Remove from skillet and set aside.

Pour in wine to deglaze pan and cook until reduced by half. Add cream and reduce by one-third. Stir in mustard and Worcestershire sauce; season with salt and pepper.

Return sausage and shrimp mixture to skillet and cook for about 2 minutes to heat well. Serve over pasta.

BOURBON-BARBECUED SHRIMP

Serves 4 to 6

*B*ourbon-laced barbecue sauce adds the fillip to these shrimp. Janet Robinson of Morgan City explains that the alcohol in the bourbon and the vinegar in the salad dressing cook out of the sauce, imparting a wonderful flavor to the shrimp. The marinade can also be laced with Tabasco sauce and used as a dip that is especially good for dunking French bread.

2 pounds jumbo shrimp
2 cups barbecue sauce (bottled or homemade)
1 16-ounce bottle zesty Italian salad dressing
3 tablespoons bourbon whiskey
6 tablespoons freshly squeezed lemon juice
2 teaspoons dill weed
2 tablespoons Worcestershire sauce
Tabasco Pepper Sauce to taste

Remove heads from shrimp, leaving shells on, and wash well. Chill in a glass baking dish for about 30 minutes.

Mix barbecue sauce, salad dressing, and bourbon and cook over low heat, uncovered, for about 10 minutes. Add lemon juice, dill weed, and Worcestershire sauce. Set aside to cool.

Pour cooled marinade over shrimp, stirring well to cover, and refrigerate at least 4 hours (the longer, the better).

Remove shrimp from marinade and toss onto fine wire mesh over a hot charcoal fire. Grill for about 5 minutes, turning frequently. Do not overcook. As soon as the shell starts to separate from the tail, remove shrimp from the grill and serve.

Add Tabasco sauce to the marinade, heat, and serve with shrimp.

SHRIMP CURRY VERSAILLES

Serves 4 to 6

*G*unter Preuss, chef and owner of the Versailles Restaurant in New Orleans, lets his imaginative palate dictate the ingredients of this unusual version of curry. It can be served with rice as a main dish or in small portions as a pleasurable beginning to a meal.

3 tablespoons butter
2 pounds shrimp, shelled and deveined
2 tablespoons sliced scallions
1 tablespoon chopped shallots
1 tablespoon chopped parsley
2 tablespoons curry powder or to taste
1½ tablespoons applesauce
1 teaspoon fine-chopped pimiento
1 tablespoon chutney
2 tablespoons sliced hearts of palm
3 tablespoons sherry
2 cups heavy cream
salt to taste

Melt butter in a heavy saucepan and add shrimp, scallions, shallots, parsley, and curry powder. Cook 3 to 4 minutes.

Add applesauce, pimiento, chutney, hearts of palm, and sherry, mixing well. Add cream, stirring slowly, and salt to taste. Simmer 10 to 12 minutes.

Serve with hot rice and additional chutney on the side.

JACKSON FAMILY SHRIMP CREOLE

Serves 16 to 18

*G*ood for a large family gathering or an informal party.

½ cup butter or margarine
½ pound bacon or ham, chopped fine
2 10½-ounce packages frozen okra
(or 2 pounds fresh okra)
8 scallions, sliced
2 medium white onions, sliced
1 large bell pepper, seeded and chopped
5 stalks celery, sliced
2 cups peeled and chopped tomatoes
2 teaspoons chopped parsley
dash of crab boil or other seafood spice
1 teaspoon sugar
½ cup tomato catsup
1 teaspoon salt
½ teaspoon pepper
3 pounds small shrimp (40 plus),
shelled and deveined
1 pound claw crabmeat
1 pound lump crabmeat
fluffy boiled rice with chopped parsley

In a large deep pot melt butter and fry bacon or ham pieces until slightly browned. Add okra and reduce heat. Simmer about 10 minutes.

Add scallions, onions, bell pepper, celery, tomatoes, and parsley. Simmer about 15 to 20 minutes, stirring occasionally. Cook until vegetables are tender but not mushy.

Add crab boil, sugar, catsup, salt, and pepper. Simmer about 10 minutes and taste to correct seasonings. Add shrimp and simmer about 5 minutes. Taste and correct seasonings if necessary. Remove from heat.

Add crabmeat, stirring gently.

Serve over parslied rice and with French bread.

Jackson Family Shrimp Creole; Bourbon-Barbecued Shrimp.

Ray Moran (right) and friends ready a tub of Head-of-Island crawfish for a Saturday feast.

THE VERSAILLES' GULF COAST BOUILLABAISSE

Serves 12 to 16

*S*ave this dish for that very special occasion when you wish to impress a V.I.P. It's loaded with a marvelous variety of seafood that yields a wonderfully rich flavor.

4 carrots, sliced
2 onions, sliced
6 ribs celery, sliced
2 leeks (white part only), sliced
2 fennel bulbs, sliced
½ cup butter, divided
2 tablespoons tomato paste
1 cup brandy
2 cups dry white wine
3 tomatoes, peeled, seeded, and chopped
½ teaspoon fine-chopped garlic
several threads of saffron, softened in 2 tablespoons hot water
3 quarts Seafood Stock (p. 203)
1 pound shrimp, shelled and deveined
1 pound fish fillets, skinned, boned, and cut into 1-inch pieces
6 medium lobster tails, cut into chunks
6 oysters, shucked
mussels in shells (optional)
salt and pepper to taste
½ pound lump crabmeat
chopped parsley
garlic croutons

Sauté carrots, onions, celery, leeks, and fennel in ¼ cup butter until well coated and beginning to brown. Add tomato paste, mixing well, and flame with warmed brandy. Extinguish the flames with white wine. Add tomatoes, garlic, and saffron, stirring to mix. Add fish stock and cook until vegetables are just done.

In a separate skillet add remaining butter and sauté shrimp, fish, and lobster for 1 minute. Add oysters and cook for 1 minute. Transfer to the soup mixture and cook over low heat until fish is done. Add mussels. Reduce heat to lowest point and add salt and pepper. Add more wine if desired.

To serve, ladle the soup into heated bowls and top with crabmeat and parsley. Discard any mussels that have not opened. Serve with croutons.

MR. B'S PASTA JAMBALAYA

Serves 4

*I*n the Brennan family of restaurants, Mr. B's in New Orleans occupies a special niche. Casual and upbeat, it is a pleasant mixture of informality and refined cuisine. Owned and managed by third-generation siblings Ralph and Cindy Brennan, it has garnered national attention in the news media. The innovative combination of jambalaya, that hallmark of Cajun cuisine, and pasta makes a truly memorable dish.

4 tablespoons butter
10 ounces chopped Andouille sausage or other smoked pork sausage
¼ pound chopped cooked duck breast
¼ pound raw chicken breast, sliced thin
1 dozen uncooked medium shrimp, shelled and deveined
½ cup chopped onions
½ cup chopped red and green bell peppers
2 large cloves garlic, chopped fine
½ cup chopped peeled tomatoes
½ cup veal stock
⅛ teaspoon red pepper flakes
1½ to 2 teaspoons Brennan's Creole Seasoning for Fish (p. 202)
1 cup cold unsalted butter, cut into 10 or 12 pieces
1 pound spinach pasta, cooked

Heat butter in a large sauté pan and add sausage, duck, chicken, shrimp, onions, bell peppers, and garlic. Sauté over high heat, stirring with a fork and shaking the pan.

When shrimp are half-cooked (about 2 minutes), add tomatoes, stock, and seasonings. Reduce by one-third. Swirl in butter pieces, one at a time, stirring with a fork and rotating the pan until all butter is incorporated. The sauce should be smooth and light.

Pour cooked pasta into a warmed bowl, pour the jambalaya over it, and serve at once.

At Grand Isle these popcorn shrimp are steamed, dried, and salted for counter sales throughout the South.

Galatoire's Pompano Meunière.

FLAME-GRILLED BLACK DRUM WITH CREOLE MUSTARD SAUCE

Serves 4

*C*reole cooking at its best is what Randolph's Restaurant in Golden Meadow has on the menu daily. This grilled fish is prepared simply with just enough seasoning to pique the imagination. The mustard sauce which enhances the dish is also good with chicken and ham. If black drum is not available, substitute redfish, tilefish, grouper, or any firm-textured white fish. Chef and third-generation owner Randolph Cheramie reminds us to be sure to bring the outdoor gas or charcoal grill to medium-high heat 15 to 20 minutes before cooking begins and to serve this dish with buttered corn on the cob, green salad, hot bread, and cold beer!

4 10-ounce black drum fillets
2 to 4 teaspoons white wine vinegar
2 to 4 teaspoons olive oil
salt
cayenne pepper
2 cloves garlic, crushed
cracked black pepper
¼ pound unsalted butter, melted

CREOLE MUSTARD SAUCE

½ cup heavy cream
½ cup sour cream
3 tablespoons Creole mustard or other
coarse-grained mustard
2 teaspoons Worcestershire sauce
1 teaspoon prepared mustard
¼ teaspoon salt
½ teaspoon cracked black pepper
¼ teaspoon dried basil
2 tablespoons honey

Place fillets in a shallow pan and drizzle lightly with wine vinegar and olive oil. Rub salt, cayenne pepper, and garlic into fillets well. Press cracked black pepper into fillets.

Brush one side of fish with butter. Place fish, buttered side down, on the clean, oiled grill and cook for 1½ to 3 minutes. Brush tops of fish with butter and turn. Cook for 2½ to 3 minutes.

To serve fillets, place on individual plates and spoon about 2 tablespoons of Creole Mustard Sauce over the fish.

To make Creole Mustard Sauce, combine ingredients in a saucepan and simmer for 10 minutes. Cool to room temperature.

MR. B'S BABY BLACK DRUM SALAD WITH ROASTED PEPPER AND TOMATO RELISH

Serves 6 to 8

*M*r. B's restaurant seasons a fish fillet with olive oil, salt, cayenne pepper, and chopped fresh thyme; then grills it over hot coals and marinates it with a piquant relish. It is served over avocado and mixed greens to make a terrific main-course salad. The relish can be made one day ahead and refrigerated until ready to use. Redfish, croaker, or other firm-textured, mild-flavored fish can be substituted for the baby black drum. The recipe is also good served with fish which has been poached rather than grilled.

ROASTED PEPPER AND TOMATO RELISH

1 green bell pepper
1 red bell pepper
1 yellow bell pepper
2 large ripe tomatoes, peeled, seeded, drained, and chopped
⅓ cup white wine vinegar
⅔ cup rice wine vinegar
1 clove garlic, crushed
2 sprigs of fresh rosemary
(or ¼ teaspoon dried rosemary), divided
½ cup olive oil
salt and pepper to taste

SALAD

6 fillets of baby black drum
6 tablespoons olive oil
salt to taste
cayenne pepper to taste
chopped fresh thyme to taste
salad greens (lettuce, chickory, watercress, raddichio, etc.)
3 avocados, peeled and sliced
grapefruit sections and mango slices (optional)

To make relish, roast peppers under broiler flame or in a very hot iron skillet until skin is charred. Place peppers in a plastic bag for 10 to 15 minutes to loosen the skin. When cool, skin, seed, and chop fine. Combine in a bowl with tomatoes. Set aside.

In a small saucepan combine vinegars, garlic, and half the rosemary. Simmer over low heat for 5 minutes. Remove from heat and strain over tomato-pepper mixture. Let stand 10 to 15 minutes. Chop remaining rosemary very fine and add to mixture. Add olive oil and salt and pepper.

To make salad, rub each fillet with olive oil and season with salt, cayenne pepper, and thyme. Grill seasoned fillets over hot coals about 3 minutes per side or until fish is just done. Remove to a platter and coat with 2 tablespoons of Roasted Pepper and Tomato Relish. Let stand for 30 minutes.

Arrange salad greens on individual plates with half a sliced avocado per serving. Dress with oil and vinegar from the relish and place a fillet over the greens. Top liberally with additional relish. Garnish with grapefruit sections and mango slices.

GALATOIRE'S POMPANO MEUNIÈRE

Serves 4

*P*ompano is one of the most traditional finfish in New Orleans. It is prepared in numerous ways and with a variety of sauces and garnishes. But perhaps this simple recipe is the best of all. Be sure to serve it with hot rice or crusty French bread to soak up the delicious buttery sauce.

4 6- to 8-ounce pompano fillets
salt and pepper
4 teaspoons vegetable oil
½ cup butter
juice of 1 lemon
1 tablespoon chopped parsley

Sprinkle fillets with salt and pepper and rub with 1 teaspoon of oil per fillet. Place in a flat oiled pan and broil for about 5 minutes or until fish flakes easily.

Meanwhile melt butter and whip continuously until brown and frothy. Add lemon juice and pour over fillets, garnishing with chopped parsley.

Morgan City fisherman Larry Lupo sorts snapper from the Atchafalaya Basin.

Jim Leonard's Grilled Redfish.

Fishermen try their luck around bridge pilings on Lake Pontchartrain.

JIM LEONARD'S
GRILLED REDFISH

*T**his is a splendid method of grilling redfish, drum, grouper, and other similar fish. Lafayette's Jim Leonard is a great outdoor cook. His ideas about fish cookery are distilled from long years of experimenting with new ways to achieve great results. In this recipe, the skin and scales of the fish are retained to keep the fish from drying out as it cooks. Simple, but absolutely mouthwatering!*

redfish, butterflied but not scaled
salt
cayenne pepper
½ cup butter, melted
juice of 1 lemon

Season fish generously with salt and cayenne pepper. Combine butter and lemon juice.

Place fish, scales down, directly on grill over a medium fire. Baste generously with butter and lemon mixture. Cover grill and cook from 7 to 10 minutes or until fish flakes.

A KNOCK-OFF CU-BEE-YON
(REDFISH STEW)

Serves 8

*A**genuine redfish court-bouillon is mighty hard to beat, but if you are not Creole or Cajun, it can be a little hard to manage. So for all us flatlanders, here is a delicious variation using all the right stuff in a slightly altered procedure. I prefer a Burgundy wine in this recipe because it is a little softer than other wines.*

½ cup vegetable oil
4 tablespoons flour
2 large onions, chopped (about 1½ cups)
2 stalks celery, chopped (about 1 cup)
2 green bell peppers, chopped (about 1 cup)
½ cup chopped parsley
12 to 14 allspice berries, crushed
½ teaspoon thyme
2 bay leaves
2 teaspoons salt
5 to 6 large tomatoes, skinned and chopped
(or 1 28-ounce can whole peeled tomatoes)
1 tablespoon Worcestershire sauce
1½ teaspoons Tabasco Pepper Sauce
2 garlic cloves, crushed
2 cups fish stock or water
1½ cups dry red wine
juice of ½ lemon
1 4-pound redfish
chopped parsley and scallions, mixed
lemon slices (optional)

In a large kettle heat oil. Add flour. Cook and stir for 2 minutes. Add onions, celery, bell peppers, parsley, allspice, thyme, bay leaves, and salt. Cover and "sweat" over low heat until vegetables are wilted. Add tomatoes, Worcestershire and Tabasco sauces, garlic, stock, wine, and lemon juice. Cover and cook over low heat for 30 minutes.

Fillet fish, reserving head and bones to make fish stock. Cut the fish fillets in large chunks (about 6 per fillet). Sprinkle with salt and pepper and dredge in flour. Sauté in hot oil just until done, and transfer to the stew. Cover and let stand about 20 minutes before serving. (If made early in the day, reheat before serving.) Garnish with chopped parsley and scallions and a lemon slice.

CREOLE COURT-BOUILLON
OR REDFISH STEW

Serves 4 to 6

*C**ourt-bouillon (pronounced cu-bee-yon) is as traditional a New Orleans creation as one can find. It is always made with redfish, tomatoes, spices, and wine. There are dozens of variations, some with a list of ingredients as long as your arm. Vernon and Evelyn Lashley, outstanding cooks and hosts, have developed this fairly simple version. Serve it with fluffy boiled rice.*

½ cup vegetable oil
3 tablespoons flour
12 allspice berries, crushed
3 sprigs of fresh thyme (or ¼ teaspoon ground thyme)
3 sprigs of parsley
3 bay leaves
2 large onions, chopped fine
1 clove garlic, chopped fine
6 large fresh tomatoes, chopped
1 teaspoon Worcestershire sauce
juice of 1 lemon
1 cup claret
4 cups water
2 teaspoons salt or to taste
½ teaspoon cayenne pepper or to taste
4 pounds whole dressed redfish, cut into steaks
(including skin and bones but not head or tail)

In a large saucepan heat oil. Add flour and cook 2 minutes to make a roux.

Add remaining ingredients except fish. Mix well and boil over high heat for 5 minutes. Reduce heat and let mixture come to a simmer.

Add fish steaks and cook for 15 minutes or until fish is just done. Taste to correct seasonings.

THE VERSAILLES'
REDFISH HERBSAINT

Serves 4

*H*erbsaint is an anise-flavored liqueur that often takes the place of absinthe in New Orleans. Pernod, anisette, or even ouzo may be substituted if Herbsaint isn't available. Gunter Preuss, chef and owner of the Versailles Restaurant, gives this Creole dish a decided European accent with its combination of julienne vegetables, cream, and butter.

½ cup plus 2 tablespoons Herbsaint, divided
½ cup dry white wine
1½ teaspoons fine-chopped shallots
2 tablespoons julienne of carrots (matchstick cut)
2 tablespoons julienne of celery
2 tablespoons julienne of leeks (white part only)
4 mushroom caps
4 4- to 6-ounce redfish fillets
1 cup cream
salt and white pepper to taste
juice of 2 small lemons
½ pound lump crabmeat
½ cup butter

In a sauté pan combine ½ cup Herbsaint, wine, shallots, carrots, celery, leeks, and mushroom caps. Bring to a boil and immediately reduce heat to low. Add fish and poach in the simmering liquid for 8 to 10 minutes. Remove fish and vegetables and keep warm.

Increase heat and reduce liquid by half. Add cream and reduce by half again. Season with salt, pepper, and lemon juice. Reduce heat to low; when liquid is simmering, add crabmeat and heat, tossing carefully to avoid breaking up crabmeat. Stir in butter, reserved vegetables, and remaining Herbsaint and serve over the warm fish immediately.

SAUTÉED FILLETS OF
SHEEPSHEAD WITH
TOMATO-SAUTERNES
BUTTER SAUCE

Serves 4

*I*t's no wonder that Chef Gerard Maras at Mr. B's in New Orleans is a culinary artist. His degree is in fine arts and his heart is in the kitchen, so the combination is pretty special. When the Louisiana Restaurant Association was researching underutilized species of Gulf Coast finfish, Chef Maras was asked to create some recipes using these forgotten varieties. In the following recipe a rich tomato sauce is spooned over sheepshead fillets that have been sautéed in clarified butter. Wilted spinach leaves and strips of tomato enhance the dish. Any of the mild-flavored varieties of fish can be substituted for sheepshead. The sauce is equally good over broiled or fried fish.

8 3-ounce sheepshead fillets
flour seasoned with salt, cayenne pepper, and paprika
5 tablespoons clarified butter
2 cups packed spinach leaves, steamed until wilted
½ cup sautéed strips of peeled tomatoes

SAUCE
¼ cup fine-chopped shallots
¼ cup white wine vinegar
¾ cup Sauternes wine
½ large tomato, peeled, sliced, and chopped
2 tablespoons cream
½ cup plus 3 tablespoons unsalted butter,
cut into small pieces
⅛ teaspoon salt or to taste
ground white pepper to taste

Heat butter in a skillet. Dredge fillets in seasoned flour, shaking off the excess. Sauté approximately 1½ to 2 minutes or until golden on each side. Drain on paper towels.

To make the sauce, combine the shallots, vinegar, and wine in a saucepan and cook over medium heat until reduced to approximately 2 tablespoons. Add tomato and reduce until no liquid remains. Add cream and bring to a boil. Reduce heat and whisk in butter, a piece at a time, until it is all incorporated. Puree sauce in blender, taste to adjust seasonings, and keep warm.

For each serving, spread about ½ cup spinach in the center of a heated plate and top with 2 fillets. Spoon sauce over the fish and garnish with tomato strips.

A rustic boardwalk meanders through the marshes at peninsular Grand Isle.

Fillet of Trout Marcus.

FILLET OF TROUT MARCUS

Serves 6

*T*he Versailles Restaurant has been garnering awards since its opening in 1971. With his background of European training Chef Preuss can prepare any delicacy from the vast repertoire of classical French menus, and New Orleanians have been quick to appreciate his talents. In this recipe, the Marcus Garnish that so richly enhances the fish fillets is also delicious with breast of chicken or quail.

6 6-ounce fillets of trout or similar fish
salt
ground white pepper
lemon juice
flour
5 eggs, beaten
¾ cup clarified butter or margarine
chopped parsley

MARCUS GARNISH

6 trimmed and cooked artichoke bottoms (if using canned artichokes, rinse well)
2 tablespoons sliced scallions
½ teaspoon chopped garlic
½ teaspoon chopped shallots
3 tablespoons small capers, rinsed and drained
½ cup dry white wine
½ cup lemon juice
1 cup butter
salt to taste
ground white pepper to taste

Sprinkle fillets with salt, white pepper, and lemon juice. Dredge in flour and shake off excess. Dip fillets in eggs and sauté in butter until edges begin to brown. Turn and cook about 5 minutes or until fish flakes easily.

To make Marcus Garnish, combine artichokes, scallions, garlic, shallots, capers, wine, and lemon juice in a heavy saucepan and bring to a boil. Divide butter into three pieces; add all at once, swirling and agitating the pan until completely incorporated into the sauce. Add salt and pepper.

Serve fillet with Marcus Garnish, topped with chopped parsley.

GALATOIRE'S TROUT MARGUERY

Serves 4

*G*alatoire's is considered by many food authorities to be among the greatest restaurants ever established in New Orleans. Founded just after the turn of this century, the restaurant is now in its third generation of family ownership. Chef David Gouch carries on the tradition of definitive classic Creole cuisine on which this landmark restaurant has made its reputation. Of this recipe, Chef Gouch says, "This dish is as old as I am and one of our most popular."

4 6- to 8-ounce fillets of trout
1 tablespoon vegetable oil
¾ cup water

SAUCE

3 egg yolks
1 cup butter, melted
1 tablespoon lemon juice, strained
12 small shrimp, cooked, shelled, and deveined
1 4-ounce package mushrooms, cooked
salt to taste
cayenne pepper to taste

Fold each fish fillet in half and place in a shallow pan. Add oil and water; cover. Preheat oven to 400 degrees and bake for 15 minutes. Drain and keep hot.

To make sauce, beat egg yolks in the top of a double boiler over simmering water. Beating constantly, gradually add melted butter. Add lemon juice gradually, beating until sauce has thickened.

Chop shrimp and mushrooms fine and add to sauce. Season with salt and cayenne pepper.

To serve, place each fillet in the center of a heated plate and spoon the sauce over it.

GALATOIRE'S TROUT MEUNIERE AMANDINE

Serves 4

*T*his classic dish is one of the simple joys of Creole cuisine. Over the years it has remained a favorite with many patrons of this famous New Orleans restaurant.

4 6- to 8-ounce trout fillets
salt and pepper
1 cup milk
½ cup flour
oil
1 cup butter
1 cup sliced toasted almonds
juice of 1 lemon
½ tablespoon chopped parsley

Sprinkle fillets with salt and pepper, dip in milk, and roll in flour. Fry in ¾ inch of hot oil in a shallow skillet until golden on both sides. Remove and keep warm.

In a separate pan melt and whip butter until brown and frothy. Add sliced almonds and lemon juice. Place each fillet on a heated plate and pour sauce over it. Sprinkle with chopped parsley.

MR. B'S TUNA STEAKS WITH GINGER-SOY BUTTER SAUCE

*S*ince most restaurants prepare individual servings to order, they customarily have a variety of sauces ready to nap a serving as soon as it has been cooked. The sauce in this recipe can be made early in the day and kept warm or reheated in a double boiler. It's wonderfully rich, so a little goes a long way. Mr. B's serves it over a grilled yellowfin tuna steak nested in a julienne of mixed steamed vegetables. Try it with shark, swordfish, or other varieties of firm-textured finfish.

1½ cups fresh orange juice
½ cup fine-chopped fresh ginger root
2 cloves garlic, chopped fine
½ cup soy sauce
½ cup rich veal stock
⅓ cup cream
1½ pounds cold unsalted butter, cut into 12 pieces
pepper to taste
2 tablespoons water
1 teaspoon butter
4 ounces julienne of mixed vegetables such as leeks,
red onions, carrots, green and yellow squash
1 8-ounce yellowfin tuna steak
salt and pepper to taste
butter

In a stainless steel saucepan mix orange juice, ginger root, and garlic; bring to a boil and cook until reduced by half. Add soy sauce and stock and reduce by two-thirds. Add cream, reduce heat, and whisk in butter, one piece at a time, until incorporated. Season with pepper, strain, and keep warm in a double boiler.

In a large sauté pan, combine water, butter, and vegetables. Season with salt and pepper. Cover pan and steam for about 1 minute.

Season tuna steaks with salt and pepper, brush with butter, and grill 2 minutes per side over a hot charcoal fire or under the broiler. Tuna should be medium rare.

To serve, place steamed vegetables on a warm plate, then top with tuna steak and sauce.

PATOUT'S EGGPLANT PIROGUES

Serves 6

*E*ggplant pirogues (the Acadian name for a type of dugout boat used in the bayous) make interesting and edible containers for seafood or vegetable stuffing. Try them with Patout's Shellfish and Eggplant Dressing (p. 99), Patout's Smothered Cajun Okra (p. 116), a seafood au gratin, or any other Cajun dish that is compatible with eggplant. It makes a great main dish when stuffed with seafood or, when filled with vegetables, a hearty accompaniment to baked or broiled fish.

3 medium eggplants
1½ teaspoons salt
2 teaspoons cayenne pepper
1 teaspoon ground black pepper
1 teaspoon ground white pepper
2 eggs
12 ounces beer or 1½ cups milk
1 cup flour
vegetable oil
1 tablespoon grated Parmesan cheese

Halve eggplants lengthwise and scoop out pulp, leaving a ½-inch shell (reserve pulp for Patout's Shellfish and Eggplant Dressing). Place shells in large bowl and cover with cold water. Set aside.

Mix salt and peppers together and set aside.

Beat eggs and beer together, adding half the salt-pepper mixture.

Place flour in a shallow pan and mix with remaining salt-pepper mixture.

Fill a large heavy pot with oil to a depth of about 5 inches and heat to 350 degrees.

Drain eggplant shells and dry well. Dip into egg batter, then in flour mixture, coating well and shaking off excess flour. Deep-fry, one or two at a time, about 8 minutes or until golden brown. Drain on paper towels.

Fill with stuffing of your choice, sprinkle with Parmesan cheese, and place under broiler to brown.

At Coteau Holmes neighbors take over the community store for a Saturday-morning jam. A dilapidated cane syrup mill sits idle near New Iberia. A stately Bayou Teche plantation preserves a remnant of Louisiana's past.

PATOUT'S MAQUE CHOUX

Serves 10 to 16

*A*t Patout's Restaurant in New Orleans this is a favorite with Liz and Ronnie Alting's customers. It uses sweet corn but transforms its taste and texture to something different. Ronnie guarantees that you'll never want corn any other way. Even corn that is too mature for "roasting ears" is ideal for this dish because of the way it is sliced off the cob. Ronnie means it when he says you don't want whole kernels for this dish.

24 ears fresh sweet corn
1 cup butter
1 medium onion, chopped fine
2 large bell peppers, chopped fine
6 large ripe tomatoes, peeled, seeded, and chopped
2 teaspoons salt
2 teaspoons pepper

Shuck corn. Hold each cob over a bowl and cut away the kernels in layers (you don't want to end up with whole kernels), then scrape the knife down the cob to "milk" it. Set aside.

Heat butter in a large heavy pot over medium-high heat. Add onion, bell peppers, and tomatoes and sauté about 15 minutes or until onion is transparent. Add salt, pepper, and reserved corn and milk from the cobs, stirring well. Reduce heat to medium, cover, and cook 20 to 30 minutes or until corn is tender. If mixture begins to dry out, add a little milk.

PATOUT'S SMOTHERED CAJUN OKRA

Serves 6 to 8

*T*his basic Cajun side dish makes a terrific accompaniment to almost any entrée. It also freezes well.

1 pound fresh okra
2 medium onions, chopped fine
2 medium bell peppers, chopped fine
6 very ripe tomatoes, peeled, seeded, and chopped
3 cups water
1 teaspoon white vinegar
salt and pepper to taste

Wash okra well and drain. Cut off stem ends and discard; slice okra thin. Place in a large heavy pot; add onions, bell peppers, tomatoes, water, and vinegar and stir well. Cover and bring to a simmer over medium heat.

Reduce heat and simmer slowly 45 minutes to 1 hour or until okra is tender.

Season with salt and pepper. Add a little water if the okra seems to be drying out; if there seems to be too much liquid, remove cover, increase heat, and allow some to evaporate.

In the morning mist an oak-canopied road winds through bayou country from New Iberia to Morgan City.

TODD GERALD'S LOUISIANA PRALINES

*T*his unusual method of preparing pralines comes from the private files of the Gerald family, owner of the group of Louisiana restaurants known as Ralph and Kacoo's. Toasting the pecan halves gives them a delicious flavor and crisp texture. The untoasted pecan pieces bind the mixture together and enhance the basic pecan flavor.

2 cups pecan halves
3 cups granulated sugar, divided
1 cup evaporated milk
¼ teaspoon salt
3 tablespoons butter
2 teaspoons vanilla extract
1½ cups broken pecan pieces

Spread pecan halves on a baking sheet. Preheat oven to 350 degrees and toast for 5 minutes. Cool and set aside.

In a small heavy saucepan, melt 1 cup sugar over low heat.

Meanwhile, place remaining sugar and milk in a large saucepan and cook until almost boiling. Add melted sugar, stirring constantly. Cook to 238 degrees on a candy thermometer or until a little of the mixture forms a firm but soft ball when dropped into cold water.

Remove from heat and add remaining ingredients. Stir until mixture begins to thicken.

Drop by tablespoons onto aluminum foil and let set. Peel off foil and store pralines in a covered container.

BREAD PUDDING SOUFFLÉ WITH WHISKEY SAUCE

Serves 8

*P*robably the most frequently requested dessert at Commander's Palace in New Orleans and at Brennan's of Houston is their famous bread pudding. An even more elegant version of this long-time favorite is an airy soufflé made from the basic pudding recipe and served with a whiskey sauce. To savor the delicate texture of this lofty dish and ensure its dramatic impact, it must be served as soon as it comes out of the oven. A soufflé waits for no diner!

BREAD PUDDING

5 eggs
2 cups whipping cream
1 cup sugar
½ cup butter, melted and cooled
1 tablespoon vanilla extract
dash of ground cinnamon
¼ cup raisins
12 1-inch-thick slices French bread (fresh or stale)

SOUFFLÉ

6 egg yolks
½ cup granulated sugar
2½ cups cooked Bread Pudding
6 egg whites
½ cup confectioner's powdered sugar

WHISKEY SAUCE

1 cup sugar
1¼ cups milk, divided
1 cup heavy cream
dash of cinnamon
1 tablespoon butter
1 tablespoon cornstarch
1 tablespoon bourbon whiskey

To make pudding, combine all ingredients except bread slices, mixing well. Pour into a buttered 9-inch square pan.

Arrange bread slices in mixture and soak for about 5 minutes. Turn slices over gently to avoid tearing and soak 10 minutes.

Cover pan with aluminum foil and set into larger pan filled with water to within ½ inch of the top. Preheat oven to 350 degrees and bake for about 45 minutes, uncovering pudding for last 10 minutes to brown the top. When done, the custard should be soft, not firm.

To make soufflé, combine egg yolks and sugar in the top of a double boiler. Over simmering water, whisk until mixture is frothy and shiny. Remove from heat and whisk into bread pudding, mixing well.

Beat egg whites until frothy. Add confectioner's sugar gradually, beating constantly until mixture stands in stiff peaks. Gently fold into pudding mixture.

Butter and lightly sugar a 1½-quart soufflé dish. Spoon soufflé mixture into dish, filling it three-fourths full. Wipe rim of soufflé dish clean. Preheat oven to 375 degrees and bake for 35 to 40 minutes.

To make sauce, in a saucepan combine sugar, 1 cup of milk, and cream. Bring to a boil and add cinnamon and butter.

Combine cornstarch with remaining milk to form a smooth paste. Pour into hot sauce, stirring until clear and thick.

Remove from heat and stir in whiskey.

Serve soufflé topped with sauce.

FLAMING MINCEMEAT SUNDAES

Serves 12

*H*ere is another recipe from the Wall family of New Orleans. John Wall recommends it for a wonderful holiday dessert. For a spectacular presentation, bring the chafing dish to the table to flame the mincemeat. Have scoops of ice cream mounded in a silver bowl and serve the plates as soon as the pyrotechnic display has finished.

1 12-ounce jar prepared mincemeat
½ cup brandy, divided
¼ cup orange juice
⅓ cup drained and chopped maraschino cherries
⅔ cup chopped walnuts
2 quarts vanilla ice cream

In a chafing dish combine mincemeat, ¼ cup brandy, orange juice, cherries, and walnuts. Cook over moderate heat until thoroughly heated and bubbly.

In a small saucepan heat remaining brandy until bubbles form around the edge of the pan. Carefully ignite brandy and pour it over the mincemeat.

Serve over ice cream.

These St. Martin Parish traildrivers sport the cowboy garb that is traditional in southwestern Louisiana.

TEXAS

*A*LONG THE SWEEPING, 375-mile curve of the Texas Gulf Coast, seafood cookery is as diverse and colorful as the geography and people of the state. The fabric of Texas history was woven by numerous ethnic groups: in its earliest days, native American tribes, French explorers, colonial Spaniards, and Mexicans. Later, Anglo settlers streamed in from Georgia, Tennessee, and Alabama; then came Germans, Czechs, Poles, Jews, and other European immigrants. In recent times, turbulent world events have brought Chinese, Japanese, Indian, Cuban, Vietnamese, and a later wave of Mexican immigrants, among others, to Texas shores.

Food shops and restaurants from Amarillo to

Spring Break crowds enjoy the sun and surf of South Padre Island. Before the days of bag limits, trotliners took a plentiful share of redfish from Texas' productive bays.

El Paso to Beaumont reflect the influence of all these ethnic traditions, offering endless inspiration for the ambitious cook. In the large cities one can browse at Chinese, Vietnamese, or Hispanic grocery stores, or at small shops that carry Indian, Indonesian, Middle Eastern, Jewish, or Italian fare—not to mention the large supermarkets with their exotic ingredients and imported products.

Natural and manmade oyster reefs dot the Texas coastline, and this popular mollusk is often the featured specialty at the corner cafe of small coastal towns, just as they are at the upscale oyster bars in urban areas. A Texan's favorite way with oysters is to dip them in seasoned cornmeal as soon out of the water as possible, fry them quickly in hot, deep fat, and serve them with a squeeze of fresh lemon juice. Catsup, tartar sauce, or remoulade sauce often accompanies them.

"Jumbo" Gulf shrimp, batter-dipped and fried to a light golden color, has long been a standard item on Texas seafood restaurant menus. But because shrimp is so versatile, it is also sautéed, steamed, and grilled, with a variety of marinades and sauces reflecting a particular cuisine.

The bays and lagoons from Sabine Pass to Brownsville support numerous species of finfish; redfish, red snapper, speckled trout, and flounder are all highly sought by sportfishermen and seafood shoppers alike. In today's health-conscious culinary climate, fish is in new demand, and Texans are showing increased interest in underutilized fish varieties. Wherever markets carry tuna, shark, swordfish, amberjack, grouper, and tilefish, creative cooks are preparing these fish in new ways that still reflect the state's rich cooking traditions.

Sandhill cranes arrive for the winter on Matagorda Island. These blue heron chicks get their first glimpses of their coastal home.

In a shallow-draft boat designed for bays, fishermen seek feeding gamefish near the rig-building industries of Port Aransas. Wildflowers thrive in the diverse habitat along the Texas coast. Moored fishing boats cast twilight reflections in tranquil Port Lavaca harbor.

Now replaced by a concrete span, the Intracoastal Canal swingbridge near High Island was the last of its kind on the U.S. Gulf. The three-story sandstone Ashbel-Smith Building, which housed the first medical school west of the Mississippi, recalls Galveston's heyday as a prosperous seaport.

A barge train chugs past Port Arthur.
The gaudy decor of this Aransas
Pass seafood stand is aimed at the
beach-bound trade. A sun worship-
per on one of Galveston's many
beaches puts her Caddie to good use.

A cattle egret gets a free ride from its host in the marshy ranching and rice-growing area of the upper Texas coast.

CRAB AND CORN BISQUE

Makes 6 cups

*I*n Texas crabmeat is available just about any time of year, but the big blue crabs are especially delicious in the summertime. And, as fortuitous culinary circumstance has it, corn is especially sweet and delicious at the same time. Succulent lumps of white crabmeat make the best soup when paired with tender kernels of corn cut and scraped from the cob. If fresh corn is unavailable, look for the tenderest frozen variety or canned shoe-peg corn.

4 tablespoons butter, divided
1 small onion, chopped
2 shallots, chopped
1 tablespoon sugar
2 tablespoons water
1 medium potato, cubed
2½ cups milk, divided
2 cups fresh corn (or 1 10-ounce package frozen corn)
2 tablespoons chopped parsley
1½ cups lump crabmeat
⅛ teaspoon paprika
salt to taste
chopped parsley

In a heavy saucepan, melt 2 tablespoons butter and add onion, shallots, sugar, and water. Cover and "sweat" until onion is tender.

Add potato and 1¼ cups milk. Cover and cook until potato is tender. Add corn and cook for about 10 minutes or until tender. Remove from heat, add parsley, and puree mixture. Return to heat and add remaining milk.

In separate pan sauté crabmeat in remaining butter; add to soup and season with paprika and salt. Cover and let stand for at least 30 minutes. Heat and garnish with additional chopped parsley.

Note: A 10 ¾-ounce can of condensed cream of potato soup plus 2 cans of milk can be substituted for the potato and milk. Add soup and 1 can of milk after the corn is cooked, puree the mixture, and add remaining milk. Proceed as directed above, omitting salt.

VIETNAMESE CRAB SOUP

Makes about 2 quarts

*H*ieu Nguyen (known as "Hill" to his customers) came to Houston in 1981 and has been in the seafood business ever since. Although he had no previous experience, his Fountainview Fish Market was an immediate success. It is a meeting place at noon for a devoted following who come to lunch on fried seafood sandwiches and platters that Hill cooks to order. This soup recipe is one prepared frequently by his wife, described by Hill as the real cook of the family. It is a delicate dish enhanced by oyster sauce, which is available in Asian markets, and by a lot of ground black pepper. Vietnamese gourmets like an abundance of pepper in this dish.

1 2½- to 3-pound chicken
water
2 pounds fresh asparagus
2 tablespoons cornstarch
5 tablespoons water
1½ teaspoons salt
1 tablespoon sugar
1 teaspoon oyster sauce
1 pound lump crabmeat
ground black pepper

Cut chicken in half, place in a large pot, and cover with water. Bring to a boil and cook about 3 minutes. Pour off water and rinse chicken and pot to remove solids that might cloud the soup.

Return chicken to pot, cover with water, and simmer until done. Remove chicken and save for another dish. Skim broth and boil until reduced to about 1½ quarts.

Wash asparagus. Cut each stalk diagonally into 2 or 3 pieces and add to broth.

Mix cornstarch and water in a small bowl. Add salt, sugar, and oyster sauce and stir well. Add to broth and cook until thick.

Stir in crabmeat carefully to preserve lumps. Sprinkle with pepper and serve at once.

FRIED CRABS

*I*f you ever get to Rockport, look up Bill Berkley and see about going out in the bay on his barge. It is a great experience. Aboard the barge Bill cooks his catch in great kettles. The smell of salty sea air adds atmosphere and flavor to the cooking aromas. Fried crabs never tasted like this on shore! Here are his directions.

Clean crabs, remove backs, and wash bodies. Crack claws with a hammer or a short piece of two-by-four. Pat crabs dry.

Put 2 gallons of cooking oil in a large heavy pot. Add crab and crawfish boil or other seasoning. Heat to about 350 degrees.

Drop crabs in hot oil and fry for about 5 to 6 minutes. Do not overcook. Seasoning will attach itself to crabs.

CRABMEAT QUICHE

Serves 4 to 6

*T*he Houston branch of Beaumont's Seafood Lover Market has expanded to include a deli with savory seafood. Susan Middleton is the chef and always seems to have something new and delectable to taste. The crabmeat quiche is one of the most popular items. Susan suggests using special-grade crabmeat, which is white body meat that has a good texture but is not as expensive as lump crabmeat.

½ cup butter or margarine, melted
½ cup milk (at room temperature)
4 eggs (at room temperature)
2 tablespoons flour

1 cup grated Swiss cheese
½ cup chopped onion
2 tablespoons chopped parsley
½ pound special-grade crabmeat,
picked through for shells
1 teaspoon lemon juice
⅛ teaspoon cayenne pepper
½ teaspoon seasoned salt
1 9-inch unbaked Basic Pastry shell (p. 208)

Combine butter, milk, eggs, and flour and mix well. Fold in cheese, onion, parsley, crabmeat, lemon juice, and seasonings.

Pour mixture into pastry shell. Preheat oven to 325 degrees and bake for 35 to 45 minutes.

Crabmeat Quiche.

125

Gulf Coast Eggplant with Crab.

GULF COAST EGGPLANT WITH CRAB

Serves 4 to 6

*I*n a beautiful and bucolic setting near Houston, nationally acclaimed herb growers Madalene Hill and her daughter Gwen Barclay are planning vegetable and herb gardens which will be tended by the residents of this rural facility for the retarded. Most of the fresh foodstuffs used for meals served at the new Willow River Farms will be grown in these gardens, and there is even a plan to market the surplus harvest of herbs as the plants become more prolific. This recipe from Madalene and Gwen illustrates their enthusiasm for fresh herbs in cooking.

3 small or 2 medium eggplants
4 tablespoons butter, divided
2 large cloves garlic, crushed
1 cup chopped scallions
1 cup sliced celery
½ cup fine-chopped or slivered red bell pepper
½ cup chopped parsley
1 to 1½ cups soft French bread crumbs, divided
2 teaspoons chopped fresh thyme
1 teaspoon chopped fresh rosemary
1 tablespoon chopped fresh oregano
1 tablespoon chopped fresh basil
2 eggs, beaten slightly
1 teaspoon salt
½ teaspoon black pepper
⅛ teaspoon cayenne pepper or Tabasco Pepper Sauce
1 pound crabmeat
(or 1 pound chopped cooked shrimp)
juice of 1 large lemon
½ cup freshly grated Romano or Parmesan cheese
chopped parsley

Wash and dry eggplants. Preheat oven to 350 degrees, place eggplants on a baking pan, and bake about 35 or 40 minutes or just until tender. Remove from oven, cut in half lengthwise, and cool. With a spoon or sharp knife, scoop out pulp, leaving a ½-inch shell. Chop or mash pulp.

While eggplants are baking, sauté garlic, scallions, celery, and bell pepper in 2 tablespoons butter until soft but not browned. Remove from heat and combine with eggplant pulp and all remaining ingredients except ½ cup bread crumbs, remaining butter, and cheese. Mix lightly and taste to correct seasonings.

Spoon filling loosely into reserved eggplant shells. Top with remaining bread crumbs and dot with remaining butter.

Arrange filled shells on an oiled shallow pan; do not crowd. Preheat oven to 350 degrees and bake about 20 to 25 minutes or until hot and lightly browned. During the last 5 to 6 minutes, sprinkle with cheese.

Serve garnished with chopped parsley.

Note: The filling in this recipe can also be baked in a buttered casserole dish instead of the eggplant shells.

CRABMEAT AU GRATIN

Serves 4 to 6

*G*aido's Seafood Restaurant has become a landmark in Galveston's restaurant scene. Founded in 1911 by S. J. Gaido, it has grown in size and fame during the past eight decades. Dishes on the menu are constantly being developed and refined. Due to the combination of formal training, on-the-job experimentation, and openness to suggestions made by employees and guests, some "trademark" recipes have emerged. The crab dish here exemplifies this cooperative spirit and is one of the most popular items on the menu.

3 tablespoons butter
3 tablespoons flour
2 cups milk
½ cup dry sherry
1 teaspoon Worcestershire sauce
1 tablespoon seasoned salt or to taste
1 pound lump crabmeat
½ cup grated cheddar cheese
½ cup Monterey Jack cheese
paprika

Melt butter in a saucepan. Add flour and stir to mix thoroughly.

Add milk, sherry, Worcestershire sauce, and seasoned salt, stirring constantly. Bring to a boil, continue stirring, and cook for 5 minutes. Remove from heat. Sauce may be refrigerated at this point if desired.

Mix sauce with crabmeat and divide among individual ramekins or spoon into a buttered ceramic baking dish. Top with a mixture of the two cheeses and sprinkle with paprika: Preheat oven to 350 degrees and bake about 15 minutes for ramekins, or 30 minutes for one large dish. Allow additional cooking time if the sauce has been refrigerated.

A Port Aransas shrimper dons a slicker for the troll.

Ferrari's Spinach-Ricotta Pasta Shells in Crabmeat Sauce.

FERRARI'S SPINACH-RICOTTA PASTA SHELLS IN CRABMEAT SAUCE

Serves 12 as hors d'ouevre, 6 as main course

F rom Ava Pereira comes this marvelous dish—shell pasta stuffed with a spinach-ricotta filling and baked in a rich crabmeat and tomato sauce. Ava's unique pasta shop in Houston, Ferrari's Pastas, makes a large variety of specialty pastas flavored with herbs, spices, and peppers.

24 jumbo Ferrari pasta shells or similar pasta
salted water

SAUCE

2 tablespoons olive oil
½ cup chopped onions
3 tablespoons fine-chopped carrot
1 35-ounce can whole peeled Italian plum tomatoes, undrained
1 tablespoon chopped fresh basil
(or ½ tablespoon dried basil)
¼ teaspoon sugar
½ teaspoon salt or to taste
⅛ teaspoon pepper or to taste
1 pound lump crabmeat

FILLING

1 tablespoon olive oil
2 tablespoons chopped onion
1 pound ricotta cheese
⅓ cup chopped cooked spinach, squeezed dry
1 teaspoon chopped fresh basil
(or ½ teaspoon dried basil)
⅓ cup grated Parmesan cheese

Fill a large kettle with salted water and bring to a boil. Add pasta shells and boil for 3 to 5 minutes (*al dente*). (If using dried pasta, cook according to directions on package.) Drain.

To make sauce, heat oil in a heavy saucepan and sauté onions and carrot until onions are translucent. Add tomatoes, basil, sugar, salt, and pepper. Simmer for 1½ hours, checking frequently. Taste to correct seasonings; they will concentrate and intensify as the sauce thickens. Remove from heat, add crabmeat, and set aside.

To make filling, heat oil in a skillet and sauté onion until translucent. Add remaining ingredients, mixing well. Pipe or spoon into cooked pasta shells.

Spoon all but ⅓ cup of the reserved sauce into a shallow baking dish. Arrange filled shells over the sauce and drizzle remaining sauce over shells to make a decorative pattern. Preheat oven to 350 degrees and bake, covered, for 25 to 30 minutes or until heated through.

RABY'S CRAB STUFFING

Makes 4 pounds

*A*t Raby's Seafood in Port O'Connor Joyce Raby and her crew of helpers prepare crabmeat-stuffed crabs, flounder, shrimp and jalapeño chilies, and a few other items that customers request from time to time. This seafood market got its start in the early 1950s when Helen ("Granny") Raby was persuaded by friends to go into the business of marketing her famous stuffed crabs. In 1981 her son, Dan, and her daughter-in-law, Joyce, took it over, enlarged it, and hired more help for the growing business. And today their son, Dennis, and daughter-in-law, Emma, are involved as well. The Rabys harvest their own seafood, which is then cleaned, cooked, and, in the case of crab, picked on the premises. The following recipe has been adapted from Granny Raby's original. It makes a large amount and may be successfully halved, if desired. However, it freezes well, providing the crabmeat has not been previously frozen, so making the whole amount is infinitely worthwhile. Then there is always some on hand to stuff any sort of seafood, mushrooms, jalapeño chilies, or whatever your imagination dictates.

½ cup water
2 tablespoons margarine
2 cups chopped celery
2 cups chopped onions
¼ cup chopped bell pepper
½ teaspoon salt
½ teaspoon pepper
⅛ teaspoon Italian seasoning
1 heaping tablespoon chopped parsley
¼ cup flour
¼ cup dry milk powder
4 tablespoons water
1 8-ounce package saltine crackers, crushed
¼ cup prepared mustard
3 generous tablespoons dill pickle relish
1 4-ounce jar chopped pimientos, undrained
2 pounds lump crabmeat

In a large pot heat water and margarine. Add celery, cover, and cook until tender but still crisp. Add onions and bell pepper, cover, and cook until tender but still crisp. Remove from heat and add salt, pepper, Italian seasoning, and parsley.

Mix flour, milk powder, and water to make a paste. Stir into vegetables and cook just until thick.

Remove from heat and mix in crackers, mustard, pickle relish, and pimientos. Cool. Fold in crabmeat.

Chill before using, particularly when stuffing small items such as shrimp, mushrooms, or jalapeños.

Bluewater shrimpers cull for jumbos after a three-hour net drag.

CATHERINE SHULT'S CRAB CASSEROLE

Serves 8

*T*his is a dish that makes its appearance at almost every party given by the friends of Ann Shult Griffith, a renowned Houston cook and hostess. Ann's mother, Catherine Shult, was a fine cook with an eye to good seasoning and to ease of preparation.

4 tablespoons butter, divided
1 cup chopped onion
1 cup chopped celery
1 8-ounce package fresh mushrooms, sliced
2 cups prepared herb stuffing mix, divided
¾ cup milk, divided
1 8-ounce can water chestnuts, drained and sliced
2 cups mayonnaise
1 tablespoon Worcestershire sauce or to taste
liberal dash of Tabasco Pepper Sauce
1½ pounds lump crabmeat

In a heavy saucepan melt 2 tablespoons butter and sauté onion, celery, and mushrooms until soft. Set aside.

Soften 1 cup of stuffing mix with ½ cup milk. Stir in vegetables and water chestnuts.

Thin mayonnaise with remaining milk and Worcestershire sauce. Add to mixture and season with Tabasco sauce. Fold in crabmeat.

Spoon mixture into a 2-quart buttered casserole dish. Sprinkle remaining stuffing mix over the top and dot with remaining butter; preheat oven to 375 degrees and bake about 45 minutes or until golden brown on top and heated through.

Tremont's Lump Crab Ravioli in Gingered Chicken Broth.

TREMONT'S LUMP CRAB RAVIOLI IN GINGERED CHICKEN BROTH

Serves 6

*C*hef John Watt at the Tremont Hotel in Galveston assures us that although this recipe may appear somewhat complicated, it is really quite simple to prepare. It consists of stuffed wonton wrappers that are poached in stock and served with a wonderful assortment of greens. Not all home cooks have access to exotic specialty items such as arugula and fresh basil. Luckily for the home gardener, both are easily grown in the warm climate along the Gulf Coast, but they are seasonal. If you need a substitute for arugula, combine spinach leaves and watercress. Or try bok choy or Chinese cabbage. Be adventurous! For fresh basil, substitute a combination of dried basil, softened in hot water, and a few spinach leaves.

1 pound lump crabmeat
zest and juice of 1 lemon
²⁄₃ cup shredded fresh basil leaves, divided
salt to taste
ground white pepper to taste
1 package wonton wrappers (16 to 20)
1 quart strong chicken stock
1 cup dry white wine
8 cloves garlic, chopped fine
2 tablespoons grated fresh ginger root
2 tablespoons olive oil
6 shiitake mushrooms
4 tomatoes, skinned, seeded, drained, and chopped
(to make 1 cup of "tomato concasse")
16 to 20 arugula leaves
½ cup grated smoked or fresh mozzarella cheese
1 teaspoon roasted red pepper flakes
6 sprigs of mint

Combine crabmeat with lemon zest and juice. Fold in ⅓ cup basil and season with salt and pepper.

Place a spoonful of the crab mixture in the center of each wonton wrapper. Wet the edge of the wrapper and fold over to make a triangle, pressing the edges with a fork to seal. Set aside.

In a saucepan combine stock, wine, garlic, and ginger. Bring to a boil, lower heat, and reduce slightly to intensify the flavor. It should have a decided ginger-garlic taste. Strain through a fine strainer and keep warm.

In a sauté pan heat olive oil, add reserved ravioli, and sauté over medium heat for 30 seconds on each side, making sure that the pasta does not stick to the pan. Add mushrooms and reserved stock. Simmer for 4 to 5 minutes.

In each of six bowls place equal portions of remaining basil and tomato concasse. Add several leaves of arugula to each bowl, followed by equal portions of ravioli. Ladle stock into each bowl.

Garnish with cheese, red pepper flakes, and mint.

KEY ALLEGRO CRAB CAKES

Serves 6

*T*o spend a weekend in Rockport at Gaye Tullos's Cooking School is a gourmet's treat. Gaye is an accomplished cook, attributing her expertise to her mother, her French grandmother, and cooking guru Madeleine Kamman. Although she specializes in French cookery, Gaye utilizes the local Gulf Coast seafood in down-home but unique dishes.

1 tablespoon butter
½ cup fine-chopped scallions
½ cup fine-chopped celery
1 pound crabmeat (claw meat is fine)
2 cups dry bread crumbs, divided
1 tablespoon chopped parsley
1 teaspoon dried thyme
1 tablespoon lemon juice
1 tablespoon Worcestershire sauce
¼ teaspoon ground white pepper
½ teaspoon salt or to taste
2 eggs
1 teaspoon dry mustard
2 cups flour
1 cup milk
¼ cup vegetable oil

Melt butter in a skillet and sauté scallions and celery until translucent. Remove from heat and cool.

In a bowl combine crabmeat, 1½ tablespoons bread crumbs, parsley, thyme, lemon juice, Worcestershire sauce, pepper, and salt.

In a separate bowl beat 1 egg with dry mustard and add to crab mixture. Refrigerate for 1 hour.

When well chilled, shape mixture into 6 flat cakes. Beat remaining egg with milk.

Dip cakes in flour, then in egg-milk mixture, and finally in remaining bread crumbs. Refrigerate 1 hour.

Heat oil in a skillet and brown cakes on each side. Serve with Cocktail Sauce for Shrimp or Oysters (p. 204) or Gaido's Tartar Sauce (p. 204)

A yellow-slickered old salt eyes the Bolivar Peninsula's East Bay for schooling redfish.

RUGGLES GRILL CRAB CAKES WITH FIRECRACKER SALSA

Makes 4 patties

*B*ruce Molzan, chef and owner of Ruggles Grill in Houston, is one of the leaders in Southwest cuisine. Bruce and his co-chef, Gary Mercer, have developed crab cakes that are wonderful with the two sauces suggested. Their Firecracker Salsa is good on just about anything.

3 tablespoons olive oil
¼ cup fine-chopped onion
2 tablespoons fine-chopped yellow bell pepper
2 tablespoons fine-chopped red bell pepper
1 teaspoon fine-chopped garlic
3 tablespoons fine-chopped celery
3 tablespoons flour, seasoned with salt and pepper
1 cup heavy cream
1 cup unseasoned bread crumbs
1 pound lump crabmeat
salt and pepper to taste
flour
2 eggs, beaten
1 cup bread crumbs, seasoned with 1 strip cooked,
chopped bacon and 1 teaspoon each of fresh
chopped basil and parsley
vegetable oil
arugula leaves

TOMATO SAUCE

6 ripe Italian plum tomatoes
2 cloves garlic, chopped fine
2 tablespoons fine-chopped shallots
2 teaspoons chopped fresh basil, divided
(or 1 teaspoon dried basil)
1 teaspoon chopped fresh thyme
(or ½ teaspoon dried thyme)
2 tablespoons olive oil
1 red bell pepper
salt and pepper to taste

FIRECRACKER SALSA

½ medium avocado, chopped
½ medium cucumber, peeled, seeded, and
chopped fine
4 medium tomatoes, peeled, seeded, and
chopped fine
1 tablespoon fine-chopped yellow bell pepper
1 tablespoon fine-chopped red bell pepper
½ teaspoon fine-chopped serrano chili
1 teaspoon fine-chopped jalapeño chili
¼ teaspoon ground black pepper
2 tablespoons shredded fresh basil
(or ½ tablespoon dried basil)
3 tablespoons olive oil
juice of 3 limes
salt to taste

Heat oil in a large skillet and sauté onion until translucent. Add bell peppers, garlic, and celery and sauté for 1 minute. Do not burn garlic.

Add seasoned flour, mixing well, and stir in cream. Cook for 2 minutes. Add unseasoned bread crumbs and crabmeat. Stir to combine. Mixture should be stiff, so more bread crumbs may be needed. Season with salt and pepper.

Divide mixture into four equal parts and mold into patties. Roll each in flour, dip in beaten eggs, and coat with seasoned crumbs.

Add about 1 inch oil to skillet and heat over medium-high heat. Cook crab cakes until golden on each side.

To make Tomato Sauce, sauté tomatoes, garlic, shallots, 1 teaspoon basil, and thyme in olive oil for 10 minutes. Cool and puree in a food mill.

Char red bell pepper in a hot skillet, then peel and seed. Puree to make ¼ cup. Add puree to tomato mixture. Season to taste with salt and pepper and stir in remaining fresh basil.

To make Firecracker Salsa, combine all ingredients and mix well. Add more serrano chilies if a hotter sauce is desired.

Serve crab cakes on a bed of Tomato Sauce with a dollop of Firecracker Salsa on the side. Garnish with arugula leaves.

VIETNAMESE SPICY CRABS

Serves 3 to 6

*S*picy crab, or salted crab, as it is sometimes called, it a favorite hors d'ouevre with Vietnamese. It is necessary to break the crabs apart and suck the meat out of the shells, but they are delicious accompanied by ice-cold beer. Hieu Nguyen of Houston's Fountainview Fish Market gives credit to the distaff side of the family for this recipe. Oyster sauce is available in Asian markets.

½ teaspoon salt
2 tablespoons sugar
1 tablespoon dark soy sauce
1 tablespoon oyster sauce
6 whole crabs, cleaned
4 tablespoons vegetable oil
1 clove garlic, peeled
ground black pepper

Mix together salt, sugar, soy sauce, and oyster sauce. Set aside.

Cut crabs into halves or quarters and pat dry with paper towels. Let air-dry a little, if necessary. There should be no moisture to cause the oil to spatter.

Heat oil in a wok and add garlic. Cook over high heat and remove as it begins to brown. Add crabs and stir-fry until red. Add reserved sauce and stir-fry until crabs are well coated. Sprinkle with ground black pepper and serve at once.

Vietnamese Spicy Crabs; Thai House Hot and Sour Fish Soup (see page 150).

GIB'S STEAMED LOBSTER TAILS

*M*y brother, Gib Thompson, is a lobster aficionado who has developed numerous ideas for preparing frozen lobster tails. Steaming is his clear preference. The flavor of the meat isn't diluted by immersing in water—as in boiling; nor is the meat dried out—as in broiling. He suggests steaming a few extra; they can be wrapped in plastic wrap and then zapped in a microwave. In fact, he claims they are even better the next day! Here are his directions.

In the bottom of a large kettle bring water to a boil, adding bay leaf, lemon slices, onion, garlic, wine—whatever seasonings appeal to you. Reduce heat and simmer 1 or 2 minutes.

Position a rack over, but not touching, the water and place thawed lobster tails on the rack. Cover tightly. A 10-ounce lobster tail will require steaming for about 14 minutes; a 6-ounce tail, about 10 minutes.

Serve with drawn butter and lemon, browned butter with a few drained capers, or one of the many sauces in "Basics and Bonuses."

Note: A kettle can be made into a satisfactory steamer by resting a rack on several tunafish cans that have been opened at both ends.

CRAWFISH ENCHILADAS

Serves 8 as first course, 4 as main course

*B*rennan's of Houston calls this "Texas Creole Cooking," combining Creole ingredients and techniques with Texas seasonings and styles. Whatever you choose to call it, it's just wonderful! This dish can also be served as a main course, with black beans and guacamole as side dishes. Call it "Tex-Mex Creole."

2 tablespoons corn oil
¼ cup chopped yellow onions
½ medium red bell pepper, chopped
½ medium green bell pepper, chopped
½ medium poblano chili, chopped
1 large clove garlic, crushed
1 Italian plum tomato, skinned and chopped
12 ounces crawfish tails, cooked and shelled
1 tablespoon chopped fresh basil
1 tablespoon chopped fresh cilantro
½ teaspoon ground cumin
4 ounces Swedish farmer's cheese, grated
salt and black pepper to taste
8 corn tortillas

TOMATILLO SALSA

10 tomatillos, roasted and seeded
1 poblano chili, roasted and seeded
1 teaspoon chopped fresh cilantro
1 cup chicken stock
salt and pepper to taste

Heat corn oil in a large skillet. Over medium heat sauté onions and peppers until soft. Add garlic and tomato, cooking slightly. Add crawfish tails, basil, cilantro, and cumin. Cook for about 3 minutes. Remove from heat and stir in cheese, mixing well. Season with salt and pepper.

In a nonstick skillet over medium heat warm tortillas on both sides to soften. Divide crawfish mixture into 8 portions and fill tortillas. Roll up, place in a shallow baking dish, and cover. Preheat oven to 350 degrees and bake for 8 minutes or until heated through.

To make Tomatillo Salsa, place all ingredients in a heavy saucepan over medium-high heat. Bring to a boil, reduce heat, and simmer for 15 minutes. Puree and keep warm.

Serve enchiladas on warm plates, topped with Tomatillo Salsa.

SEAFOOD LOVER'S
CRAWFISH SALAD

Serves 2 to 4

*T*he Seafood Lover Market had its beginnings in Beaumont when the Edwards family, encouraged by Texas A&M University, brought its seafood expertise into operation in a market that specializes in a variety of fresh seafoods. The family has raised catfish and crawfish on their Catfish Acres farm for many years, so fresh fish is the only fish they acknowledge. It is still a family-owned business with a second market now in Houston. One can always find the newly popular varieties, such as amberjack, tilefish, and grouper, as well as long-time favorites. Here is the family recipe for crawfish salad.

1 cup Mustard Sauce
1 cup fine-chopped celery
3 hard-cooked eggs, chopped fine
1 pound shelled crawfish tails, cooked in water seasoned with crab boil
2 tablespoons chopped scallions
2 tablespoons chopped salad olives
Tabasco Pepper Sauce to taste
salt to taste

MUSTARD SAUCE

1¼ cups Creole mustard or other coarse-grained mustard
⅔ cup mayonnaise
4 teaspoons prepared horseradish
¼ teaspoon cayenne pepper

Combine all ingredients. Cover and refrigerate until thoroughly chilled.

To make Mustard Sauce, mix all ingredients well and refrigerate until ready to use.

A Port Bolivar fisherman relaxes after a satisfying day on the water. These dock house workers display some of the catch scored by Port Bolivar's tiny but successful fleet.

BRENNAN'S SAUTÉ OF LOUISIANA CRAWFISH

Serves 4

*B*rennan's of Houston, under the able leadership of Alex Brennan-Martin and Dick Brennan, Jr., serves the same fine cuisine one finds at Commander's Palace in New Orleans, another Brennan restaurant. This is not at all surprising since they grew up under the tutelage of Alex's mother, Ella Brennan, and her brother, Dick Brennan, Sr. Indeed some of the recipes are shared by both restaurants, and the chefs of each work together and with the families who own these fine establishments. This crawfish recipe, served over angel hair pasta or rice, is rich and satisfying and needs only a green salad and some good white wine to make a grand meal.

½ cup butter, divided
1 pound cooked crawfish tails, shelled and deveined
1 cup chopped scallions, including green tops
1 tablespoon Brennan's Creole Seasoning
for Fish (p. 202)
1 tablespoon Worcestershire sauce
salt to taste
angel hair pasta or rice

Melt 2 tablespoons butter in heavy pan and add crawfish, scallions, Creole seasoning, and Worcestershire sauce. Sauté until hot, stirring constantly. Add remaining butter, about 2 tablespoons at a time, tossing mixture until butter forms a creamy sauce. Add salt.

Serve at once over pasta or rice.

CHINESE STEAMED OYSTERS

Serves 3

*D*orothy Huang, author of Dorothy Huang's Chinese Cooking, has taught more than 10,000 students over the past fifteen years—quite a record in anyone's book. She develops and tests recipes for major companies, and when I asked her to create something new for this book, she enthusiastically responded with the following recipe. Since the juices collected during steaming are so delicious, Dorothy suggests serving bread to soak them up or adding them to a side dish of rice. The Chinese salted black beans and oyster sauce are available in Asian markets.

1 pint fresh oysters
12 pods of snow peas
1 tablespoon corn oil
1 strip bacon, chopped
1 tablespoon chopped garlic
1 teaspoon fine-chopped ginger root
1 tablespoon Chinese salted black beans, rinsed and chopped
1 tablespoon chopped scallions
2 tablespoons oyster sauce
1 lemon, cut into 6 wedges

Drain oysters well. Dry with a paper towel and divide among six 3-inch ramekins. Set aside.

String snow peas and make a small V-cut at one end. Blanch in boiling water for 30 seconds, drain, and freshen in cold water. Drain and pat dry. Set aside.

Heat oil in a wok over high heat. Add bacon, garlic, ginger root, black beans, and scallions. Stir-fry for 30 seconds. Transfer to a bowl and mix in oyster sauce. Spoon mixture over reserved oysters.

In a Chinese steamer bring 3 quarts water to a boil over high heat. Place dishes of oysters in the steamer tray and steam for 1½ minutes or until oysters are heated through. Arrange the dishes of oysters on a serving platter and garnish each dish with 2 snow pea pods. Serve with lemon wedges.

TONY'S FEDELINI AL BUCANIERA

*T*he reputation of Tony's Restaurant in Houston for the best in classic Italian cuisine can surely be confirmed with one bite of this mixed shellfish dish with pasta. Briny shellfish, fresh tomatoes with a hint of herbal fragrance, and freshly cooked pasta will transport you to the sunny Italian seashore for a memorable dinner.

2 cloves garlic, chopped
1 teaspoon red pepper flakes
7 tablespoons olive oil, divided
1 pound tomatoes, peeled and chopped
¾ cup shelled and deveined shrimp (about ½ pound)
½ cup fresh shelled clams
salt and pepper to taste
1 pound fedelini or thin spaghetti
¼ cup mixed chopped parsley and basil
½ pound lump crabmeat

Sauté garlic and red pepper flakes in half the olive oil. Add tomatoes and cook for 15 minutes. Set aside.

In a separate pan sauté shrimp and clams in remaining oil. Cook just until done, then add reserved tomato sauce. Season with salt and pepper and set aside.

In a large pot of boiling water cook fedelini just until done, or *al dente*. Drain, sprinkle with parsley and basil, and mix with reserved sauce. Add crabmeat and heat through. Serve at once.

The fully restored Lydia Ann Channel Lighthouse at the tip of San Jose Island dates back to the 1850s.

Chinese Steamed Oysters.

SHRIMP AND APPLE CURRY

Serves 6

*M*y friends from India call this sort of dish a "colonial curry"—the type of curry loved by Westerners who are certain that it must be the "real thing" because it contains curry powder. No matter that it is a dish whose origin is unknown; it is just plain delicious and easy to serve to a crowd. When increasing the recipe, however, avoid overseasoning when multiplying the amount of Worcestershire sauce, nutmeg, and peppercorns.

¾ cup butter, divided
½ cup chopped onion
3 tablespoons chopped celery
½ cup chopped, peeled green apple
6 peppercorns
1 bay leaf
½ cup flour
1½ teaspoons curry powder or to taste
¼ teaspoon sugar
⅓ teaspoon grated nutmeg
2½ cups milk
2 teaspoons lemon juice
½ teaspoon Worcestershire sauce
1½ pounds shelled cooked shrimp

Melt ⅓ cup butter in a heavy saucepan. Add onion, celery, apple, peppercorns, and bay leaf; cook over medium heat until onion is golden. Blend in flour, curry powder, sugar, and nutmeg, mixing well.

Remove from heat and add milk, mixing well. Return to heat and cook until thick.

Add lemon juice and Worcestershire sauce, mix, and remove from heat. Cool, remove bay leaf, and blend sauce in a blender.

Heat remaining butter in a skillet and add cooked shrimp, coating with butter. Heat through but do not cook. Add sauce and heat well.

Serve over plain rice or saffron rice, accompanied by condiments such as chutney, blanched slivered almonds or chopped peanuts, chopped cucumber, raisins, diced banana, chopped hard-cooked eggs, grated coconut, chopped tomatoes, and yogurt mixed with chopped cilantro.

Houston's hazy city skyline towers beyond a docked freighter.

SAUTÉED SHRIMP WITH GINGER, GREEN CHILE, AND CILANTRO

Serves 4

This is a popular appetizer at Ruggles Grill in Houston. Co-chef Gary Mercer advises having all ingredients chopped, measured, and ready to use. The preparation of the dish should take no longer than 5 minutes and everything happens quickly. Remember, he adds, sauté means to turn! Be careful not to overcook the shrimp. Each of the cooking steps only takes a short time, but together they are sufficient to cook them through.

olive oil
12 cloves garlic, crushed
1 whole jalapeño chili
16 jumbo shrimp, shelled and deveined
3 tablespoons grated fresh ginger root
2 tablespoons fine-chopped shallots
⅓ cup white wine
¼ cup Seafood Stock (p. 203)
¼ cup heavy cream
4 tablespoons fine-chopped jalapeño chilies
¼ cup chopped cilantro leaves, loosely packed
7 tablespoons unsalted butter, softened
salt and white pepper to taste
juice of 1 or 2 limes or to taste

In a sauté pan large enough to hold shrimp in one layer, add just enough olive oil to cover the bottom. Add garlic and jalapeño. Brown on all sides over high heat, turning often to prevent burning. Remove with a slotted spoon and discard.

Add shrimp, ginger, and shallots, tossing and stirring to coat with oil. Continue to sauté about 45 seconds or until shrimp begin to turn opaque. Drain off oil.

Deglaze pan with wine and continue to toss shrimp over high heat until wine almost evaporates.

Add Seafood Stock and cream and cook over high heat until reduced by about one-third. Add chopped jalapeños and cilantro and immediately stir in butter, 1 tablespoon at a time.

Remove from heat; add salt, pepper, and lime juice. Serve at once.

SHRIMP AND SNOW PEA SALAD

Serves 6 as a first course

A light, crisp salad with more than a hint of Chinese cuisine, this can be served as a first course or as a lunch dish accompanied by sliced ripe tomatoes and crusty French bread. My Cuban friend, Andrea Buxton, is a fabulous cook who puts her personal touch on the dishes she prepares. She suggests adding marinated roasted red peppers, mixing them with the rest of the ingredients just before serving. Included is her recipe for the peppers, which is also a marvelous accompaniment for grilled fish or chicken.

½ pound snow peas (about 2 cups)
1½ cups mushrooms, sliced
⅔ pound shrimp, shelled, cooked, and split
½ cup water chestnuts, sliced
2 tablespoons chopped parsley
1 teaspoon fresh ginger root, minced
2 tablespoons garlic chives or scallion tops
3 tablespoons olive oil
1½ teaspoons white wine vinegar
1 tablespoon dry vermouth
salt to taste

MARINATED ROASTED RED PEPPERS

2 large red bell peppers
¼ cup olive oil
1 tablespoon raspberry vinegar
1 teaspoon water
½ teaspoon black pepper
⅛ teaspoon salt
dash of sugar
½ cup chopped fresh basil

Blanch snow peas in boiling water for about 2 minutes, then refresh immediately in ice water. Mix with mushrooms, shrimp, water chestnuts, parsley, ginger root, and chives.

In a small bowl mix oil, vinegar, and vermouth. Immediately before serving, toss pea and shrimp mixture with the dressing and salt to taste. Serve at room temperature. (Do not toss salad with dressing ahead of time because the salt and vinegar will discolor the snow peas if allowed to stand.)

To make Marinated Roasted Red Peppers, bake peppers in a 500-degree oven for 20 minutes. When cool enough to handle, skin, seed, and slice. Mix remaining ingredients and pour over the pepper strips. Refrigerate overnight.

Sautéed Shrimp with Ginger, Green Chile, and Cilantro.

Close-hauled to catch Galveston Bay breezes, sailors tack for regatta buoys off the Clear Lake Channel.

SHRIMP WITH JALAPEÑO CREAM SAUCE

Serves 4

*C*hurrascos Cocina Sud America in Houston, popularly known as Churrascos, is typical of a South American steakhouse and grill, featuring the "Sunday cuisine" of Latin America. Co-owners Michael and Glen Cordua are originally from Nicaragua. Michael, an economics graduate of Texas A&M University, is the menu developer. With Glenn, whose doctorate in psychology is from Brown University, he investigates the foods of Latin America, adapting and improving new recipes as well as recreating those favorites of childhood memories. Glenn's passion for wines has inspired one of the most unique wine lists in the area, featuring South American and California wines not found elsewhere in Houston. A fruity Chardonnay goes well with this dish.

½ cup butter
1 medium onion, cut into julienne strips
1 green bell pepper, cut into julienne strips
1 red bell pepper, cut into julienne strips
3 jalapeño chilies, seeded and sliced
⅛ teaspoon salt
ground black pepper
1 clove garlic, crushed
36 large shrimp, shelled and deveined
1 cup sour cream

Melt butter in a large skillet and sauté onion and peppers until they are soft but still crunchy. Add salt, pepper, and garlic. Add shrimp and sauté until pink. Stir in sour cream and heat but do not boil. Taste to correct seasonings. Serve over white rice.

Shrimp with Jalapeño Cream Sauce.

SEAFOOD LOVER'S SHRIMP MOUSSE

Serves 6 to 8 as a first course

*T*his mousse is usually available to taste at the Houston branch of the Seafood Lover Market, but you have to get there before noon or the samples will be all gone. Chef and owner Susan Middleton says this dish will serve 20 to 25 people as a cocktail party spread, but it is so good that I like it as a first course. It's rich, so small servings are adequate.

2 tablespoons unflavored gelatin
¼ cup water
1 10 ¾-ounce can condensed cream of tomato soup
1 8-ounce package cream cheese, softened
¾ cup chopped onion
½ cup chopped celery
1 cup mayonnaise
1 teaspoon lemon juice
1 teaspoon salt
1 pound cooked shrimp, shelled, deveined, and chopped

Soften gelatin in water. In a saucepan heat soup. Stir in softened gelatin until completely dissolved. Remove from heat.

Add cream cheese and mix well, using an electric mixer.

Stir in remaining ingredients and pour into an oiled 1-quart mold. Refrigerate until set. Unmold and serve. Or serve in individual ramekins as a first course or a luncheon dish.

The Victorian architecture of Galveston's East End historic district stands in contrast to the modern presence of the University of Texas Medical Branch.

TONY'S SHRIMP MOUSSE

Serves 4

*F*rom the files of Tony's Restaurant in Houston comes the following silky mousse. It's a wonderfully rich dish which needs no further embellishments; it's great for a lunch dish or a first course preceding a light dinner. If fresh tarragon is not available, Mexican mint marigold is a good substitute.

1 pound shrimp
3 cups water
1 envelope unflavored gelatin
¼ cup white wine
¼ cup dry sherry
3 tablespoons brandy
2 tablespoons fine-chopped fresh tarragon
½ cup mayonnaise
salt and pepper to taste
½ cup heavy cream

Shell and devein shrimp and set aside. In a saucepan cover shrimp shells with water and boil for about 15 minutes. Strain and continue cooking until reduced to 2 cups. Add shrimp and cook 2 to 3 minutes or just until tender. Remove shrimp and set aside. Reduce broth to 1¼ cups.

Soften gelatin in wine and sherry and add to shrimp broth. Heat until gelatin has dissolved and the broth is clear.

Mix broth, reserved shrimp, and brandy and process in a food processor until smooth. Transfer to a bowl and cool.

Combine cooled shrimp mixture with tarragon, mayonnaise, salt, and pepper.

Whip cream until it forms soft peaks and fold into shrimp mixture. Spoon into an oiled mold or individual molds and refrigerate overnight.

SHRIMP WITH LOBSTER SAUCE

Serves 4

*M*y friend Gertrude Yang grew up in Shanghai and came to the United States to attend college. She has remained here since graduation and is a charming ambassador of good will between China and all her American friends. I was fortunate to be able to go with her to China on her first return visit there. It was an overwhelming experience—cultural, visual, and culinary. Gertrude is a fine cook and taught Chinese cooking for several years, so she planned each meal as meticulously as the itinerary itself. We ate our way through some of the most delicious food in China on that trip. Here is one of her most popular recipes, which—despite the title— contains no lobster. The fermented black beans are available in Asian markets and some specialty markets.

1 pound raw shrimp (16 to 20 count)
¼ cup peanut oil, divided
2 slices fresh ginger root
1 tablespoon dry sherry
2 teaspoons fermented black beans, chopped
2 cloves garlic, crushed
¼ pound lean ground pork
1 tablespoon soy sauce
1 teaspoon salt
½ cup unsalted chicken stock
(if using salted stock, omit salt)
2 tablespoons cornstarch, dissolved in
3 tablespoons cold water
1 scallion, chopped
2 eggs, lightly beaten

Shell and devein shrimp, leaving tail section intact. Slice lengthwise along center of underside of shrimp, but do not cut entirely through the flesh. Flatten with a knife or cleaver.

In a wok heat 2 tablespoons oil and ginger. Add shrimp and stir-fry for 1 minute. Add sherry and stir. Remove shrimp and set aside.

Add remaining oil. Stir in fermented black beans and garlic. Add pork and stir-fry until no longer pink. Stir in soy sauce, salt, chicken stock, and cornstarch mixture. Add reserved shrimp and scallion, stirring until thick. Pour in eggs in a slow stream, stirring slightly. Remove from heat and serve at once.

SHRIMP SOUP

Serves 6 to 8

*O*ne of the most seductive seafood soups I have tasted is this marvelous chupe de camarones from Churrascos in Houston. It calls for fish stock, which is available in packaged form or, better, easily made at home (see Seafood Stock, p. 203). Michael Cordua, chef and co-owner of the restaurant, uses a lobster base to enhance the flavor further, but it is equally good with a well-flavored fish stock. The recipe calls for panela cheese, a Mexican low-fat cheese. Any low-fat cheese can be substituted, but be sure it is really low in fat. A cheese with a high fat content gets stringy in hot broth, spoiling the texture of this dish.

1 tablespoon butter
1 large or 2 small chayote squash, peeled
and cut into ¼-inch cubes
1 8-ounce can baby corn ears, cut into ¼-inch slices
6 cups Seafood Stock (p. 203)
4 ounces lobster base (optional)
1 pound small shrimp, shelled and deveined
(45 + count)
1 pound panela cheese or other low-fat cheese,
cut into ¼-inch cubes
1 cup heavy cream
salt to taste

Melt butter in a heavy saucepan and sauté squash until slightly softened. Do not overcook. Add corn and toss to coat with butter. Add Seafood Stock and lobster base. Heat to simmering and add shrimp, cheese cubes, cream, and salt. Taste to correct seasonings. Heat to simmering and serve at once.

SHRIMP IN MUSTARD SAUCE

Serves 10 as a first course, 4 to 6 as a main course

*F*ormer Houstonians Martha and John Culbertson returned to California a few years ago to oversee the family business of making sparkling wines. Their Culbertson's Winery makes a variety of "cuvées"—all delicious. Martha's Cafe Champagne at the winery has won accolades from visitors who come from all over the country to sample the wines and food and to attend her cooking classes. This is one of many popular recipes there.

4 tablespoons vegetable oil
30 large shrimp, shelled and deveined
salt and pepper
2 shallots, chopped fine
2 tablespoons chopped fresh tarragon
½ cup Culbertson Brut champagne
½ cup cream
½ pound unsalted butter, cut into small pieces
2 tablespoons Dijon mustard
salt and pepper to taste
1 tablespoon chopped chives

In a heavy skillet heat oil and sauté shrimp 6 to 7 minutes or just until done. Sprinkle with salt and pepper and remove from pan. Set aside and keep warm.

In the same pan sauté shallots until tender. Add tarragon and heat through.

Deglaze pan with champagne, scraping up any browned bits. Add cream and boil until reduced and thickened. Whisk in butter, one piece at a time, to form an emulsion. Whisk in mustard. Do not let sauce come to a boil again. Season with salt and pepper.

Return shrimp to pan to heat through. Garnish with chives.

As a main course, serve over rice or pasta.

SMOKED SHRIMP MARINATED IN SUN-DRIED TOMATO VINAIGRETTE

Serves 4

*G*alveston's Tremont Hotel is one of the most picturesque buildings in the restored Strand area. The old hotel has been refurbished in the style of the late nineteenth century and houses a popular restaurant with an outstanding menu. Under the talented hands of Executive Chef John Watt, classic dishes are prepared in new ways to attract gourmands from the mainland as well as the island itself.

24 medium to large shrimp, shelled, deveined, and
smoked over mesquite in a smoker, according to
manufacturer's directions
Sun-Dried Tomato Vinaigrette
lollo rosso or other ruffled salad greens
cracked black pepper
lemon slices

SUN-DRIED TOMATO VINAIGRETTE

1 cup balsamic vinegar
1 cup fresh lemon juice
½ teaspoon salt
¼ teaspoon ground black pepper
1½ cups extra-virgin olive oil
16 fine-chopped sun-dried tomatoes, marinated
in olive oil for 24 hours
16 cloves garlic, chopped fine
4 serrano chilies, seeded and chopped fine

Marinate smoked shrimp in 2 cups of Sun-Dried Tomato Vinaigrette for 4 hours.

To make Sun-Dried Tomato Vinaigrette, mix vinegar, lemon juice, salt, and pepper together until salt has completely dissolved. Whisk in olive oil. Stir in remaining ingredients, mixing well.

To serve, arrange greens on four serving plates. Drizzle with Sun-Dried Tomato Vinaigrette and place 6 shrimp in the center of the plate. Sprinkle with cracked black pepper and serve with a lemon slice.

Smoked Shrimp Marinated in Sun-Dried Tomato Vinaigrette.

PICKLED SHRIMP

Serves 12 to 15 as an hors d'oeuvre

*T*his popular cocktail party dish never fails to please a crowd, and there is never any left over. The fact that it should be made at least a day in advance is a big bonus when planning a party, and the proportions can be increased to serve any number of guests. Remember to go easy on the salt when increasing the recipe.

3 pounds shelled and cooked shrimp
3 onions, sliced very thin
7 or 8 bay leaves
1¼ cups salad oil
¾ cup white vinegar
½ tablespoon salt
2½ teaspoons celery seeds
2½ tablespoons undrained capers
generous dash of Tabasco Pepper Sauce
1 garlic clove, crushed

Alternate layers of shrimp and onions in a shallow glass dish.

Combine remaining ingredients and pour over shrimp. Cover and refrigerate for 24 hours or longer.

Drain off marinade and serve icy cold in a bowl (a large shell looks great) with a small container of toothpicks to spear the shrimp.

SHRIMP EMPANADAS

Makes enough filling for 6 to 8 empanadas

*E*mpanadas de camarones *is a favorite first course at Churrascos Cocina Sud America in Houston, although it can also be a grand lunch dish when accompanied by a green salad or a dish of guacamole. The restaurant serves it piping hot, sans sauce. Note that the filling, which contains raisins and olives, is unlike some of the Mexican recipes for similar dishes. It should be baked in pastry dough rather than in tortillas. The seafood glacé is unsalted fish stock which has been reduced until it is thick and syrupy. Do not reduce commercially prepared stock: the amount of salt will render it unpalatable. You may substitute a small amount of a seafood bouillon seasoning cube, but remember that one cube usually contains enough salt for 2 cups of water, so go slowly!*

2 medium onions, cut into julienne strips
⅔ cup raisins
⅔ cup stuffed green olives
4 ounces seafood glacé
1 teaspoon olive oil
2 tablespoons Tio Pepe liqueur
½ teaspoon ground cumin
¼ teaspoon red pepper flakes
1 teaspoon paprika or achiote paste
½ pound small shrimp, shelled and deveined
Basic Pastry (p. 208)

Mix onions, raisins, olives, glacé, olive oil, and liqueur. Simmer over low heat for 1 minute. Add cumin, red pepper flakes, and paprika or achiote paste. Continue to simmer about 25 minutes or until onion is wilted. Add shrimp and cook for another 3 minutes or until pink.

Roll out Basic Pastry dough and cut into 6-inch circles. Fill each pastry circle with about ⅓ cup filling. Fold over and seal edges well. Place on an ungreased baking sheet. Preheat oven to 420 degrees and bake 30 minutes or until lightly browned.

ANGEL HAIR PASTA WITH SHRIMP, CRAB, AND SCALLOPS

Serves 6

*F*ormer Houstonian Martha Culbertson oversees the cuisine of Cafe Champagne, located at the Culbertson Winery in California. Martha says this popular dish is marvelous when made with Gulf Coast shrimp and crab. It is also a boon for the hostess since a great part of it can be made ahead of time. Cook the shrimp, make the shrimp stock base, and set aside. When ready to serve, add cream and proceed with the recipe from this point on.

1½ pounds unshelled medium shrimp
3 tablespoons olive oil
1 tablespoon cognac
1 medium carrot, chopped
1 onion, chopped
1 stalk celery, chopped
1 red bell pepper, chopped
½ cup Culbertson Brut champagne
dash of cayenne pepper
1½ cups water
1 cup heavy cream
½ pound scallops
½ pound lump white crabmeat
1 pound fresh angel hair pasta
fresh basil leaves

Shell and devein shrimp and set aside. In a saucepan heat oil, add shrimp shells, and sauté over high heat. Add cognac and flame the shells. Add carrot, onion, celery, red bell pepper, champagne, and cayenne pepper and mix well. Add water and bring to a boil. Reduce heat and simmer for 30 minutes.

Process mixture in a blender to chop shells. Strain through a fine sieve, pressing to extract the juices. Return liquid to a saucepan and reduce to 1 cup.

Meanwhile cook reserved shrimp in salted water until pink. Drain and set aside.

In a saucepan heat cream and reduce by about one-fourth. Add scallops and cook for 2 to 3 minutes or just until done. Add boiled shrimp, reduced stock, and crabmeat and heat through.

Cook pasta *al dente*, drain, and combine with sauce. Serve garnished with basil leaves.

Family pride reflects in this shrimp boat built in a Bolivar backyard.

VIETNAMESE SPRING ROLLS

Makes 8 to 12 rolls

*S*pring rolls as they are prepared in Vietnam are not to be confused with Chinese egg rolls. The Vietnamese roll contains pork, shrimp, lettuce, and cooked rice sticks in a very thin wrapper of rice paper. Although the filling is cooked, the wrapper is not. Sauce flavored with peanut butter and chopped peanuts as well as a hot sauce, such as Tabasco, accompany the rolls. Sprigs of fresh mint are also traditional with the dish. Hieu Nguyen, chef and owner of Fountainview Fish Market in Houston, shares this family recipe. Rice sticks, rice paper, and Hoisin sauce are available in Asian markets.

½ teaspoon salt
½ whole lemon
1 slice onion
1 pound medium shrimp (45 to 50 count)
1 pound pork tenderloin
½ package rice sticks
1 head leaf lettuce
3 teaspoons peanut butter
6 tablespoons sweet Hoisin sauce
6 tablespoons water
3 tablespoons sugar
1 to 2 tablespoons chopped unsalted peanuts
8 to 12 circles of rice paper (12-inch diameter)
Tabasco Pepper Sauce

Fill a saucepan with enough water to cover shrimp and bring to a boil. Add salt, lemon, and onion. Reduce heat and simmer for 5 minutes. Drop in shrimp and remove from heat. Let stand until shells are pink. Drain, shell, and devein shrimp. Set aside. (This method keeps the shrimp from curling up—not a desirable shape for spring rolls.)

Place pork in a pot of salted water which almost covers it. Bring to a boil, cover, reduce heat, and simmer about 30 minutes or to an internal temperature of 170 degrees. Discard water and cool. Slice in very thin slices. Set aside.

Cook the rice sticks in boiling water according to directions on package. Drain and set aside.

Wash lettuce, remove any stems, and reserve the leafy green part. Drain well and set aside.

In a small saucepan combine peanut butter, Hoisin sauce, water, and sugar. Bring to a boil, reduce heat, and simmer until sugar is dissolved and peanut butter is thoroughly incorporated. Transfer to a serving bowl and top with chopped peanuts. Set aside.

Wet hands and brush just enough water on both sides of each piece of rice paper to soften it. About 3 or 4 inches from the bottom edge of the circle, place two pieces of rice stick. Lay three shrimp over the rice sticks, followed by two or three slices of pork. Cover with shredded lettuce. Fold the bottom of the rice paper circle over the filling. Fold each side toward the center and over the bottom flap to make an envelope. Starting at the bottom, roll the spring roll carefully toward the top of the circle. It will seal itself.

Serve at once with the Hoisin sauce and Tabasco sauce. Rice paper dries quickly and will break if allowed to dry out.

Rolling with eight-foot seas, snapper anglers from Freeport try their luck around an offshore rig platform. Bringing home the fish is less strenuous at the brimming Kemah and Seabrook markets near Galveston Bay.

BRENNAN'S GRILLED MAKO SHARK WITH GREEN GAZPACHO SALSA

Serves 4

*C*ousins Alex Brennan-Martin and Dick Brennan want the cuisine of their restaurant, Brennan's of Houston, to reflect the best of the local Texas flavors and seasonings as well as the Creole style of their heritage. With the cooperation of Chef Carl, the three have combined their talents to produce some very interesting interpretations of local ideas. Shark is a mild, firm-textured fish with a welcome lack of bones, but swordfish is an equally delicious substitute.

4 6-ounce Mako shark steaks
Brennan's Creole Seasoning for Fish (p. 202)
vegetable oil
sprigs of cilantro

TOMATILLO SALSA

10 tomatillos, husked
½ poblano chili, seeded
leaves from about 15 sprigs of cilantro
1 cup chicken stock
½ cup chopped onion

GREEN GAZPACHO SALSA

1 cup Tomatillo Salsa
½ cup peeled, seeded, and diced cucumbers
¼ cup fine-chopped onion
¼ cup fine-chopped celery
3 tablespoons chopped bell pepper
1 tablespoon thin-sliced scallions (green tops only)
½ teaspoon chopped cilantro leaves
½ teaspoon fresh lime juice
¼ jalapeño chili, seeded and chopped fine
¼ teaspoon fine-chopped garlic
dash of Tabasco Pepper Sauce

Sprinkle fish with seasoning powder and rub with vegetable oil. Set aside.

To make Tomatillo Salsa, combine all salsa ingredients in a heavy saucepan. Bring to a boil, reduce heat, and simmer for 15 minutes. Puree in a blender or food processor. Chill.

To make Green Gazpacho Salsa, combine all salsa ingredients. Taste to correct seasonings. Chill well.

Grill fish steaks over hot coals until just barely done. Place on a warm plate and top with chilled Green Gazpacho Salsa. Garnish with sprigs of cilantro.

BILL BERKLEY'S FRIED FISH

Serves 8 to 10

3 pounds fish (any kind, saltwater or freshwater)
3 cups milk
1 egg
2 tablespoons Dijon mustard
2 tablespoons Tabasco Pepper Sauce
3 cups yellow cornmeal
2 teaspoons ground white pepper
2 tablespoons seasoned salt
2 teaspoons garlic powder
cooking oil

Cut fish into fillets about ¾ inch thick. Set aside. Mix milk, egg, mustard, and Tabasco sauce together. Set aside. Mix cornmeal and seasonings together. Set aside.

Dip fillets in batter and then in cornmeal mixture, coating well. Shake off excess. Fry in hot oil at 350 degrees or until crisp and golden. Drain on paper towels.

POACHED FISH CARILLON

Serves 6 as main course, 10 to 12 as first course

*T*his was a favorite way of preparing Gulf fish at Hilltop Herb Farm's Restaurant in Houston's Carillon Center. Although the restaurant is now only a memory, this is a particularly useful recipe because the method works for just one or two servings or for a crowd. The dish works well with grouper, snapper, redfish, and tilefish. Thin fillets such as flounder or sole should be rolled or folded so that they remain moist while cooking. The Lemon Thyme Butter Sauce is delicious on fish or poultry as well as steamed vegetables. It keeps well in the refrigerator for several days, and the recipe can be doubled or tripled.

6 6-ounce fish fillets
1 cup dry white wine
1 cup water
1 large yellow onion, cut into 2-inch slices
1 lemon or lime, cut into 6 to 8 slices
2 large bay leaves, broken into 1-inch pieces
1 rib celery, cut into 2-inch pieces
3 to 4 sprigs each of several mild fresh herbs (such as lemon thyme, marjoram, basil, mint, or parsley)
2 tablespoons butter or oil
3 cups julienne of mixed vegetables of various colors and textures (such as yellow and green squash, carrots, snow peas, green beans, red bell peppers)
½ cup thin-sliced scallions
1 tablespoon each of chopped fresh lemon thyme, sweet marjoram, and oregano
½ teaspoon salt or to taste
1 tablespoon lemon juice
chopped parsley and sprigs of other fresh herbs

Bill Berkley's Fried Fish.

LEMON THYME BUTTER SAUCE

½ cup butter or margarine
2 tablespoons fine-chopped yellow onion
1 teaspoon pureed or fine-chopped garlic
⅓ cup dry white wine
1 tablespoon chopped fresh lemon thyme
3 egg yolks, slightly beaten
2 teaspoons lemon juice
salt and ground white pepper to taste

Rinse fish fillets and pat dry. In a large stainless skillet or other shallow dish, combine wine, water, onion, lemon, bay leaves, celery, and herbs. Bring to a boil, reduce heat, and simmer for 5 to 6 minutes. Press lemon slices with back of spoon to release flavor.

Add fish fillets and spoon hot liquid over them to moisten thoroughly. Cover with a tight-fitting lid and poach about 8 to 10 minutes per inch of thickness or until fish is opaque. Do not overcook!

Meanwhile, in a large skillet sauté vegetables in butter or oil, adding vegetables a handful at a time. When heated through, add herbs, salt, and lemon juice and remove from heat. Keep warm.

To make Lemon Thyme Butter Sauce, heat butter in a small, heavy, noncorrosive saucepan and sauté onion and garlic until soft but not brown. Add wine and cook over medium heat until reduced by half. Add lemon thyme, mixing well.

Remove from heat and add 1 or 2 tablespoons to the egg yolks, mixing well. Whisk warmed egg yolks into the butter-wine mixture and return to heat. Cook, stirring constantly, about 1 minute or until sauce is thick. Remove from heat, season with lemon juice, salt, and pepper, and keep warm over hot water until ready to use. (If egg yolks become grainy, process sauce in a blender for a few seconds until smooth.)

Divide among individual plates or arrange on a serving platter. Remove fish fillets from poaching liquid and place on top of vegetables. Spoon Lemon Thyme Butter Sauce over fillets and garnish with chopped parsley and herbs.

A catch of redfish and black drum is proudly exhibited at the Lydia Ann Channel jetties.

THAI HOUSE HOT AND SOUR FISH SOUP

Serves 2 to 3

*K*nown as Tom Yam Pla, this popular fish soup at the Thai House Restaurant in Houston is also excellent with shrimp instead of fish. If Kaffir leaf is unavailable, omit it or substitute a lemon or lime leaf. *Thai shrimp-chili paste and Thai fish sauce (nam pla) are available at ethnic markets.*

2 cups well-seasoned chicken broth
1 1-inch piece lemon grass, sliced diagonally
1 Kaffir leaf
1 tablespoon Thai shrimp-chili paste
4 ounces fish cubes
2½ teaspoons fresh lime juice
1½ teaspoons Thai fish sauce
2 scallions, chopped
2 to 3 sprigs of cilantro

Combine broth, lemon grass, Kaffir leaf, and shrimp-chili paste in a saucepan. Bring to a boil, reduce heat, and simmer 1 minute.

Add fish cubes and simmer 2 minutes or until done. Stir in lime juice and fish sauce.

Ladle soup into warmed serving bowls and top with scallions and cilantro.

At this Rockport bait stand the inventory runs low after a day of catering to Aransas Bay anglers.

GOA FLOUNDER CURRY

Serves 8

*O*n the coast of the Arabian Ocean lies Goa, one of the most important areas in India for seafood. The seafood dishes from this region take many forms, most of them spicy with chilies, nuts, and herbs. In this curry recipe pomfret, a beautifully flavored fish, is traditionally used. Suneeta Vaswani, a talented cook, teacher, and historian now living in Houston, uses flounder as a substitute since it is the Gulf of Mexico variety that most closely resembles pomfret in texture. The coconut milk used in this recipe is available in Asian markets.

12 whole dried red chilies, seeded
2 serrano chilies, seeded
15 to 18 garlic cloves, peeled
½-inch piece of ginger root, peeled
2 teaspoons cumin seed, roasted
2 teaspoons poppy seeds
4 tablespoons raw cashew nuts
2 to 4 tablespoons vinegar
1 teaspoon powdered turmeric
6 to 8 tablespoons vegetable oil
2 medium onions, pureed
1 14-ounce can unsweetened coconut milk
3 pounds flounder fillets (about 1½ inches thick)
juice of 2 lemons
lemon wedges

CACHUMBER SALAD

1 ripe tomato, chopped
1 medium onion, chopped
2 serrano chilies, seeded and sliced thin (optional)
juice of 1 lemon or lime

Combine chilies, garlic, ginger root, cumin seed, poppy seeds, cashew nuts, vinegar, and turmeric. Blend in a blender (not a food processor) to form a paste. Set aside.

Heat oil in a large skillet and fry onions until golden, stirring frequently. Add spice paste and mix well. Fry 6 to 8 minutes or until the oil begins to separate.

Add coconut milk, mixing well, and bring to a boil. Lower heat and simmer for 6 to 8 minutes.

Add fillets and bring to a boil again. Lower heat and cook about 8 minutes or until fish is cooked. Do not overcook. Remove from heat, add lemon juice, and let stand for 30 minutes.

To make Cachumber Salad, mix all ingredients and refrigerate until ready to serve.

Serve curry hot with plain boiled rice, lemon wedges, and Cachumber Salad.

Workers line up to peel and grade shrimp at Freeport.

GROUPER BAKED WITH VEGETABLES

Serves 8 to 10

*B*ill Berkley, airline pilot by profession, fisherman by choice, and chef by talent and inclination, created this recipe for an almost effortless baked fish dish. The juices of the fish baste the potatoes, and both are flavored by the mélange of vegetables layered over it all. Any mild-flavored, firm-textured fish will be delicious prepared this way.

3 pounds potatoes, parboiled
5 to 6 pounds whole dressed fish or large fillets
5 bell peppers (any color)
3 large onions
5 ribs celery
2 pounds fresh mushrooms
2 pounds tomatoes
seasoned salt
ground black pepper
garlic powder
1½ cups butter
Worcestershire sauce
juice of 2 lemons
2 lemons, sliced thin
1 bunch of parsley, chopped

Cut potatoes in half if very large and place in the bottom of a large baking pan. Place fish over potatoes.

Cut bell peppers, onions, and celery into thick slices. Clean mushrooms and quarter tomatoes.

Layer vegetables over the top of the fish, seasoning each layer with salt, pepper, and garlic powder. Cube butter and layer over vegetables. Sprinkle with Worcestershire sauce and lemon juice.

Layer lemon slices over vegetables. Sprinkle with parsley.

Cover the dish with foil and bake on an outdoor smoker (or in a 350-degree oven) until the fish flakes easily. The cooking time will depend on the size of fish or fillets.

GROUPER WITH NASTURTIUM SAUCE

Serves 4

*T*his imaginative dish comes from the kitchen of Madalene Hill and Gwen Barclay, the mother-daughter team of Hilltop Herb Farm in Cleveland. It's a real beauty, with its colorful sauce and flower garnish. The leaves and blossoms of the nasturtium are delicious, with a peppery bite similar to that of watercress. In fact, watercress may be substituted for nasturtiums, with marigold petals added for color and additional flavor. Other fish varieties with similar texture and flavor can be substituted if grouper isn't available.

1 cup heavy cream
½ cup dry white wine
1 tablespoon lemon juice
½ cup butter, cut into tablespoon-size pieces
1 clove garlic, chopped fine
1 ounce nasturtium leaves, chopped
(about 15 leaves)
½ ounce nasturtium flowers, chopped
(about 12 to 14 blossoms)
1 tablespoon chopped fresh parsley
2 teaspoons chopped fresh lemon thyme
salt to taste
4 6- to 8-ounce grouper fillets
flour seasoned with salt and white pepper
butter, vegetable oil, olive oil, or a combination
additional nasturtium flowers and chopped parsley

Combine cream, wine, and lemon juice in a small noncorrosive saucepan and simmer over low heat until reduced to ½ cup, stirring often. Remove from heat and whisk in butter, one piece at a time. Add garlic, nasturtium leaves and flowers, parsley, and thyme. Add additional salt or lemon juice if needed. Keep warm.

Dredge fillets in seasoned flour, shaking off excess, and sauté in butter or oil.

To serve, top each fillet with sauce and garnish with additional nasturtium flowers and parsley.

DOROTHY HUANG'S HOISIN GROUPER

Serves 2

*T*he sweet piquancy imparted to seafood dishes by Hoisin sauce is one of the hallmarks of Chinese cuisine. Houston's Dorothy Huang, cookbook author and cooking teacher, recommends this recipe for grouper, amberjack, snapper, or similar fish. Hoisin sauce is available in Asian markets.

⅛ teaspoon ground white pepper
1 tablespoon rice wine or dry sherry
1 tablespoon cornstarch
½ tablespoon soy sauce
1½-pound grouper fillet, boned, skinned, and cut
into ¾-inch cubes
3 tablespoons corn oil, divided
1 red bell pepper, cut into 1-inch pieces
1 tablespoon shredded fresh ginger root
1 teaspoon red pepper flakes
2 scallions, cut diagonally into 1-inch pieces
1 tablespoon Hoisin sauce
1 tablespoon soy sauce
1 cup toasted sliced almonds

Combine white pepper, wine, cornstarch, and soy sauce. Add fish and mix, coating evenly.

In a wok heat 1 tablespoon oil over high heat. Stir-fry bell pepper for 1 minute. Remove and set aside.

Rinse and dry the wok. Heat remaining oil over high heat. Add ginger root, red pepper flakes, and fish cubes. Stir-fry for 1 to 2 minutes or until fish is done. Add scallions, Hoisin sauce, soy sauce, and reserved bell pepper. Stir to mix well. Transfer to a serving platter and garnish with almonds.

BROILED GROUPER FILLETS WITH SPICY TOPPING

Serves 4

*S*uneeta Vaswani's cooking classes are fun and very informative. She keeps up a running dialogue on Indian history, politics, and culture with her students and at the same time demonstrates Indian cooking techniques and recipes. This broiled fish recipe is from the area around Goa, located on the coast of the Arabian Ocean. It can be prepared with any "meaty" fillet. The Indian red chili powder and tamarind concentrate are available in Asian markets.

1 medium onion
½ medium tomato
⅓ cup cilantro leaves
6 to 8 garlic cloves
6 to 8 serrano chilies
1 tablespoon vegetable oil
1 teaspoon ground coriander
¾ teaspoon ground cumin seed
½ teaspoon powdered turmeric
¼ teaspoon Indian red chili powder
¼ teaspoon salt
1 teaspoon tamarind concentrate
4 8-ounce grouper fillets

Puree onion, tomato, cilantro, garlic, and chilies in a food processor.

Heat oil in a small skillet and sauté pureed mixture 3 to 4 minutes over medium heat. Add coriander, cumin, turmeric, chili powder, and salt. Sauté 2 minutes.

Add tamarind concentrate, mixing well. The mixture should be thick and fairly dry.

Rub a broiler tray with vegetable oil and place fillets on the tray. Spread spice mixture over fillets. Broil in a preheated broiler for 10 to 15 minutes or until fish flakes easily.

Windsurfers veer through the white-caps at Corpus Christi.

This sportfisherman is baited up and ready for the redfish run through Galveston Island's San Luis Pass.

KINGFISH BACKSTRAP SALAD

Serves 4

*T*he kingfish, or king mackerel, is a streamlined, fast fish that can provide a real challenge for sportfishermen. Its firm-textured flesh has a more pronounced flavor than most other Gulf Coast varieties, which perhaps explains why it isn't widely available in fish markets. However, those in the know regard it as a delicious fish if prepared properly. At her cooking school in Rockport, Gaye Tullos demonstrates this method of utilizing the "backstrap," that portion of the fillet near the backbone that can be popped out of a cross-section steak like a ball. Fresh tuna can be substituted if kingfish isn't available.

¼ cup vegetable oil
2 tablespoons red wine vinegar
1 clove garlic, crushed
½ onion, chopped
1 teaspoon Worcestershire sauce
fresh herbs such as thyme, oregano, or savory
1 pound kingfish backstrap, cut into large chunks
8 scallions, chopped fine
½ cup fine-chopped sour pickle
2 teaspoons drained capers
½ cup mayonnaise (preferably homemade)
2 tablespoons fine-chopped celery
½ teaspoon lemon juice
salt and pepper to taste
shredded red and green cabbage (optional)

Combine oil, vinegar, garlic, onion, Worcestershire sauce, and herbs. Add fish chunks and marinate at least 1 hour.

Drain fish and pat dry. Grill over hot coals just until done. Cool and combine with remaining ingredients except cabbage, tossing to mix well. Serve at room temperature on a bed of shredded cabbage.

MANSFIELD CLUB'S REDFISH ON THE HALF-SHELL

*A*t the end of a successful day of deep-sea fishing, sportfishermen bring their redfish catch back to the Mansfield Club in Port Mansfield to be prepared for an ambrosial dinner. They usually ask to have it "on the half-shell." Fillets are cut from the fish, leaving the skin and scales on. When cooked over a hot charcoal fire, the scales and skin form a shell from which the meat can easily be scooped out. The chef says not to worry about the burned scales. It won't affect the taste of the fish.

To prepare the fillets, brush the flesh side of each fillet with melted butter and oyster sauce (available at any Asian market). Sprinkle with lemon pepper. Cover loosely with aluminum foil and grill, skin side down, over a very hot fire for 15 to 20 minutes or until the flesh flakes. (Grilling time will vary according to the thickness of the fillet.)

A Galveston Bay shrimper heads back to port at Kemah.

THE RIVOLI'S REDFISH AND CRAB IN PUFF PASTRY

Serves 6

*T*his is one of the most popular dishes on the menu at Ed Zelinsky's Rivoli Restaurant in Houston. Prepared puff paste dough is available in certain bakeries and in the frozen-food section of fine supermarkets. Phyllo pastry can be substituted, but the dish will not be quite the same.

6 4-ounce redfish fillets
salt and pepper
1-pound package puff paste dough
½ pound lump crabmeat
1 egg, beaten

DILL SAUCE

1 tablespoon butter
1 tablespoon flour
½ cup fish stock
¼ cup dry white wine
¼ cup cream
salt and pepper to taste
5 to 6 drops lemon juice
1 tablespoon chopped fresh dill
(or ½ tablespoon dried dill)

Season fillets with salt and pepper and set aside.

Divide dough into 6 pieces. On a floured surface, roll each into a rectangle big enough to completely envelop a fillet and a dollop of crabmeat.

Divide crabmeat into 6 portions and place a portion into each of the dough rectangles. Place a fillet on top of the crabmeat.

Pull the sides together to make a seam down the center of the top, pinch together to seal, and brush with beaten egg. Turn seam side down and brush the top with beaten egg. Make "scales" with a melon baller or sharp-edged spoon and put the finished packet on a buttered baking sheet. Repeat with each packet.

To make Dill Sauce, melt butter in a saucepan, add flour, and cook 1 minute. Add stock and wine, stirring constantly, and cook for 2 minutes. Add cream, mixing thoroughly. Add remaining ingredients. Taste to correct seasonings.

Preheat oven to 375 degrees and bake packets on the middle rack for 15 to 20 minutes or until pastry is well browned. Serve hot, topped with Dill Sauce.

CAFE ANNIE'S GULF SNAPPER WITH AVOCADO AND TOMATILLO SAUCE

Serves 4

*T*his recipe comes from owner and chef Robert Del Grande of Cafe Annie in Houston. The Avocado and Tomatillo Sauce is useful in many dishes and can be prepared ahead of time.

4 7- to 8-ounce snapper fillets
¼ cup olive oil
sprigs of fresh oregano
(or ⅛ teaspoon dried oregano)
salt and pepper
1 avocado, chopped
1 lime, quartered
4 sprigs of cilantro

AVOCADO AND TOMATILLO SAUCE

5 tomatillos, husked
2 serrano or jalapeño chilies, stemmed
1 shallot, peeled
2 cloves garlic, peeled
1 cup water
1 tablespoon vinegar
1 ripe avocado, peeled and seeded
1 bunch of cilantro leaves, chopped
juice of 1 lime
½ cup butter, cut into small pieces
salt and pepper to taste

Marinate fillets in olive oil and oregano for about 1 hour. Sprinkle with salt and pepper.

Heat a nonstick pan over moderately high heat and sauté fish just until heated through and still slightly translucent in the center.

To make Tomatillo Sauce, combine tomatillos, chilies, shallot, garlic, water, and vinegar in a saucepan. Bring to a boil, reduce heat, and simmer for about 30 minutes.

Transfer ingredients with ½ cup of the liquid to a blender. Add avocado, cilantro, and lime juice and blend for about 30 seconds or until smooth. Do not overblend. If mixture is too thick, add additional liquid.

Transfer sauce to a saucepan and heat until warm. Stir in butter, salt, and pepper.

Spoon warm Tomatillo Sauce onto each of four dinner plates. Place fillets in the sauce and garnish each with chopped avocado, a lime wedge, and a cilantro sprig. Serve with Tomato Rice (p. 165).

A sunbather basks in the Padre Island sun.

BAKED SNAPPER WITH COMINO

Serves 6 to 8

*W*hen I met Bob Parvin (whose wonderful photographs enhance this book) and his wife Ellen, we immediately began to exchange fish ideas. He's a dedicated fisherman and conservationist as well as a talented chef, so it was only natural to include one of his delicious dishes. The marvelous flavor of the fish really shines through this combination of Southwest seasonings.

5- to 6-pound snapper, grouper, or similar fish
salt to taste
½ cup vegetable oil
2 tablespoons crushed cumin seeds
1 teaspoon paprika
1 clove garlic, chopped fine
½ cup chopped parsley
½ teaspoon salt
¼ teaspoon pepper
1 lemon, sliced thin

Rub fish inside and out with salt and let stand for 15 minutes. Rinse and pat dry.

Combine oil, cumin seeds, paprika, garlic, parsley, salt, and pepper. Place fish on a sheet of heavy aluminum foil and rub inside and out with the mixture. Fold foil over fish and seal. Preheat oven to 400 degrees and bake 40 to 50 minutes. Open the foil and continue to bake another 15 minutes. Remove to warm platter and garnish with lemon slices.

BAKED SNAPPER
IN COCONUT SAUCE

Serves 6

*W*hole fish can make a dramatic presentation when beautifully garnished and presented. This fish dish from Suneeta Vaswani, Houston's expert on Indian cuisine, is equally good when prepared with several small fish. Just be certain to adjust the baking time accordingly. The masala paste recipe given below is a very typical one. Masala is the name for a paste made of spices, herbs, and other seasonings which have been ground or pounded together. It is the base for all Indian curry sauces. When coconut milk or yogurt is added, it is called a ''wet'' masala.

1 4-pound whole fish, including head and tail
½ teaspoon salt
2 tablespoons vegetable oil
1 teaspoon Indian red chili powder
1½ teaspoons ground cumin seed
2½ teaspoons ground coriander
1 teaspoon fine-chopped garlic
1 teaspoon peeled and fine-chopped ginger root
¼ cup fine-chopped tomatoes
3 to 4 sprigs of cilantro

MASALA PASTE

¼ cup unsalted cashews
1 tablespoon poppy seeds
1 teaspoon cumin seeds
2 dried red chilies
2 2-inch pieces of cinnamon
4 cloves
2 tablespoons water

SAUCE

1½ tablespoons vegetable oil
1½ teaspoons mustard seeds
1 teaspoon peeled and fine-chopped ginger root
1 teaspoon fine-chopped garlic
8 to 10 fresh curry leaves, if available
Masala Paste
1 14-ounce can unsweetened coconut milk
juice of 1 lemon or lime
3 tablespoons chopped cilantro leaves

Wipe fish dry, score both sides with deep diagonal cuts, and place on an oiled baking sheet.

Mix salt, oil, chili powder, cumin, coriander, garlic, and ginger. Rub into fish well and refrigerate several hours or let stand for 15 minutes at room temperature.

Wrap head and tail in foil. Preheat oven to 350 degrees and bake 30 to 40 minutes or until fish flakes easily.

Meanwhile, prepare Masala Paste. Mix and grind all ingredients except water in a blender or spice grinder. Add water to make a thick paste. Set aside.

To make sauce, heat oil in a skillet with a tight-fitting lid until almost smoking. Add mustard seeds

Key Allegro, a canal development, sprawls over a section of Rockport's coast. This rookery and surrounding wetlands near the Texas-Louisiana border offer a safe haven for migratory fowl.

and cover immediately. When popping stops, lower heat and uncover. Add ginger, garlic, and curry leaves and fry 30 seconds. Add Masala Paste and sauté 4 to 5 minutes, stirring constantly. Do not burn. If sauce sticks to the bottom of the pan, sprinkle with 1 to 2 tablespoons water and continue to sauté until slightly darker in color with a faint aroma.

Add coconut milk slowly, mixing well. Cover and simmer 10 minutes. Remove from heat and add lemon juice and chopped cilantro.

Place baked fish on a serving platter, pour sauce over fish, and garnish with tomatoes and cilantro sprigs.

RUGGLES GRILL
BAKED RED SNAPPER WITH
GARLIC AND ROSEMARY

Serves 2 generously

*T*his simple recipe uses marvelously different seasonings that perfume the delicate flesh of snapper. Chef Gary Mercer of Ruggles Grill in Houston suggests baking it with the head (the thickest part of the fish) toward the back of the oven, where the temperature is hotter. He also suggests drizzling a little white wine around the fish if it sticks to the pan or starts to burn.

1 3½-pound red snapper, dressed and scaled
(with head on)
8 cloves garlic
5 sprigs of fresh rosemary
olive oil
juice of 1 lemon
salt and pepper to taste
1 lemon, sliced

Score fish twice on each side with two deep diagonal cuts all the way to the bone.

Crush garlic and place two cloves into each of the four incisions. Reserving 1 stem of rosemary for garnish, push 2 stems from the front cut through the flesh of the fish and out the back cut on each side of the fish.

Rub fish generously with olive oil and place on an oiled or nonstick baking pan. Drizzle with lemon juice and season with salt and pepper.

Preheat oven to 375 degrees and bake 10 minutes for each inch of thickness at the thickest part. When the flesh in the cut nearest the head has turned opaque around the bone, the fish is done.

To serve, remove fish to a platter, place the reserved rosemary in the mouth, cover the eye with a lemon or olive slice, and arrange the lemon slices around the fish in a decorative manner.

RED SNAPPER NUECES

Serves 4 to 6

*C*hef Ray Vargas shared the recipe for this popular dish at the Water Street Oyster Bar in Corpus Christi. He added this bit of whimsy to my copy of the recipe: "Nueces is Spanish for nuts. There are no nuts in the recipe. You figure it out." The flavor of the brandy, sherry, and seasonings blend beautifully to create a tantalizing "nutty" flavor—maybe that's it!

⅓ cup sherry
⅓ cup brandy
1⅓-ounce cube fish-flavored stock base
1⅓ cups water
4 tablespoons butter
4 tablespoons flour
1 large clove garlic, crushed
⅛ teaspoon ground black pepper
⅛ teaspoon ground white pepper
⅛ teaspoon cayenne pepper
1 pound small shrimp, shelled and deveined
½ pound lump white crabmeat
2 to 2½ pounds snapper, grouper, or flounder fillets
flour seasoned with salt and pepper
butter

Combine sherry and brandy in a small saucepan and cook over high heat until reduced by half. Set aside.

Combine fish stock base and water. Set aside.

In a separate saucepan, melt butter, add flour and garlic, and cook for 5 minutes. Add reserved liquor and stock base, stirring constantly until thickened. Add ground peppers.

Stir in raw shrimp and cook until opaque, then fold in crabmeat.

Dredge fish in seasoned flour and sauté in butter until fish is golden brown and flakes easily. Serve with sauce spooned over the fish.

SPINACH-STUFFED SNAPPER

Serves 4

6 tablespoons butter, divided
4 shallots, chopped
1½ 10-ounce packages frozen spinach, thawed
1 cup soft bread crumbs
2 tablespoons heavy cream
⅛ teaspoon salt or to taste
⅛ teaspoon ground white pepper
large pinch of nutmeg
½ teaspoon lemon juice
2 carrots, chopped
2 onions, chopped
2 ribs celery, chopped
1 4-pound red snapper, cleaned (with head and tail)
salt and pepper
vegetable oil
1 cup vermouth or dry white wine
parsley

In a heavy saucepan melt 3 tablespoons butter. Add shallots and sauté until soft. Add thawed spinach, cover, and cook until tender. Uncover and cook until liquid is evaporated.

Mix in bread crumbs, cream, salt, pepper, nutmeg, and lemon juice. Set aside.

In a skillet melt remaining butter. Add carrots, onions, and celery and sauté for 5 minutes to make a mirepoix. Line a large baking pan with heavy aluminum foil, extending the ends a little to facilitate removing the cooked fish from the pan. Spread mirepoix evenly over the foil.

Sprinkle fish inside and out with salt and pepper and rub oil over the head and tail. Cover tail with foil.

Stuff reserved spinach mixture in cavity, lay fish over mirepoix, and pour vermouth over fish. Preheat oven to 375 degrees and bake for 10 minutes per pound, or until fish flakes when pierced gently with the point of a knife. Baste frequently while cooking.

To serve, remove fish carefully to a warm platter, remove foil from tail, and cover the eye with a slice of stuffed pimiento or lemon. Garnish platter with lots of parsley.

RED SNAPPER VERACRUZ

Serves 6

*R*ay Vargas, chef at Bud Lomax's Water Street Oyster Bar in Corpus Christi, has a good instinct for what his customers like in seafood. His concern is to prepare their favorite dishes with the freshest and most flavorful ingredients, concentrating on a smaller menu that is outstanding in every respect. The Red Snapper Veracruz recipe is his interpretation of an all-time favorite with gourmets around the Texas and Mexican Gulf Coast.

3 tablespoons vegetable oil
1 small onion, chopped
3 cloves garlic, chopped
4 cups peeled and chopped tomatoes
2 bay leaves
½ teaspoon dried oregano
½ teaspoon dried thyme
⅓ cup chopped parsley
½ teaspoon salt
½ teaspoon sugar (if tomatoes are very acidic)
3 tablespoons drained capers
12 large pitted green olives
2 pickled jalapeño chilies, sliced
2 pounds snapper fillets
flour seasoned with salt and pepper
butter or oil

Heat oil in a saucepan and add onion. Cover and sauté until translucent. Add garlic, tomatoes, herbs, salt, and sugar. Cook over high heat to evaporate some of the tomato juice. Sauce should be chunky and not too thin. Add capers, olives, and chilies and heat through.

Dredge snapper fillets in seasoned flour and sauté in hot butter or oil until golden brown. Do not overcook. Serve with sauce spooned over fillets.

Rockport's tiny, picturesque harbor caters to anglers and artists.

Spinach-Stuffed Snapper.

A blue winter night envelops the Corpus Christi jetties.

DONG TING'S STEAMED RED SNAPPER

Serves 2

*D*eep in the romantic lake district of central China lies the largest lake in Hunan Province, Dong Ting. Specially prepared fish from its waters have long been one of the province's culinary delights. Family recipes that have been adapted to the fish varieties from Gulf waters are among the most popular dishes at Houston's Dong Ting restaurant. The fermented black bean is available in Asian markets.

1 12-ounce red snapper, scaled and cleaned
(with head and tail)
2 teaspoons salt
2 teaspoons fermented black bean
1 jalapeño or other hot chili, sliced
4 slices of ginger root, shredded
2 whole scallions, cut into 1-inch strips
1 tablespoon rice wine
½ teaspoon ground white pepper

Cut three or four diagonal slashes ¼ inch deep on each side of the fish and rub well with salt. Set aside.

Mix together fermented black bean, jalapeño, ginger root, and scallions. Spread half of the mixture on a large platter. Place the fish over the mixture and spoon the other half over the top. Sprinkle wine and white pepper over the dish and place in a steamer over boiling water. Cover and steam for about 15 minutes. Serve at once.

DONG TING'S SPICY SQUID

Serves 4

*T*he Hunan-style cuisine of Dong Ting Restaurant in Houston is spicier and more intensely flavored than that of the traditional Chinese dishes of Canton. In many ways it resembles the fiery cooking of nearby Szechuan, where it is believed that the demon responsible for arthritis can be driven out by the heat of the chilies used in cooking. The specialties of the restaurant are based on ancestral recipes handed down in the families of San and Jo Hwang, the owners.

12 ounces baby squid
3 tablespoons vegetable oil, divided
2 tablespoons fine-chopped garlic
1 tablespoon fine-chopped jalapeño chili
(or other hot variety)
1 tablespoon soy sauce
2 tablespoons thin-sliced scallions
1 teaspoon rice wine
½ teaspoon sesame oil

Place squid flat on a cutting board. Holding the body with one hand, pull out the clear inner "quill" with the other hand. Peel off the spotted skin and cut off the tentacles. Cut the cleaned sacs into ½-inch slices. Wash well and drain.

Heat 1 tablespoon oil in a wok or large saucepan over high heat. Add squid and stir-fry about 1 minute or until it begins to turn white. Remove squid and drain in a colander.

Heat remaining oil. Stir in garlic, jalapeño, and soy sauce and heat until fragrant. Add reserved squid and scallions and stir-fry for another minute. Sprinkle with rice wine and sesame oil; serve at once.

SWORDFISH SCALLOPINI

Serves 6

*S*usan Middleton, who, with her brother Chris, is one of the best purveyors of seafood in Houston, suggested this method of preparing a dense fish such as swordfish or tuna. When prepared this way, swordfish takes on an entirely different taste and texture. The trick is to cook the scallopini for a few seconds at high heat. This seals in the juices and makes a crisp crust. There are endless sauces that can be served with the scallopini—the one suggested here has a piquant flavor that complements the delicate taste of the swordfish.

6 swordfish steaks (about ⅜-inch thick)
salt and pepper
oil
1 cup fine dry bread crumbs
thin slices of lime

SAUCE

⅔ cup olive oil
4 tablespoons lime juice
zest of 1 lime
3 tablespoons fine-chopped parsley
2 tablespoons fine-chopped fresh oregano
¼ teaspoon salt
1 small clove garlic, crushed

Sprinkle swordfish steaks with salt and pepper and refrigerate for 1 hour or longer. Rub with oil and coat with bread crumbs.

Heat oil in a skillet and sauté steaks about 45 seconds on each side or just until done. Remove to a heated platter and keep warm.

To make sauce, combine all ingredients and mix well. Let stand at least 1 hour.

Serve steaks garnished with lime slices and topped with sauce.

FILLET OF TROUT WITH GREEN PEPPERCORN SAUCE

Serves 8

*T*he basic poaching technique used in this recipe can be adapted for almost all fish fillets. The poaching liquid can be made in advance and kept in the refrigerator for a day or so before using. Simply bring it to a boil and use as directed. Fish fillets can be poached, cooled in the poaching liquid, and served cold with a seasoned mayonnaise dressing. And the poaching liquid itself can be used as a base for sauces incorporating tomatoes, herbs, fennel, and many other vegetables and herbs that are compatible with fish. With a little imagination on the part of the cook, there is a lot of mileage here!

2 cups clam juice
1 cup water
1 cup dry white wine
1 carrot, sliced
1 onion, sliced
½ bay leaf
1 sprig of thyme (or ⅛ teaspoon dried thyme)
1 teaspoon salt
8 parsley stems
8 peppercorns (white or black)
1½ to 3 pounds trout fillets

SAUCE

3 tablespoons butter
2 teaspoons flour
1½ cups poaching liquid
2 teaspoons Dijon mustard
1 cup heavy cream
2 to 3 tablespoons green peppercorns

In a saucepan combine clam juice, water, wine, carrot, onion, bay leaf, thyme, salt, parsley, and peppercorns and bring to a boil. Reduce heat and simmer for 30 minutes. Remove from heat and strain.

Butter a large shallow baking dish. Arrange fish fillets in a single layer and add hot liquid. Cover with buttered foil. Preheat oven to 350 degrees and poach for 15 to 20 minutes or until fish is opaque and flakes easily. Remove fillets to a platter and keep warm.

To make sauce, melt butter in a saucepan, add flour, and stir to make a roux. Stir in poaching liquid, mustard, and cream, mixing until smooth. Strain and add peppercorns. Heat through and pour over fish fillets. Serve any extra sauce in a sauceboat.

South Padre Island's Ila Loetscher, affectionately known as the "Turtle Lady," helps preserve the endangered Ridley sea turtle.

MANSFIELD CLUB'S TROUT LAGUNA AND TROUT MANSFIELD

*T*he Mansfield Club in Port Mansfield is a sportsman's haven with fishing and hunting opportunities as varied as any along the Gulf Coast. In the evenings, the chef prepares the catch for dinner according to the guest's wishes. The ingredients for the following trout recipes are given for individual servings, but they can be multiplied easily to accommodate any number. Neither dish needs an accompanying sauce. Try any mild-flavored fish if trout isn't available.

TROUT LAGUNA

1 trout fillet
prepared jalapeño sauce
½ teaspoon dill weed
¼ teaspoon lemon pepper
garlic powder to taste
flour
olive oil

TROUT MANSFIELD

1 cup flour
1 tablespoon Creole seasoning powder
1 teaspoon garlic powder
1 tablespoon lemon pepper
1 trout fillet
1 egg, beaten
olive oil

To make Trout Laguna, spread fillet with jalapeño sauce and wrap in plastic wrap; marinate for at least 20 minutes and preferably 1 hour. Sprinkle fillet with dill weed, lemon pepper, and garlic powder, then dredge in flour. Sauté in olive oil until fish is browned and flakes easily, turning once.

To make Trout Mansfield, mix flour and seasonings. Dip each fillet in beaten egg, dredge in seasoned flour, and sauté in olive oil until fish is browned and flakes easily, turning once.

Migrant field workers harvest the cabbage crop in the Lower Rio Grande Valley. Dense subtropical vegetation characterizes much of the South Texas coastal plain. A young gardener lends a hand on the family farm in the Winter Garden region of South Texas.

BARBECUE-SPICED TUNA WITH ROASTED TOMATO-BUTTER SAUCE AND MANGO GARNISH

Serves 4

*T*he ever-imaginative Robert Del Grande, chef and owner of Cafe Annie in Houston, creates marvelously flavored dishes using Texas seafood as well as wild game. The recipe is in four basic parts that all come together for the final presentation. Barbecue Spice can be made anytime and used as needed for chicken and beef as well as fish. The Roasted Tomato-Butter Sauce can be made early on the day it is to be used, leaving only the mango garnish to prepare and the tuna to grill.

4 7-ounce yellowfin tuna steaks
Barbecue Spice to taste
oil
2 mangoes, peeled
4 sprigs of cilantro

BARBECUE SPICE

8 ancho chilies
1 tablespoon cumin seeds, lightly toasted in a hot skillet
1 teaspoon coriander seeds, lightly toasted
1 teaspoon ground cinnamon
2 tablespoons brown sugar
2 tablespoons kosher salt
1 teaspoon grated orange zest (optional)

ROASTED TOMATO-BUTTER SAUCE

4 ripe Italian plum tomatoes
2 shallots, peeled
2 cloves garlic, peeled
¼ small yellow onion, chopped
2 small serrano chilies
1 cup chicken stock
1 small bunch of cilantro leaves, chopped fine
4 tablespoons butter, cut in small pieces
juice of 1 lime
1 teaspoon cracked black pepper
1 teaspoon kosher salt (less if using salted stock)

Heat a heavy skillet until very hot. Dust tuna fillets with Barbecue Spice. Add a little oil to the skillet and sear fillets over high heat, keeping them medium rare.

To make Barbecue Spice, wash chilies, pat dry, and remove stems and seeds. Spread on a pan, preheat oven to 300 degrees, and bake for 15 to 20 minutes or until lightly toasted and dry. In a food processor combine chilies with remaining ingredients and blend to form a coarse powder. Cover and refrigerate until ready to use.

To make Roasted Tomato-Butter Sauce, place tomatoes, shallots, garlic, onion, and chilies in a small roasting pan. Preheat oven to 350 degrees and roast for 45 to 60 minutes or until tomatoes are blistered and well cooked. Transfer to a food processor and blend to form a coarse puree. Transfer to a saucepan.

Add stock and bring to a boil. Lower heat to simmer, add cilantro, and whip in butter one piece at a time. Add lime juice, pepper, and salt. Keep warm.

To make mango garnish, slice mangoes in ⅛-inch slices that are parallel to the flat side of the seed. Cut slices into very small cubes.

Spoon some Roasted Tomato-Butter Sauce onto four dinner plates. Scatter mango garnish over the sauce and place a tuna fillet in the center of each plate. Garnish with a sprig of cilantro.

GRILLED TUNA STEAKS WITH MANGO SAUCE AND THREE-PEPPER CHUTNEY

Serves 6

*C*hef John Watt at Galveston's Tremont Hotel combines some interesting flavors in this recipe for grilled tuna.

6 6- to 8-ounce tuna steaks
cilantro

MANGO SAUCE

2 mangoes
1 cup dry white wine
4 tablespoons fresh orange juice

THREE-PEPPER CHUTNEY

2 cups fine-chopped red bell pepper
2 cups fine-chopped yellow bell pepper
4 serrano chilies, seeded and chopped fine
1 tablespoon brown sugar
1 tablespoon champagne vinegar
1 tablespoon grated ginger root
1 tablespoon fine-chopped garlic
¼ cup extra-virgin olive oil
juice of 2 limes
salt and pepper to taste

Grill tuna steaks over hot coals until just done but still slightly pink in the middle.

To make Mango Sauce, peel mangoes and discard seed. Chop and puree in a blender with wine and orange juice. Set aside.

To make Three-Pepper Chutney, combine peppers, brown sugar, and vinegar in a saucepan and sweat over low heat until peppers are slightly transparent. Stir in ginger and garlic. Cook for 1 minute. Remove from heat and cool.

Stir in remaining ingredients, mixing well.

Spoon a little Mango Sauce onto the center of a serving plate and swirl plate until sauce coats the bottom. Place a grilled tuna steak in the center and top with slightly warm Three-Pepper Chutney. Garnish with cilantro.

At a Port Isabel photo concession, a lifesize "Jaws" gobbles tourists for the price of a Polaroid.

VEGETABLE STEW

Serves 4 to 6

*A*round the first part of June, all the summer vegetables in our garden seem to ripen at the same time. So it seemed inevitable that they should be combined in a mélange of wonderful flavors and textures. This makes a very good dish to serve with broiled or baked fish that isn't sauced.

1 large onion, sliced
2 cloves garlic, crushed
3 tablespoons olive oil
2 large tomatoes, peeled and chopped
2 ribs celery, cut into chunks
1 medium eggplant, cut into cubes
2 small zucchini squash, sliced
¼ pound whole baby okra
1 teaspoon salt
1 teaspoon chopped fresh oregano

Combine onion, garlic, and olive oil in a large heavy pan. Sauté until transparent but not brown.

Add tomatoes and cook 10 minutes. Add remaining ingredients, cover, and simmer over low heat until vegetables are very soft. Taste to correct seasonings.

COLD GRAPEFRUIT SOUP

Serves 8

*T*exas is known the country over for its sweet grapefruit, but don't limit it to breakfast. Try this on a hot summer day—it's refreshingly different and makes a wonderful beginning to a cold seafood dinner. In a pinch, frozen unsweetened pink grapefruit juice (not canned) can be substituted for the fresh-squeezed juice.

3 large or 4 small avocados, peeled and pitted
2½ cups fresh-squeezed grapefruit juice, divided
juice of 1 lemon
1 teaspoon salt
2 teaspoons sugar
¼ teaspoon ground allspice
¼ teaspoon ground cinnamon
2 cups ice water

Mix avocados in blender with 2 cups grapefruit juice and blend until smooth. Add lemon juice, salt, sugar, allspice, cinnamon, remaining grapefruit juice, and water. Blend thoroughly. Serve ice cold.

CELERY CHABLIS

Serves 6

*C*elery is seldom prepared as a hot vegetable, but it makes a very good side dish for broiled fish.

1 whole stalk of celery, cut into 2-inch pieces
½ cup water
½ cup Chablis wine
salt to taste
3 tablespoons butter
3 tablespoons flour
¾ cup chicken stock
salt and white pepper to taste
Parmesan cheese
paprika

In a saucepan poach celery with water, Chablis, and salt. When almost done, remove with a slotted spoon and transfer to a buttered 4-cup casserole. Reserve liquid.

In a separate saucepan melt butter and add flour, mixing to make a roux. Stir in chicken stock and ½ cup reserved cooking liquid, stirring until thick. Season with salt and pepper.

Pour over celery and sprinkle with Parmesan cheese and paprika. Preheat oven to 400 degrees and bake about 20 minutes.

HERBED POTATOES

Serves 12

*H*erbed potatoes make a good dish to serve with smoked fish steaks or grilled fish. It's a nice change from the more usual potato salad and, since it contains no mayonnaise, a good choice for summertime picnics.

3½ pounds boiling potatoes
⅓ cup cider vinegar
¾ cup olive oil
½ teaspoon salt or to taste
2 cloves garlic, crushed
2 tablespoons fresh rosemary, minced
1 tablespoon mint, chopped fine
¼ cup parsley, chopped fine

Boil potatoes until tender, peel, and cube. Mix vinegar, oil, and salt and add to warm potatoes. Gently fold in remaining seasonings. Let stand, covered, at room temperature for 1 hour or longer. Taste to correct seasonings before serving. Serve at room temperature.

VEGETABLE-TOMATO SAUCE FOR FISH, SHRIMP, OR PASTA

Serves 6 to 8

This sauce give more than a slight nod to anyone who counts calories and cholesterol. It has only 3 tablespoons of olive oil or vegetable oil, is full of fresh vegetables and herbs, and can take endless variations, depending on just what happens to be in the refrigerator. The trick is to simmer it for several hours to reduce and concentrate the tomato while developing that rich, spicy flavor that only long cooking with herbs and spices can produce. It is excellent over grilled or broiled fish, or over pasta with grated Parmesan cheese sprinkled over the top. Or try adding a couple of pounds of shelled and cooked shrimp to the sauce and serving it over rice.

3 tablespoons olive oil
3 onions, sliced (about 2 cups)
2 bell peppers, sliced (about 2 cups)
3 carrots, sliced thin (about 1 cup)
2 ribs celery, sliced (about 1 cup)
3 large cloves garlic, crushed
1 teaspoon salt
6 large, very ripe tomatoes, peeled and chopped
(or 1 14½-ounce can peeled whole tomatoes)
half of 3-ounce can tomato paste
1 bay leaf
1 tablespoon fresh oregano leaves
(or ½ teaspoon dried oregano)
½ teaspoon fresh thyme leaves
(or ¼ teaspoon dried thyme)
4 tablespoons chopped parsley
2 tablespoons balsamic vinegar
1 cup water
½ cup sliced stuffed green olives
2 tablespoons drained capers
1 8-ounce package fresh mushrooms, sliced

Combine olive oil, onions, bell peppers, carrots, celery, garlic, and salt in a heavy saucepan. Cover and cook over low heat until vegetables are about half-cooked. Add tomatoes, tomato paste, herbs, vinegar, and water. Cover and cook over very low heat for about 2 hours, adding more water only if necessary.

Add olives, capers, and mushrooms. Cover and cook for 1 hour or until sauce is thick. Taste to correct seasonings.

TOMATO RICE

Tomato Rice, the creation of Robert Del Grande at Houston's Cafe Annie, accompanies a snapper dish at the restaurant, but it is also good with many other fish and poultry entrées.

1 cup uncooked rice
4 ripe Italian plum tomatoes, stemmed and chopped
½ yellow onion, chopped
2 tablespoons butter
salt and pepper to taste

Cook rice according to directions on the package. Combine tomatoes and onion in a blender and puree, adding a little water if necessary.

Stir puree and butter into cooked rice and cook until liquid has evaporated but rice is still moist. Add salt and pepper, remove from heat, and cover to keep warm. Place a folded paper towel or two under the lid to absorb the steam.

BAKED ZUCCHINI PUDDING

Serves 4 to 6

A casserole such as this zucchini pudding complements fish dishes that are prepared with tomatoes or tomato sauce. The mild flavor of zucchini combined with cheeses and egg points up the sharpness of a tomato sauce and enhances the delicate flavor of the fish.

4 cups grated zucchini
1½ teaspoons chopped mint
2 tablespoons chopped parsley
5 scallions, chopped (including tops)
2 teaspoons chopped oregano
1 teaspoon salt
¼ teaspoon ground white pepper
dash of cayenne pepper
4 eggs, beaten
⅔ cup grated Gruyère, baby Swiss,
or other mild cheese
⅔ cup flour
8 tablespoons bread crumbs
2 tablespoons grated Parmesan cheese
4 tablespoons butter

Mix zucchini, mint, parsley, scallions, oregano, salt, white pepper, and cayenne pepper together. Add beaten eggs and cheese and mix well. Sift flour into the mixture a little at a time, mixing well after each addition.

Spoon into a buttered 6-cup casserole dish. Top with bread crumbs and Parmesan cheese; dot with butter. Preheat oven to 350 degrees and bake 30 minutes or until set.

*Shorebirds feast on morsels left by
the early-morning tide.*

CHURRASCOS' CHEESE FLAN

Makes 8 cups

I thought I had tasted most of the great flans of Latin America, but this one takes the blue ribbon—silky, sensuous, and rich, rich, rich! It's absolutely marvelous. The recipe makes a large quantity and might be halved satisfactorily, but the whole amount doesn't last very long at our house. It is reminiscent of a Yucatecan Queso de Napoles (Napolitano cheese dessert) but with the addition of cream cheese. The cooking time of the flan is determined by the size of the mold. Small molds, the ⅓- to ½-cup size, take less than an hour, and a 2-quart baking dish takes a little over an hour—not as much variance as one might think. The important thing is to watch the flan for the last 10 to 15 minutes of cooking; when it stops "shivering" when moved, it is done. It will continue to firm up as it cools. The time-honored method of inserting a knife blade into the center until it comes out clean is also a good test.

A Port Isabel souvenir shop displays its wares for the tourist trade. On South Padre Island, monolithic resort hotels dominate what is still one of the longest and least populated barrier islands in the world.

6 large eggs
5 egg yolks
2 14-ounce cans sweetened condensed milk
2 cans whole milk (use empty condensed milk cans)
4 tablespoons vanilla extract
10 ounces cream cheese
2 cups sugar
¼ cup water
whipped cream
lemon and lime slices (or berries)

Mix eggs, egg yolks, condensed milk and whole milk, vanilla extract, and cream cheese in a blender or mixer. Blend until the cream cheese has been thoroughly incorporated. Push mixture through a sieve and set aside.

In a heavy saucepan melt sugar and heat until golden brown. Add water a little at a time and stir to combine. (This should be done with *extreme caution*. The sugar will boil up as water is introduced, so be very careful that it does not splatter on your hands.)

Pour a little of the caramel into individual ovenproof flan molds. Divide the flan mixture evenly among flan molds and set the containers in a pan of water. Water should come up about halfway on the molds. Preheat oven to 300 degrees and bake, uncovered, for 1 hour.

Remove from oven and cool at room temperature about 1 hour. Run a knife around edges of each dish to loosen. Refrigerate until chilled. Turn each mold out on a serving plate, along with the syrup that has collected at the bottom. Garnish with whipped cream, lemon and lime slices, or berries.

COLD DAIQUIRI SOUFFLÉ

Serves 10 to 12

*T*his dish is fairly rich but tastes light. A small serving of this tart-sweet soufflé is a perfect ending to a summertime dinner.

6 egg yolks
1 cup sugar
1 cup lime juice
grated zest of 3 limes
pinch of salt
2 envelopes unflavored gelatin
½ cup rum
10 egg whites
2 cups whipping cream
crushed pistachio nuts (optional)
2 packages frozen sweetened raspberries
or strawberries, thawed

Beat egg yolks until light and fluffy. Add sugar gradually and beat until light in color. Add lime juice, zest, and salt, mixing well.

In a heavy saucepan over low heat (or in the top of a double boiler) cook mixture, stirring, until thick; do not boil.

Meanwhile, soak gelatin in rum to soften. Add to hot egg mixture and stir until completely dissolved. Cool to room temperature.

While custard is cooling, wrap an oiled wax paper collar around the top of a 6-cup soufflé mold and tie with string. It should extend about 2 inches above the rim of the dish. Set aside.

Beat egg whites until they form soft peaks but are not dry.

Whip cream to form soft peaks. Fold beaten egg whites into custard, then fold in whipped cream. Spoon into prepared soufflé dish and chill several hours or until firm.

Before serving, run a knife around the paper collar and untie string to remove collar. Press crushed pistachio nuts gently into soufflé exposed above the rim of the dish.

Puree thawed raspberries or strawberries in a food mill. Serve over soufflé.

FIGS IN MADEIRA

Serves 6

Not too many years back there was a fig tree in every backyard in Texas! During the season, usually in late June and early July, we got out early in the morning to pick the juicy sweet fruit before the birds got there. Today our landscaping plans don't include these wonderful trees, but sometimes a friend who still has an old tree will share. And dried figs also do very well in this recipe.

36 large figs
2 cups sweet Madeira
1 cup heavy cream, whipped
1 teaspoon vanilla extract
½ cup toasted slivered almonds

In a saucepan combine figs and Madeira; bring to a boil, reduce heat, and simmer, covered, for 5 minutes. Remove from heat and allow to stand for at least 30 minutes or until figs have absorbed Madeira and are very tender.

Whip cream to form soft peaks. Add vanilla extract.

Garnish figs with whipped cream and almonds and serve with Madeira syrup.

PEARS POACHED IN SAUTERNES

Serves 6

Slightly underripe pears should be used in the following recipe—they're easy to find in any supermarket. If you have access to hard cooking pears, this is a delectable way to prepare them. Just add a little more sugar and cooking time. Sauternes, Gewürztraminer, and fruity California whites are all wonderful wines in which to poach the fruit.

6 whole pears, peeled and cored (halved, if desired)
1½ cups Sauternes or other white wine
1 cup light brown sugar
12 to 18 thin strips of lemon peel
1 teaspoon lemon juice
3 tablespoons butter
½ cup light rum, warmed
1 cup whipped cream, slightly sweetened and flavored with vanilla extract

Arrange pears, wine, brown sugar, lemon peel, lemon juice, and butter in a shallow nonmetallic pan. Cover pan and poach pears over low heat until tender (time will vary according to variety of pear). Transfer to a chafing dish.

Cook liquid until syrupy and pour over pears. (The dish can be prepared to this point early in the day.)

At serving time heat pears in syrup in the chafing dish. Pour warmed rum over fruit and ignite. When flames die out, serve pears with cold whipped cream.

PECAN CRUNCH PIE

Surely the most requested recipe at Gaido's in Galveston, this is an unusual version of a pecan pie, really an upside-down pie that is decorated on the top with additional pecans. During baking, the crumbs from the crust rise to the top to combine with pecans, making a good crunchy topping. This top becomes a good crunchy bottom when the pie is inverted. The pie should not be completely cooled when inverted because it will be difficult to turn it out of the mold intact. Incidentally, it is even better the next day, served cold.

CRUST

1½ cups fine graham cracker crumbs
7 tablespoons sugar
7 tablespoons butter, melted

FILLING

5 eggs
1½ cups sugar
1¾ cups light corn syrup
2 teaspoons vanilla extract
¼ teaspoon salt
2½ cups toasted pecan pieces

TOPPING

2½ cups toasted pecan halves
¼ cup light corn syrup
vanilla ice cream (optional)

To make crust, combine ingredients and press into a well-buttered 10-inch springform pan.

To make filling, mix all ingredients and pour into the prepared pan. Preheat oven to 300 degrees and bake for approximately 1 hour. The pie is done when it is soft to the touch in the center and firm around the outside edge.

Remove from oven and cool on a wire rack for about 1 hour and 15 minutes. While pie is still warm, invert on a serving dish, removing the sides and bottom of the pan.

To make topping, mix together pecans and syrup. Cover the top and sides of the pie with pecan mixture, making a decorative pattern on top and standing the pecans vertically around the side. The syrup will hold the pecans to the pie.

Slice and serve while still a little warm. Vanilla ice cream is wickedly delicious as a garnish.

RUBY RED PIE

Serves 8

Ruby Red grapefruit is unique to the Texas Rio Grande Valley and is thought to be a sport from the original white variety. Ruby Reds are sweet, with little of the bitterness that one sometimes finds in other varieties. Pink grapefruit is another popular and delicious variety from the Valley, having the same characteristics as their red cousins. Frozen unsweetened pink grapefruit juice (not canned) can be substituted for the fresh-squeezed juice; reconstitute it with slightly less than the suggested amount of water.

2 envelopes unflavored gelatin
1½ cups fresh-squeezed Ruby Red or pink grapefruit juice, divided
2 large or 3 medium eggs, separated
¾ cup sugar
½ teaspoon grapefruit zest
½ cup fruity white wine
⅛ teaspoon salt
1 cup heavy cream
1 baked 9-inch pastry shell
12 sections of fresh grapefruit

Soften gelatin in ¾ cup grapefruit juice and heat over low heat until completely dissolved. Set aside.

Beat egg yolks with sugar until thoroughly mixed and light in color. Combine with reserved gelatin mixture and cook over low heat until mixture has thickened slightly, stirring constantly. Remove from heat, fold in zest and wine, and cool until mixture is slightly thickened but not set.

Beat egg whites with the salt to form soft peaks. Beat cream to form soft peaks.

Fold cream into the custard mixture, then fold in egg whites carefully to preserve the maximum volume. Chill mixture in the refrigerator or over a bowl of ice water until it begins to mound and hold its shape. Spoon into the baked pie shell, piling up the center. Garnish with grapefruit sections. Chill several hours before serving.

BRENNAN'S FAMOUS STRAWBERRY SHORTCAKE

Serves 6

This has become a signature dish for the Houston restaurant, rivaling the famous bread pudding for which Brennan's and its sister restaurant in New Orleans, Commander's Palace, are known. Each portion is baked to order so that the rich shortcakes are a meltingly warm contrast to the chilled strawberry filling and smooth whipped cream. Executive Chef Carl Walker has these tips: assemble and serve it right out of the oven; don't overwhip the cream, just be sure that it forms soft peaks so that it coats the berries; substitute fresh peaches or raspberries if the strawberries aren't in tip-top shape. Blueberries or mangoes are pretty tasty, too.

SHORTCAKES

3 cups cake flour
1 cup sugar
1½ tablespoons baking powder
1 teaspoon salt
¾ cup shortening
3 eggs
½ cup milk
2 tablespoons vanilla extract

FILLING

3½ pints strawberries, washed, hulled, and divided
1 cup sugar
2 tablespoons Grand Marnier
2 cups heavy cream whipped with ¼ cup sugar
powdered sugar
mint sprigs

To make shortcakes, mix all dry ingredients. Cut in shortening with a fork until mixture consists of pea-size pieces.

Whip eggs, milk, and vanilla together and add to flour mixture, blending until smooth. Refrigerate for at least 30 minutes.

Place chilled dough on a well-floured surface. Roll or pat with hands to flatten. Cut with a biscuit cutter into six 4-inch shortcakes. Place on an oiled baking sheet. Preheat oven to 350 degrees and bake for 12 minutes. Remove from oven and keep warm.

To make filling, slice 2½ pints strawberries and place in a large bowl. Puree remaining berries with sugar and Grand Marnier. Pour over sliced berries and fold together.

Slice warm shortcakes in half. Spoon filling over bottom half, top with whipped cream, and cover with top half of shortcake. Dust with powdered sugar and garnish with a mint sprig.

Highlighted by the rising sun, the Rio Grande meanders lazily toward the Gulf of Mexico.

MEXICO

*T*HE UNIQUE COOKERY OF MEXICO draws equally from Old World and New World traditions. The native cuisine, based on chilies, beans, tomatoes, squashes, corn, and chocolate, gradually incorporated foods brought over by the Spanish, such as rice, onions, garlic, cinnamon, and pork. The result is some of the most distinctive food in the western world.

Mexico's coastline along the Gulf is dotted with the cities of Tampico, Veracruz, Campeche, and Cancún, as well as smaller communities in between. Because of comparative isolation from each other as well as differences in terrain, each area has its own seasonings that define the cooking of that immediate vicinity. For example, annatto seeds ground into

Fishing boats line the smooth beaches of Poza Rica del Mar, the site of Cortés's first New World outpost. Huichol Indians tune their instruments in the Tampico market.

171

a paste with herbs and spices becomes *achiote*, a seasoning for which the Yucatán is known. Olives and capers play an important part in the preparation of dishes from Tampico and Veracruz. Even certain chili varieties used in a dish may reveal its origin.

Shrimping is the most important seafood industry along this part of the Gulf Coast, with fleets of shrimp boats going out from Campeche, Veracruz, and Tampico to harvest the briny crop. Much of it is exported to the United States, but a certain quantity is dried for use in traditional dishes prepared in inland cities. Sportfishing is becoming an important tourist attraction, especially in the Cancún area, where fish from the Caribbean join the Gulf Coast varieties.

Seafood markets in larger coastal towns offer shrimp, oysters, crabs, and spiny lobsters in addition to dozens of types of fish. Pompano is a great delicacy in Veracruz. Red snapper (*huachinango*) and snook (*robalo*) are probably the most popular finfish along the Gulf Coast. The Yucatecans revere the dogfish shark, harvested at a small size, which they call *cazón*. *Sierra*, a kind of mackerel, turns up in many places in Mexico.

Once unfamiliar north of Mexico, *ceviche* (*cebiche, seviche*), a cold salad of raw fish pieces "cooked" in lime juice, is now common on menus from the Florida Keys to Yucatán. Conch meat is sometimes substituted for the fish.

Other seafoods are prepared in distinctive ways. In Tabasco, the large moro crabs are stuffed and then heated through in a sauce made of pumpkin seeds and *achiote*. In Cozumel, a delicious lobster soup is seasoned with toasted oregano, onion, and a roasted head of garlic, while the broth is thickened with masa and colored with *achiote*.

An authentic, unbeatable way to enjoy fish along the Mexican coast is to grill it whole or filleted, right out of the water, over a smoky seaside fire and sprinkle it with a squeeze of fresh *limón* or *citrón*. *Es fantástico*.

Rust-busters scrape a freighter loading at Tampico, Mexico's busiest Gulf port.

The graceful arcades over the side-
walks of downtown Tampico reflect
the Spanish Colonial influence.
The sons of shark fishermen in Laguna de Tamiahua await the return
of the village fleet. A Tampicaneo
finds a restful spot on the main city
plaza.

Papantla's steep streets offer a view of the surrounding hills and citrus orchards. The striking features of this Veracruz native reflect the rich ethnic heritage of the 400-year-old port. A sun-baked adobe facade exemplifies much of the region's timeless quality.

A Las Casitas Islander commutes to work in a dugout canoe while a fisherman's son uses a similar craft for a secret hideout. At the Port of Veracruz, boys dive for tourists' pesos flipped from the docks. The Rio Tecolutia, which drains the region, is fished for giant prawns.

Crab and Shrimp Nachos.

A Totonac Indian heads for the
market at Papantla, once the
vanilla capital of the world.
At La Pesca (right), a young
child waits for her mother to buy
groceries.

CRAB QUESADILLAS VERACRUZ STYLE

*A*lthough it is possible to prepare Quesadillas de Jaiba à la Veracruzana with prepared tortillas, the result will be a different dish because in this recipe the "raw" tortilla is stuffed and then fried. And the liquid used in the tortilla dough is chicken or beef broth, which will add flavor to the final dish. If a tortilla press is not available, roll the dough out between sheets of waxed paper and cut into circles with a large cookie cutter. Epazote is a smoky-flavored weed that grows wild in most of the Southwest—it is shoulder high around the corral at our farm. It is added to beans in Mexican and Indian cuisines and is thought to diminish flatulence.

TORTILLAS

2 cups masa harina
2 tablespoons all-purpose flour
1 cup chicken or beef broth (or more if necessary)
½ teaspoon salt

FILLING

¼ cup vegetable oil
1 onion, chopped fine
1 tomato, skinned, chopped fine, and drained
1 jalapeño chili, seeded and chopped fine
1 pound crabmeat (claw or body)
several leaves of epazote, chopped (optional)
salt and pepper to taste
vegetable oil

Prepare the tortilla dough by mixing the flours well. Add broth and salt and knead until dough is pliable and leaves the sides of the bowl fairly clean. Cover and let rest.

To prepare the filling, heat oil in a skillet and add onion, tomato, and jalapeño. Cook until onion has softened and mixture has dried a little. Fold in crabmeat, add epazote, and season with salt and pepper.

Press out tortillas and put about 1 tablespoon of stuffing in the middle of the tortilla. Fold in half and press edges together to seal. Repeat until all the stuffing has been used. If rolling out the tortillas between sheets of waxed paper, it is fairly easy to peel the paper off one side, fill the tortilla, and use the other sheet of paper to help fold the tortilla dough around the filling. If using prepared tortillas, see the directions for cooking in the recipe for Shrimp Quesadillas (p. 182).

To fry, heat about ½ inch of vegetable oil in a heavy skillet and fry quesadillas on each side and on the bottom side until golden brown. Drain on paper towels and serve at once with Guacamole (p. 197).

To toast, heat a *comal* or heavy iron griddle to medium hot. Toast the quesadillas on all three surfaces. Do not have the griddle so hot as to burn the tortilla before the filling is cooked. It will take a little practice.

CRAB AND SHRIMP NACHOS

Makes 40 nachos

*T*his tasty finger food disappears quickly at a cocktail party. The tortillas can be fried ahead of time and kept in a tightly sealed tin, then recrisped in the oven. The shellfish filling can also be made ahead of time.

vegetable oil
10 6-inch corn tortillas
2 tablespoons butter
½ pound shrimp, shelled, deveined, and chopped
½ pound crabmeat (claw or special grade)
1 8-ounce carton sour cream
½ teaspoon cumin seeds, toasted and crushed
⅛ teaspoon salt or to taste
3 cups grated Chihuahua or Monterey Jack cheese
10 pickled jalapeño chilies, seeded and sliced
Charred Tomatillo Salsa (p. 194)
and Avocado Salsa (p. 194)

In a large skillet heat oil to a depth of ½ inch. Cut the tortillas in quarters and fry each piece for a few seconds or until crisp. Drain on paper towels.

In another skillet melt butter and sauté chopped shrimp until barely pink. Remove from heat and cool. Stir in crabmeat, sour cream, and cumin seeds. Season with salt. Place about 1 tablespoon of the mixture on each tortilla piece and cover with grated cheese.

Place nachos on a large flat pan and broil about half a minute or until cheese is melted. Top each nacho with a slice of jalapeño. Serve with side dishes of Charred Tomatillo Salsa and Avocado Salsa.

STUFFED CRABS TAMPICO STYLE

Serves 8 to 10

*H*ere is a typical way of preparing stuffed crabs in the Tampico area. When my friend Chata DuBose was translating this recipe, jaibas rellenas tampiquena *sounded so good to her that she prepared them for dinner that very evening! Jalapeño lovers can add as many of the fiery peppers as desired.*

4 tablespoons olive oil
1 onion, chopped
1 clove garlic, crushed
2 pounds tomatoes, skinned, chopped, and drained
2 to 3 tablespoons chopped parsley
2 hard-cooked eggs, chopped fine
1 large canned pimiento, chopped
12 almonds, blanched and chopped
12 stuffed olives, chopped
1 canned jalapeño chili, chopped
1 cup dry bread crumbs, divided
1 pound special-grade crabmeat
salt and pepper to taste
3 tablespoons butter

Heat oil and sauté onion until transparent. Add garlic and tomatoes and fry well, drying out the mixture a little. Add parsley, eggs, pimiento, almonds, olives, jalapeño, and ½ cup bread crumbs. Mix well. Fold in the crabmeat and season with salt and pepper.

Fill individual crab shells or ramekins or spoon the mixture into a buttered casserole dish. Top with remaining bread crumbs and dot with butter. Preheat oven to 325 degrees and bake until well heated and browned on top.

SOFT-SHELL CRABS WITH TOMATO SALSA

Serves 1

butter
2 large soft-shell crabs
flour seasoned with salt and pepper
1 medium tomato, skinned, seeded, and chopped fine
1 large tablespoon sun-dried tomatoes
¼ small clove garlic, crushed
1 scallion, chopped fine (including top)
¼ teaspoon pink peppercorns
1 tablespoon chopped basil
2 tablespoons fish stock
salt and ground white pepper to taste

Heat butter until bubbly. Dust crabs with seasoned flour and sauté. Remove and keep warm.

Add remaining ingredients except fish stock and salt and pepper. Heat through.

Add stock; heat and season to taste. Spoon salsa over the crabs and serve.

As a variation, grill the floured crabs over hot coals, about 1 minute each side. Pour 2 tablespoons tequila over salsa and flame. Spoon over the grilled crabs.

SCALLOP SEVICHE

Serves 8

*T*hat wonderful dish called seviche—seafood cooked by the acidity of lime or lemon juice—has become one of the most fashionable first courses on today's menus. *Traditionally, snapper is the star of this dish, but adventurous cooks are using shellfish and a variety of other finfish to produce some mouth-watering versions of this Mexican favorite.*

1½ pounds bay scallops
½ cup plus 3 tablespoons fresh lime juice
½ teaspoon salt
1 tablespoon chopped cilantro
3 avocados, peeled, seeded, and cubed
3 small tomatoes, skinned, seeded, and sliced thin
⅓ cup vegetable oil
salt to taste

Combine scallops, ½ cup lime juice, salt, and cilantro in a glass bowl; toss to mix. Cover and refrigerate overnight. When ready to serve, drain and add avocados, tomatoes, oil, and 3 tablespoons lime juice. Mix gently and add salt. Serve on lettuce leaf cups or in small ramekins or dishes.

Scallop Seviche.

Paella.

PAELLA

Serves 12

*O*f Spanish origin, paella is served in various local versions throughout the coastal regions of Mexico. It is always a crowd-pleaser, and, believe it or not, it can be partially cooked ahead of time and finished after the guests arrive. Don't be intimidated by the list of ingredients. Once they are assembled, it's a simple matter to prepare them for the finished dish. Purists may think this is taking too many liberties with this famous Spanish dish, but purists have always eaten it with gusto at our house.

8 tablespoons olive oil, divided
3 pounds chicken pieces
1 pound shrimp, shelled and deveined
salt and pepper
2 or 3 links of chorizo or other seasoned pork sausage
½ pound lean pork, cut into cubes
¼ pound ham, cut into strips (optional)
1 large onion, chopped
2 cloves garlic, crushed
1 red bell pepper, cut into strips
1 large tomato, peeled, seeded, and chopped
1 teaspoon chopped oregano
1 cup rice
2½ cups chicken stock
1 teaspoon saffron
2 tablespoons hot water

1 package frozen artichoke hearts
1 package frozen peas
12 mussels, scrubbed and "de-bearded"
1 can snails (optional)
chopped parsley

Heat 4 tablespoons olive oil in a heavy skillet. Season chicken and shrimp with salt and pepper. Brown chicken pieces in the oil and remove. Brown shrimp in the oil and remove.

Brown whole sausages, remove, and cut into pieces. Brown pork and ham. Add onion, garlic, bell pepper, tomato, and oregano. Cook, stirring frequently, until most of the liquid has evaporated. Set aside.

Heat remaining oil in a paella pan or other shallow ovenproof pan. Add rice and fry until transparent. Add pork and ham mixture, chicken stock, and saffron softened in the hot water. Bring to a boil over high heat; taste to correct seasonings. Remove from heat.

Add thawed artichoke hearts, mixing well. Sprinkle thawed peas over the top and arrange chicken and sausage pieces, mussels, and snails over the top. (The dish can be prepared in advance to this point.)

Cover loosely with foil. Preheat oven to 375 degrees and bake for about 25 minutes or until liquid is absorbed. Do not stir. Remove from oven and discard any mussels that have not opened. Add reserved shrimp and cover loosely with a towel.

Let rest for 10 minutes. Sprinkle with chopped parsley and serve directly from the pan.

LIME SOUP WITH SHRIMP

Serves 8

6 corn tortillas, cut into ⅜-inch strips
vegetable oil
1 large onion, chopped
6 Italian plum tomatoes, peeled,
seeded, and chopped
3 10 ¾-ounce cans chicken broth
3 cans water (use empty broth cans)
juice and rinds of 2 limes
2 teaspoons chopped fresh oregano
(or 1 teaspoon dried oregano)
2 pounds medium shrimp, shelled, deveined, and
halved lengthwise
¼ teaspoon ground white pepper
leaves from 8 sprigs of cilantro
1 8-ounce package cream cheese, cut into small cubes

Heat oil to a depth of ½ inch in a large heavy skillet. Fry tortilla strips a few at a time for about 30 seconds or until crisp. Drain on paper towels.

Pour off all oil except 2 tablespoons and add onion. Cook until soft. Add tomatoes and cook for 2 or 3 minutes. Add chicken broth, water, lime juice and rinds, and oregano; simmer for about 5 minutes.

Remove lime rinds and add shrimp. Cook until shrimp is just barely done. Add pepper.

Serve in heated bowls garnished with cubes of cream cheese, cilantro leaves, and tortilla strips.

BAKED SHRIMP
WITH PEPPERS AND ONIONS

Serves 6

*B*ecause it's easy and really good, Camarones al Queso con Pimientos y Cebollas is a favorite with the pupils of Chata DuBose, a native of Mexico and now a cooking teacher in Houston. Oaxaca and manchego cheeses are available in Mexican markets. Muenster is a possible substitute for these stringy and slightly acidic cheeses.

¾ cup olive oil
½ cup butter
3 white onions, sliced on the diagonal
5 red bell peppers, roasted, seeded, and
sliced in strips
5 green bell peppers, roasted, seeded, and sliced
½ teaspoon salt
¼ teaspoon ground black pepper
2 pounds medium shrimp, shelled and deveined
8 ounces Oaxaca, manchego, or
Muenster cheese, grated
8 ounces Monterey Jack cheese, grated

Snook with Chile Ancho Sauce (see page 191); Soft-Shell Crabs with Tomato Salsa (see page 178); Lime Soup with Shrimp.

Heat oil and butter in a skillet and brown onions. Add peppers and cook over low heat for 15 minutes. Season with salt and pepper. Stir in shrimp and cook for 5 minutes. Taste to correct seasonings.

Spoon mixture into a casserole dish and cover with grated cheeses. Preheat oven to 325 degrees and bake for 20 minutes or until cheeses have melted.

SHRIMP SOUSED WITH TEQUILA

Serves 1

*T*his is a favorite way to serve shrimp in the Yucatán. Kathy Ruiz, chef at Otto's Grill in Cancún, makes her own jalapeño-lime pasta to accompany the shrimp, but prepared spinach, tomato, or other flavored pastas are also good. For another variation, chill the cooked shrimp and add about 2 tablespoons of chopped tomato for each serving and garnish with cilantro. This makes a good salad for a first course. My friends Lynn Herbert and Sarah McMurrey, who are great cooks and love to experiment, have tried this recipe with similar variations. They suggest flaming the shrimp, then adding the rest of the ingredients, with some chopped tomato, to the pan to heat. Lynn served the shrimp over tomato pasta and added a bit of cilantro. Sarah served it for a first course with crusty bread.

6 large shrimp, shelled (with tail section intact)
salt to taste
vegetable oil
2 tablespoons tequila
juice of 1 lime
zest of ¼ lime
6 thin slices jalapeño chili or to taste
1 large tablespoon chopped scallions (including tops)

Split shrimp lengthwise to devein and butterfly shrimp. Season with salt. Sauté in hot oil until barely done. Pour tequila over the pan and flame. Remove shrimp to a dish. Mix remaining ingredients and pour over shrimp.

On the count of three, netters lined up across a neck of the Laguna de Tamaihua toss for small fish migrating with the tide.

Shrimp Quesadillas.

SHRIMP QUESADILLAS

Makes 6

*T*his is one of the most popular dishes at Otto's Grill in Cancún. Kathy Ruiz, the restaurant's chef, prepared it for me in her home one evening, and I have attempted to recreate it here from memory.

4 tablespoons butter
1 large onion, chopped fine
1 or 2 cloves garlic, crushed and chopped fine
2 poblano chilies, roasted, peeled,
seeded, and chopped
1 pound shrimp, shelled and deveined
oil
1 3-ounce package cream cheese
salt to taste
12 thin flour tortillas
¼ pound Chihuahua or mild cheddar cheese
Charred Tomatillo Salsa (p. 194), Red Pepper and
Jicama Salsa (p. 194), or a fresh tomato salsa
sliced avocado

Melt butter in a heavy skillet and sauté onion and garlic until soft but not brown. Add chilies and heat through. Set aside.

Brush shrimp with oil and grill over hot coals just until done. Cool and chop into medium-sized pieces; add to onion mixture with enough cream cheese to bind the mixture. Add salt. Divide mixture over half the tortillas, sprinkle with grated cheese, and top with remaining tortillas to make a "sandwich."

On a medium-hot comal or heavy iron skillet, cook quesadillas on each side until the cheese has melted and the tortillas are crisp.

Divide in quarters and serve with a variety of salsas.

YUCATECAN SHRIMP COCKTAIL

Serves 6

*T*he following is a refreshing change from the more usual catsup-based shrimp cocktail sauce. It is part salad and part cocktail and makes a light first-course dish.

1 pound shelled, cleaned, and cooked shrimp
½ red onion, chopped fine
1 jalapeño chili, seeded and chopped fine
2 medium tomatoes, peeled, seeded, and chopped
¼ cup chopped cilantro
4 tablespoons white wine vinegar
½ cup olive oil
½ teaspoon salt
ground white pepper to taste

Combine shrimp, onion, jalapeño, tomatoes, and cilantro. Mix together vinegar, oil, salt, and pepper and pour over shrimp, tossing to mix well. Serve in chilled individual ramekins or lettuce leaf cups.

FRIED SHRIMP
WITH AVOCADO SALSA

Serves 4 as a first course

¾ cup fine-grind masa harina
1 teaspoon salt
½ teaspoon paprika
¼ teaspoon cayenne pepper
1 teaspoon powdered cumin or to taste
1 pound medium or large shrimp, shelled and
deveined (with tail section intact)
oil
sour cream
cilantro

AVOCADO SALSA

1 avocado, peeled, seeded, and chopped
1 tomato, peeled and chopped
1 small fresh jalapeño chili, seeded and chopped fine
juice of ½ lime
1 tablespoon chopped cilantro
1 scallion, chopped
salt to taste

Combine masa harina, salt, paprika, cayenne pepper, and cumin. Dredge shrimp in masa harina mixture, coating well.

Heat about 3 inches of oil to 350 degrees. Drop in shrimp one by one and fry until golden. Drain on paper towels.

To make Avocado Salsa, combine all ingredients, mixing well but keeping chunky texture. Let stand about 30 minutes before serving.

Serve shrimp with salsa and a dollop of sour cream. Garnish with a sprig of cilantro.

SHRIMP-STUFFED EMPANADAS WITH ACHIOTE

Makes about 20

*T*his recipe for Empanadas con Camarones y Achiote comes from the areas around Campeche and the Yucatán, where achiote is a popular seasoning spice. It is used in a interesting way in the tortilla dough in this dish. Prepared flour tortillas can also be used with this filling, although the dish will not be quite the same. Pastry dough can be substituted for the tortilla dough to produce delicious empanadas that are more like the South American variety. The recipes for Crab Quesadillas (p. 177) and Shrimp Quesadillas (p. 182) show other methods of stuffing tortillas.

TORTILLAS

1 pound masa harina
½ cup flour
1 tablespoon Achiote Paste (p. 192)
6 tablespoons vegetable oil
2 cups warm water

FILLING

½ cup olive oil
1 white onion, chopped fine
4 cloves garlic, crushed
2 jalapeño chilies,
seeded and chopped fine
2 tomatoes, peeled and pureed
1 tablespoon Achiote Paste (p. 192)
1 teaspoon ground allspice
1 teaspoon dried oregano, crushed
1 teaspoon salt or to taste
2 pounds shrimp, shelled, deveined, and chopped

To prepare tortilla dough, mix together masa harina and flour. Dissolve achiote paste in vegetable oil and mix with 1 cup water. Add to flour mixture, along with additional water to make a dough. Knead dough until pliable; cover and set aside.

To make filling, heat oil in a skillet and add onion and garlic. Cook until transparent. Add jalapeños, tomato puree, achiote paste, allspice, oregano, and salt. Cook until mixture is dry. Add chopped shrimp and stir until shrimp is pink. Set aside to cool.

Make tortillas in a press or roll out balls of dough between sheets of waxed paper and trim to make even circles. Spoon filling into tortillas, fold in half, and seal the edges.

Heat oil in a heavy skillet to a depth of about ½ inch. Fry empanadas until golden brown on all sides. Drain on paper towels and serve at once with Guacamole (p. 197).

A Totonac Indian sells his produce on a Papantla sidewalk.

MIXED SEAFOOD SALAD WITH ORANGE

Serves 4 to 6

I went for lunch one day out from Cancún to a little seafood restaurant called Mi Casa. It was on a long and fairly uninhabited stretch of beach, looking out over the incredibly blue water to Isla de Mujeres on one side and Cancún in the distance on the other side. Among the dishes I sampled during a wonderful four hours of hedonistic pleasure was a fish salad unlike others I had encountered. I have tried to recreate it here from those memories.

¾ pound very small shrimp,
shelled, deveined, and cooked
⅔ pound fish fillets (grouper, snapper, etc.),
cooked and flaked
⅔ cup fine-chopped jicama or water chestnuts
2 tablespoons jalapeño chilies,
seeded and chopped fine
2 tablespoons chopped cilantro leaves
2 tablespoons chopped parsley
1 teaspoon fine-shredded orange zest,
blanched and drained
¾ cup sour cream
2 to 3 tablespoons orange juice or to taste
juice of 1 lime
1 teaspoon salt or to taste
dash of cayenne pepper (optional)

Combine shrimp, fish, jicama, jalapeños, cilantro, parsley, and orange zest. Toss to mix. Fold in sour cream, citrus juices, salt, and cayenne pepper. Refrigerate overnight before serving.

GROUPER BAKED IN ACHIOTE MARINADE

Serves 6

*T*he dish known as Tikin Xik is found throughout the Yucatán peninsula. Made with fish, pork, or chicken, it is an outstanding example of tipico Yucatecan cuisine. Here the fish is marinated in a paste made of pulverized annatto seeds, various herbs, spices, and sour orange or lime juice. It is then wrapped in banana leaves and grilled over hot coals, making it wonderfully flavorful. It is served with hot tortillas and side dishes of avocado, tomato, pickled onions, and radishes. There are probably as many recipes for Tikin Xik as there are cooks who prepare it. One of the most successful of these was prepared for me in Cancún by Daniel Sauri Gonzalez, agriculture inspector for the Mexican government and an avid fisherman and talented cook. The achiote paste he used was commercially prepared, and to it he added chopped garlic, onion, chilies, lime juice, beer, and rum! The paste is usually available in Mexican and Cuban markets as well as in the specialty sections of some supermarkets. However, if unavailable, you can easily find annatto seeds in those same markets and make your own.

2 2½-pound whole groupers or snappers
4 tablespoons Achiote Paste (p. 192) or to taste
½ cup sour orange juice or lime juice
½ cup beer, rum, or tequila
6 Italian plum tomatoes, sliced
2 large onions, sliced
4 banana peppers, seeded and sliced
4 habanero chilies, seeded and sliced
banana leaves or foil

Open fish out flat, removing the backbone, head, and tail. Mix achiote paste, citrus juice, and liquor together until smooth and rub into the fish on the flesh side. Divide tomatoes, onions, and peppers between the fish and scatter them over the flesh. Wrap in banana leaves or foil and grill over hot coals for 20 minutes or until done. It can also be baked in a 350-degree oven for about 30 minutes. (The fish can be prepared and wrapped ahead of time, leaving the cooking until later.)

Serve with side dishes of sliced avocado, tomato, radish, and Pickled Onion Rings (p. 196). Though not traditional, sprigs of fresh cilantro are delicious as a garnish.

Near Anton Lizardo a fisherman hauls in gill nets left overnight in the surf.

YUCATECAN BOUILLABAISSE

Serves 2 generously

I had this soup in the kitchen of the Hotel Camino Real in Cancún. Chef Jean Pierre Van Assche had all the ingredients laid out and in a matter of a few minutes produced this delicious Mexican-style bouillabaisse. Van Assche is a classically trained chef, having apprenticed his way through some of the great kitchens in France. His use of local Mexican ingredients, combined in the classic style, makes for some really fine dishes. The Pernod can be served in a separate carafe so that those who don't fancy the licorice taste can enjoy the soup without it.

1 tablespoon butter
1 tablespoon olive oil
1 clove garlic, crushed and chopped
1 small tomato, peeled, seeded, and chopped fine
1 bay leaf
¼ cup julienne of leek
¼ cup julienne of carrot
¼ cup julienne of celery
⅛ cup julienne of onion
½ cup dry white wine
2 cups fish stock or chicken stock
1 4-ounce fillet of snapper or similar fish
4 shrimp, shelled and deveined
(with tail section intact)
2 slices lobster tail
4 oysters
4 ounces eel, cut into 4 pieces (optional)
salt to taste
2 tablespoons Pernod
chopped parsley

Melt butter in a heavy pot, add olive oil, and heat. Add garlic, tomato, bay leaf, and vegetables; cover and sauté 1 minute. Add wine and cook for 1 minute.

Add stock and fish. Cook for 5 minutes. Add shellfish and eel; cook 5 minutes. Add salt.

Remove bay leaf. Add Pernod, garnish with chopped parsley, and serve.

Grouper Baked in Achiote Marinade.

CHARCOAL-BROILED MAHI-MAHI

Serves 6

6 6- to 8-ounce mahi-mahi fillets (with skin on)
juice of 2 limes
juice of 1 orange
2 tablespoons garlic salt
1 tablespoon cayenne pepper or to taste
1 teaspoon ground black pepper
6 ripe bananas
½ cup vegetable oil, divided
paprika
cilantro or parsley

Place fillets on a plate, skin side down. Mix citrus juices and spoon over fillets. Sprinkle with garlic salt, cayenne pepper, and black pepper. Marinate for 30 minutes.

Rub banana skins with oil.

Place bananas on grill approximately 12 inches above hot coals and cover with grill lid or large piece of foil. Cook about 15 minutes and move to side of grill.

Drizzle remaining oil over fish fillets and rub a little on the skins to keep them from sticking. Put fish on grill, skin side down, sprinkle with paprika, and cover. Cook about 8 to 10 minutes, or until fish flakes. Do not overcook.

Remove fillets to heated plates. Place a banana on each plate, split the skin, and butter it. Garnish with a sprig of cilantro or parsley.

REDFISH OR SNAPPER WITH CILANTRO

Serves 4

*T*his dish can also be prepared in individual packets by placing the fish and jalapeño mixture in oiled aluminum foil, sealing the foil well, and then grilling over hot coals or baking in the oven as directed below. Be sure to wear rubber gloves when working with jalapeño chilies.

2 tablespoons olive oil
1 large onion, quartered and sliced thin
1 jalapeño chili, seeded and chopped
juice and grated zest of 1 lemon
½ cup chopped cilantro
4 6-ounce redfish or snapper fillets

Heat oil and sauté onion for about 2 minutes. Add jalapeño, lemon juice and zest, and cilantro. Cook for 1 minute. Remove from heat.

Place fish fillets in a shallow baking dish. Spread jalapeño mixture over each fillet. Sprinkle with a little salt and cover. Preheat oven to 350 degrees and bake for about 15 to 20 minutes or until fish flakes easily. Serve with Citrus Rice (p. 197).

PESCADO EN TIKIN XIK

Serves 4

*I*n Cancún the Tikin Xik at Hotel Camino Real is unlike the barbecued fish that home cooks prepare. Chef Jean Pierre Van Assche makes a beautiful presentation of the dish using individual bouchinette (hog snapper) opened out to resemble a butterfly. After it is cooked in an achiote paste marinade, each fish is placed on a banana leaf cut to fit the plate. It is further garnished with onions, tomatoes, and radishes, with a timbale of yellow rice to accompany. The chef cooks each portion separately, as is usual in a restaurant kitchen. I have adapted his recipe to serve four. If you have access to banana leaves, try creating your own special presentation.

4 fillets of grouper, snapper, tilefish, or similar fish
salt to taste
3 tablespoons annatto seeds
3 allspice berries
¼ teaspoon black peppercorns
¼ teaspoon salt
½ teaspoon ground oregano
2 large cloves garlic, crushed
¼ cup orange juice
¼ cup lime juice
½ cup vegetable oil
1 large onion, sliced
2 tomatoes, sliced
2 jalapeño chilies, seeded and cut into thin strips

Place fillets in a shallow dish in a single layer and salt lightly. In a spice grinder or blender combine annatto seeds, allspice berries, peppercorns, and salt and grind well. Transfer to a small bowl and mix with oregano, garlic, and citrus juices. Rub into fillets on both sides and let stand for 1 hour.

Spread the bottom of a skillet or other shallow cooking utensil with a little oil, add fillets, and pour over the marinade. Cover fish with onion and tomato slices, scatter the jalapeño slices over the top, and drizzle with remaining oil. Cook over low heat until fish flakes, basting frequently.

Serve with Yellow Rice with Saffron and Peas (p. 54).

Rows of jumbo-size pineapples festoon a roadside stand near Alvarado. Citrus groves carpet the verdant hills of northern Veracruz. A Mayan market vendor awaits customers at Izamal in Quintana Roo Province.

SNAPPER STUFFED WITH SHRIMP DRESSING

Serves 4

*W*hen Tony Diec prepared this dish in Cancún on a wild and stormy night, I was intrigued by the undefinable taste and texture of the leafy layers in which the fish was wrapped. The leaf had a strong anise flavor and the consistency of mustard greens. It grows in Tony's garden and is called hoja santa or acuyo and is used in the Yucatán to flavor certain dishes. Pernod is a fairly close substitute for this marvelous flavor.

1 3- to 4-pound snapper, grouper, or similar fish
⅓ cup extra-virgin olive oil
½ cup Pernod
½ teaspoon salt
1 clove garlic, crushed
2 Italian plum tomatoes, chopped
¼ teaspoon Fines Herbs
salt and pepper to taste
1 pound cooked shrimp, chopped
3 scallions, chopped (including tops), divided

Scale and clean fish, retaining the head. Combine olive oil, Pernod, and salt and rub into the fish, inside and out. Marinate for about 1 hour.

In a saucepan combine all remaining ingredients except shrimp and scallions and cook until mixture is dry enough to hold its shape. Fold in shrimp and half the scallions.

Spoon mixture into the cavity of the fish, wrap in foil (or banana leaves, if available), and place in a shallow pan. Preheat oven to 350 degrees and bake for about 40 minutes.

Remove to a hot platter and garnish with remaining scallions.

SNAPPER FILLETS OLÉ!

Serves 6

*S*napper is one of the most popular fish found in the Gulf of Mexico. There are many varieties of snapper, but the most familiar type is red snapper. The meat is white, medium- to large-flake, and sweet. It adapts easily to saucing as well as to grilling, baking, or broiling with just salt and butter.

2 pounds red snapper fillets
salt and pepper
juice of 1 lemon
1 garlic clove, crushed
2 medium onions, sliced
4 tablespoons olive oil
1 14½-ounce can peeled tomatoes
4 tablespoons chopped ripe olives
2 to 3 tablespoons drained capers
2 to 4 fresh jalapeño chilies, seeded and chopped fine

Season fish with salt and pepper, sprinkle with lemon juice, and set aside.

In a large skillet sauté garlic and onions in olive oil until limp. Add tomatoes, olives, capers, and jalapeños and simmer until thick. Add fish fillets, cover with sauce, and cook just until fish is flaky.

Remove fish to a hot platter and cook sauce quickly over high heat to thicken again, stirring constantly.

Spoon sauce over fish and serve with saffron rice.

BAKED SNAPPER FILLETS TAMPICO

Serves 6

*W*hile growing up in Mexico City, Chata DuBose was inspired by the superb cooking of her mother and sisters. And her father owned a restaurant there, so she was exposed to the theory and practice of preparing good food from all family members. Since moving to Houston, she spends the majority of her time researching and developing authentic Mexican dishes to be used in teaching classes or to be served at parties. She crafts dietetic dishes for a weight reduction center, always making sure that the flavor of Mexico is there. This recipe for Pescado en Su Jugo exemplifies the best of Tampico flavors as well as healthful, low-calorie food.

juice of 1 lime
2 pounds fish fillets (redfish, snapper, snook)
½ teaspoon salt
¼ teaspoon ground black pepper
⅓ cup olive oil
2 large tomatoes, sliced
1 large onion, sliced
2 cloves garlic, chopped
2 bay leaves, broken into pieces
⅓ cup sliced stuffed olives
⅓ cup drained capers
4 jalapeño chilies, seeded and cut into strips
2 tablespoons chopped parsley

Squeeze lime juice over fillets and sprinkle with salt and pepper.

Using a small amount of olive oil, grease a shallow casserole dish. Place fish on bottom. Layer remaining ingredients over fish and drizzle remaining oil over the top.

Cover with foil, preheat oven to 350 degrees, and bake about 30 minutes or until fish flakes easily. (If the fillets are in several layers, increase the cooking time.)

At a communal fishing village in northern Veracruz province, a net mender readies gear for the morning catch.

Shrimp boats dock gunwale to gunwale at this pier near Isla Mujeres.

Naranjo ranch hands prepare for the roundup.

TONY DIEC'S BAKED SNAPPER

Serves 4 to 6

*T*ony Diec is a man who loves to cook. Born in Merida, he has studied the cuisines of the Yucatán as well as the Mexican Gulf Coast regions. His career as a travel agent takes him all over the area, so he is continually gathering ideas for new dishes. The following recipe is from Veracruz.

4- to 5-pound snapper, grouper, tilefish, or
similar fish
2 to 3 cloves garlic
2 teaspoons salt, divided
½ teaspoon pepper
juice of 4 limes
4 poblano chilies
3 green bell peppers
1 cup blanched almonds
⅔ bottle dry white wine, divided
lime slices

Clean and scale fish, retaining the head. Mash garlic with 1½ teaspoons salt and pepper to form a paste. Add lime juice and rub the mixture over the entire fish, inside and out.

In a heavy iron skillet char peppers; transfer to a plastic bag to steam for 10 minutes. In the same manner, char bell peppers and transfer to a plastic bag. Cool.

Skin, seed, and chop peppers. Mix with almonds and a little wine and blend to a smooth consistency in a food processor or blender. Add remaining wine and remaining salt, pour over fish, and marinate overnight.

Wrap fish in foil, along with marinade. Preheat oven to 400 degrees and bake for 35 to 40 minutes or until fish flakes easily. Remove to a heated platter, pour sauce over fish, and garnish with sliced limes. (If cooking two 3-pound fish, the cooking time will be about 30 minutes.)

SNOOK WITH CHILE ANCHO SAUCE

Serves 6

*I*n this flavorful veracruzana dish, *Robalo Adobado*, the fish can be poached early in the day and covered with the adobo sauce. The final baking will take about 20 minutes—just long enough to heat the fish—and can be done just before serving. Lettuce dressed with vinaigrette provides a nice crunch and interesting accompaniment to the fish. As in most recipes, other fish can be substituted for snook—try tilefish. As a variation, poblano chilies can be substituted for ancho chilies to make a very good sauce. There is nothing subtle about the resulting dish, but it is very good when eaten with the shredded lettuce, which cools the heat of the sauce.

2 bay leaves
2 sprigs fresh thyme (or ⅛ teaspoon dried thyme)
2 sprigs fresh marjoram
(or ⅛ teaspoon dried marjoram)
½ teaspoon salt
water
2 pounds fillets of snook
heart of romaine lettuce
Basic Vinaigrette Dressing (p. 207)

CHILE ANCHO SAUCE

6 ancho chilies
1 cup cider vinegar
2 cups hot water
2 cloves garlic, peeled
¼ teaspoon dried oregano
4 black peppercorns
salt to taste
3 tablespoons vegetable oil

CHILE POBLANO SAUCE

3 large poblano chilies
2 red bell peppers
1 small jalapeño chili or more to taste
2 or 3 large cloves of garlic, peeled
6 black peppercorns
6 sprigs of oregano (leaves only)
½ cup vinegar
1 cup water
4 tablespoons vegetable oil
salt to taste

In a skillet large enough to hold the fish combine bay leaves, thyme, marjoram, salt, and enough water to cover fish. Bring to a boil, reduce heat to a simmer, add fish, and poach about 10 minutes or until almost done. Remove fish and place on an oiled ovenproof platter.

Pour Chile Ancho Sauce (or Chile Poblano Sauce) over fish, preheat oven to 325 degrees, and bake about 20 minutes.

To serve, garnish platter with shredded lettuce drizzled with vinaigrette.

To make Chile Ancho Sauce, roast anchos over an open flame or in a hot skillet just long enough to soften them. Remove seeds and veins. Combine with vinegar and hot water and set aside.

Heat a skillet and char garlic. Add oregano and peppercorns and heat 1 minute more. In a blender mix soaked anchos, roasted garlic mixture, 1 cup vinegar water, and salt. Blend to a smooth consistency.

Heat oil in a skillet and fry sauce, stirring constantly, about 10 minutes or until sauce thickens.

To make Chile Poblano Sauce, char poblanos, bell peppers, and jalapeño in a heavy skillet. Transfer to a plastic bag to "sweat" for 10 minutes. In the same skillet char the garlic, peppercorns, and oregano. Transfer to a blender jar.

Rub the charred skin from the peppers, seed them, and put them in the blender jar. Add half of the vinegar and water and blend to make a puree. Add more liquid as necessary to make a medium-textured mixture.

In the same skillet heat oil and add puree, stirring and frying for 10 minutes or until thickened and dried a bit. Add salt. Use as directed above.

The ornate architecture of cathedrals dominates the inland town of Coatepec.

SNOOK IN CAPER SAUCE

Serves 4

*I*n the cuisine of Tampico as well as other cities along Mexico's east coast, capers and almonds are frequently used to accent and enhance the flavors of certain dishes. This recipe for *Robalo en Salsa de Alcaparras* is typical of the Tampico area. Red snapper or similar fish can be substituted for snook, and if almond meal is not available, blanched whole almonds (about ⅔ cup) can be ground to make the meal. I skin the fish after poaching, leaving the head and tail intact. An olive slice covers the eye of the fish, and the sauce is poured over the body. Not a traditional way to serve this dish, but one more aesthetically pleasing for me.

2 carrots, sliced
2 turnips, sliced
½ small onion, sliced
2 bay leaves
1 teaspoon salt
12 peppercorns
juice of ½ lime
4 cups water or enough to cover fish
1 3- to 4-pound whole snook, red snapper, or similar fish
1 head leaf lettuce
1 pound potatoes, steamed, sliced, and salted
1 large tomato, cut into sections
1 small onion, sliced thin

CAPER SAUCE

⅓ cup drained capers
½ cup almond meal
2 tablespoons chopped parsley
1 tablespoon wine vinegar
2 cloves garlic, peeled
⅓ cup olive oil
salt to taste

Combine carrots, turnips, onion, bay leaves, salt, peppercorns, lime juice, and water in a saucepan and simmer for 30 minutes. Set aside to cool.

Place fish in a poacher or other large vessel and pour the reserved liquid over it. Bring to a boil, reduce heat, and simmer about 30 minutes or until fish is done. Remove from liquid, place on a heatproof platter, and keep warm. Strain and reserve cooking liquid.

Meanwhile make sauce by combining capers, almond meal, parsley, vinegar, garlic, and ½ cup reserved poaching liquid. Blend in a blender until smooth, adding more liquid if necessary.

Heat oil in a skillet over medium heat. Transfer sauce from the blender and cook for 1 minute. Gradually add about 1 cup poaching liquid, stirring well. Simmer about 10 minutes and add salt if desired. The sauce should be a little thicker than heavy cream. Pour over fish and cover the head and tail with foil. Preheat oven to 325 degrees and bake 20 minutes.

To serve, transfer fish to a heated platter. Arrange lettuce leaves around fish, with potato slices on top of the lettuce and tomato sections between the potatoes. Sprinkle potatoes with chopped parsley and scatter onion rings over the top.

TUNA WITH CHILIES AND TOMATO

Serves 4 to 6

6 large tomatoes
3 red chilies
4 tablespoons olive oil
4 cloves garlic, chopped
1 jalapeño chili, seeded and chopped fine
¼ teaspoon ground coriander
¼ teaspoon sugar
½ teaspoon salt or to taste
ground black pepper to taste
1 pound tuna steaks, grilled

Heat a heavy iron skillet over highest heat. Char tomatoes on all sides to blister the skins. Remove and cool; skin and chop the pulp. In the same skillet char chilies on all sides. Remove and place in a plastic bag to cool and "sweat." Skin, remove seeds, and chop fine.

Heat olive oil and sauté garlic for 1 minute. Add tomatoes, red chilies, jalapeño, coriander, sugar, salt, and pepper. Simmer until thick. Flake tuna and stir into the mixture, heating well. Turn the mixture into a bowl, cover with plastic wrap, and chill overnight. Serve accompanied by crusty bread and garlic olive oil to pour over the bread if desired.

ACHIOTE PASTE

6 tablespoons annatto seeds
water
3 allspice berries
½ teaspoon black peppercorns
2 cloves
2 tablespoons dried oregano or 3 tablespoons Mexican oregano, toasted
2 large cloves garlic
½ teaspoon salt
3 tablespoons lime juice
3 tablespoons vegetable oil

In a saucepan cover annatto seeds with water and bring to a boil. Reduce heat and simmer about 5 minutes. Remove from heat, cover, and let cool.

Drain annatto seeds and combine with remaining ingredients in a blender jar. Blend at high speed, scraping down the sides as necessary. Add more oil, if necessary, to produce a smooth paste. Cover and refrigerate. (This will keep several weeks.)

Cancún's luxurious waterfront hotels and azure waters attract tourists from around the world.

A COLLECTION OF FIVE SALSAS

*K*athy Ruiz, the chef at Otto's Grill in Cancún, has some excellent ideas for cooking fish. Her favorite way to prepare fish is to grill it, seasoning only with lime juice, salt, and flour. The flour absorbs the heat and moisture well and does not spatter as oil or butter does. The fresh taste of the fish comes through, clean and briny. Her repertoire of salsas for fish are wonderful with chicken and pork as well.

FRESH MANGO-JICAMA SALSA

Makes about 2½ cups

1 cup chopped mango
1 cup chopped jicama
juice of 6 limes
1 whole poblano chili
2 tablespoons chopped cilantro
⅛ teaspoon salt

Mix mango and jicama with lime juice. Set aside. In a very hot iron skillet char poblano on all sides. Remove to a plastic bag and let steam for 10 minutes. When cool, rub the charred skin off, remove seeds and membrane, and chop fine. Mix with mango and jicama mixture; add cilantro and salt. Allow to stand for about 3 hours. Serve at room temperature.

CHARRED TOMATILLO SALSA

Makes about 1½ cups

10 tomatillos, husked
2 serrano chilies or less to taste
1 large clove garlic, crushed
pinch of salt

Heat a large skillet very hot and roast tomatillos about 15 minutes or until the skins are charred on all sides. Remove.

Add serranos and roast 5 minutes or until charred on all sides, pressing with a spatula. Remove.

Blend tomatillos (including skin), serranos (including skin and seeds), garlic, and salt in a food processor or blender, leaving some small pieces for texture. Serve at room temperature. This sauce is *very* hot.

AVOCADO SALSA

Makes about 2 cups

2 Italian plum tomatoes
1 small jalapeño chili
2 to 3 avocados
juice of 1 lime
½ cup onion, chopped fine
¼ teaspoon salt

In a very hot iron skillet roast tomatoes. Cool and chop fine, including the charred skin. Set aside. Wearing gloves, cut jalapeño in half and remove seeds and membranes. Chop fine and add to tomatoes. Peel and seed avocados. Chop fine, squeeze lime juice over the pieces, and toss to mix. Mix all ingredients together with onion and season with salt. Serve at room temperature.

POBLANO AND MANGO SALSA

Makes 1 to 1½ cups

2 poblano chilies
1 large firm mango
juice of 1 lime
grated zest of ½ lime
1 teaspoon maple syrup
½ teaspoon salt

In a very hot iron skillet roast poblanos until charred on all sides. Transfer to a plastic bag to steam for 10 minutes.

Meanwhile, peel and seed mango and cut into thin strips. Add lime juice and zest, maple syrup, and salt, mixing well. Skin and seed poblanos under cold running water. Pat dry and cut into thin strips. Toss with mangos; correct seasonings. Allow to stand for 30 minutes. Serve at room temperature.

RED PEPPER AND JICAMA SALSA

Makes about 1 cup

1 large red bell pepper
½ jalapeño chili or more to taste
½ cup thin jicama strips
½ cup chopped onion
2 tablespoons chopped cilantro
juice of 1 lime
grated zest of ½ lime
¼ teaspoon salt

In a very hot iron skillet char bell pepper on all sides. Transfer to a plastic bag to steam.

Wearing rubber gloves, halve, seed, and chop jalapeño fine. Combine with remaining ingredients.

Skin, seed, and cut bell pepper into thin strips. Add to mixture. Taste to correct seasonings. Serve at room temperature.

Washday at Zempoala reveals the bright colors of handwoven textiles.

Four salsas from a collection (clockwise from upper left): Avocado Salsa; Charred Tomatillo Salsa; Fresh Mango-Jicama Salsa; Red Pepper and Jicama Salsa.

Flamingos flock to the brine flats of Rio Lagartos in the northern Yucatán.

MEXICAN CHEESE PUDDING

Serves 4 to 6

2 whole eggs
2 egg yolks
½ cup heavy cream
1 cup grated Chihuahua cheese
1 cup grated Parmesan cheese
2 tablespoons fine-chopped onion
1 teaspoon chopped fresh basil
(or ½ teaspoon dried basil)
⅛ teaspoon cayenne pepper
16 salted soda crackers, broken into pieces
paprika

Beat eggs, egg yolks, and cream together. Stir in cheeses, onion, basil, and cayenne pepper.

Butter a 5" x 9" baking dish and layer half the crackers on the bottom. Cover with half the cheese mixture, add layer of remaining crackers, and top with remaining cheese. Sprinkle with paprika. Preheat oven to 350 degrees and bake for 30 minutes or until brown and puffy.

PICKLED ONION RINGS

A dish of pickled onions is one of the traditional accompaniments to Tikin Xik as well as many other dishes prepared with achiote. They will keep for several weeks in the refrigerator in the unlikely case that there are any left.

2 tablespoons olive oil
2 large purple onions, sliced thin
12 peppercorns
½ teaspoon chopped fresh oregano
1 bay leaf
1 clove garlic, crushed
1 teaspoon salt
1 cup white wine vinegar (or ½ cup distilled
vinegar and ½ cup water)

In a heavy skillet heat oil and sauté onion rings for about 2 minutes. Remove from heat and add remaining ingredients. Marinate in the refrigerator for 2 days before using.

FRESH TOMATO
AND CUCUMBER SALAD

Serves 4 to 6

T his salad is especially for those fortunate gardeners who are overwhelmed with bumper crops of cucumbers and tomatoes in the summer. If you are using regular cucumbers, you will need to peel them. The hybrid English variety (so-called "burpless") really works best in this dish. It is a cool and extremely low-calorie salad.

½ cup thin-sliced onions
2½ cups thin-sliced cucumbers
2 tablespoons fine-chopped green bell pepper
2 tablespoons fine-chopped red bell pepper
3 tablespoons white vinegar
½ teaspoon salt
1 teaspoon toasted cumin seed
1½ cups halved cherry tomatoes
1 tablespoon cilantro leaves

Place onions in a colander and hold under running hot water for a minute or two to remove the strong oils. Refresh in cold water and pat dry. (This will keep onions white and sweet.)

Combine onions, cucumbers, bell peppers, vinegar, salt, and cumin seed in a bowl and toss to mix thoroughly. Cover and refrigerate for 1 hour or longer. When ready to serve, drain off accumulated liquid and toss cucumber mixture with tomatoes and cilantro. Add more salt if desired. Serve in lettuce cups or as is.

GUACAMOLE

Makes 3 to 4 cups

uacamole is traditional with many Mexican dishes. It may be used as a salad, a dip for toasted tortilla chips, or as a sauce to accompany almost anything.

2 medium tomatoes, chopped fine
¼ medium onion, chopped fine
1 to 2 tablespoons chopped cilantro
juice of 2 limes
4 avocados, peeled, seeded, and mashed
1 small jalapeño chili, seeded and chopped fine
½ teaspoon salt
ground pepper to taste

Mix tomatoes, onion, cilantro, and lime juice together. Stir in avocados and jalapeño. Add salt and pepper. Let stand for 30 minutes.

CITRUS RICE

Serves 1

1 cup hot cooked rice
½ teaspoon grated lime or lemon zest
1 teaspoon lime or lemon juice
1 teaspoon chopped parsley
dash of salt
1 teaspoon olive oil

Mix all ingredients together and serve at once.

A Tuxpan torteria sports alfresco seating for passersby.

CHOCOLATE TORTILLA DESSERT

Serves 4

his luscious Cancún dish is a treat for the eye as well as for the palate. Airy chocolate "tortillas" filled with strawberries and sweetened cream cheese float on a bed of warm white wine sabayon. It's devilishly tricky to make the tortillas, but well worth the effort. Adding flour makes them easier to manage while cooking.

"TORTILLAS"

3 eggs
3 tablespoons sugar
½ cup chocolate syrup
½ teaspoon vanilla extract
1 tablespoon flour (optional)
5 teaspoons butter

FILLING

6 ounces cream cheese
6 teaspoons sugar
milk
1 pint strawberries
additional sugar

SABAYON

4 egg yolks
¼ cup sugar
½ cup white wine

To make "tortillas," mix eggs and sugar, beating well. Add syrup and vanilla extract. Sprinkle flour over the top and beat to incorporate well. Over medium heat melt about ½ teaspoon butter in a nonstick crepe pan or skillet and pour ¼ cup batter into heated pan. Cook until set on top. Turn carefully with an oiled spatula and cook briefly on the other side. Remove from pan, add more butter, and repeat the procedure with remaining batter (it should make 8 to 10 "tortillas"). Stack with a piece of waxed paper between each. Set aside.

To make filling, mix cream cheese and sugar together, adding enough milk to thin to the consistency of very heavy cream. Set aside. Wash and hull berries, halving the very large ones. Sprinkle lightly with sugar and set aside.

To make sabayon, beat egg yolks with sugar in a large metal bowl or sabayon pan over simmering water. Add wine, a little at a time, beating constantly as the sauce thickens. When fluffy and thick, remove from heat. Do not overcook.

To serve, spoon about ½ cup of sabayon on each plate. Place two "tortillas" over the sauce and fill with strawberries. Cover with sweetened cream cheese and fold over the tops of the tortillas. Spoon a little cream cheese over the tops and sprinkle with strawberries. Serve at once.

FLAN

Serves 8

*I*n the minds of most North Americans flan is the traditional dessert of Mexico. Indeed, some variation of this basic baked custard can be found in the cuisines of most Latin American countries. It is also known as crème caramel in France and as caramel custard in English-speaking countries. The caramelized sugar makes a sauce for the custard.

1½ cups sugar, divided
6 eggs, slightly beaten
¼ teaspoon salt
1 teaspoon vanilla extract
4 cups milk

In a heavy pot or skillet melt ½ cup sugar until it is syrupy and brown. Do not burn. Pour the syrup into a 2-quart baking dish (or 8 individual custard cups), covering the bottom evenly. Set aside to cool and set.

Combine remaining sugar with remaining ingredients, mixing well. Pour through a strainer into the baking dish and place in a pan of hot water about 1 inch deep. Preheat over to 325 degrees and bake about 1 hour (or 35 minutes for individual servings) or until a knife inserted in the center comes out clean. Remove from oven and cool in the hot water until custard reaches room temperature. Chill if desired.

If serving at room temperature, invert on serving dish to unmold. If serving chilled, place dish in warm water to loosen custard, then invert on serving dish.

FAUX FLAN

Serves 8

*N*o time to cook a dessert? Try this when you are looking for a chilled pudding. It's not really a flan substitute, but will certainly fill the bill deliciously. The dessert can be served in individual dishes topped with an enormous sugared strawberry.

2⅓ cups light cream or half-and-half
1 cup sugar
1 envelope unflavored gelatin
2 cups sour cream
1 teaspoon vanilla extract
sugared fruit (optional)

Heat the cream, sugar, and gelatin together over low heat until the sugar and gelatin have dissolved. Fold in sour cream and vanilla. Pour into 8 individual custard cups (or stemmed wine glasses). Chill several hours. Serve plain or with sugared fruit.

FLAMED MANGOES

Serves 2

*R*olandi's Restaurant, in the heart of a new shopping mall in Punta Cancún, is well known for its great cuisine and for the pyrotechnics that showcase its spectacular desserts. Deft and talented waiters seem to be able to flame almost anything: cake, fruits, coffee, you name it. One of the best is the Mango Flambeado. There is nothing quite like a mango with its silky texture and intriguing flavors, and when flamed with citrus and liqueurs, it is outstanding. The following recipe is an adaptation of the original.

2 tablespoons butter
3 tablespoons brown sugar
2 or 3 strips lime zest
1 mango, peeled, seeded, and sliced in thick slices
2 tablespoons Cointreau or Triple Sec
⅓ cup light or dark rum
nutmeg to taste
vanilla ice cream or sour cream

In a chafing dish melt butter. Add sugar and lime zest and stir until sugar has melted. Add mango slices and sauté until thoroughly heated.

Pour Cointreau into pan and shake pan to distribute it. Add rum, shake pan, and flame mangos. Sprinkle with a little nutmeg and serve with ice cream or sour cream.

FRESH MANGO FREEZE

Serves 4 to 6

*T*he subtle taste of a fresh mango is hard to describe: sweet, slightly tart, velvety, juicy, and always delicious. Combined with the sharpness of yogurt in this frozen dessert, it makes a memorable finale to any meal.

4 cups mango pieces, frozen
1½ cups yogurt (low-fat is fine)
6 tablespoons powdered sugar
zest of 1 lime (about ½ teaspoon)

In a food processor puree mango until pieces are pea-sized. Add yogurt, sugar, and lime zest and process until smooth and creamy. Transfer to a covered container and freeze 1 or 2 hours before serving.

The massive walls of Izamal's central cathedral rise from the remains of a sprawling Mayan pyramid. Pristine, identical fishing boats lie beached at Puerto Chicxulub. A boat handler at Tecolutla awaits a tourist charter.

BASICS AND BONUSES

A FEW FISH FACTS

*T*he table gives some tips about the fish varieties used in the recipes. To simplify things, the experts at the University of Florida who prepared the chart have used 5 percent as the dividing line between fat and lean fish: any fish with a fat content of less than 5 percent is considered lean; above 5 percent, fat. Keep in mind that a fat fish is suited to broiling or baking, will have a stronger flavor, and will usually have a bloodline or an area of darker flesh that should be removed before eating. A lean fish has a more delicate flavor, needs to be basted with oil or butter during cooking, and generally takes well to saucing.

GUIDELINES FOR AVERAGE SERVING PORTIONS

6- to 8-ounce fillet = 1 serving
2 pounds fillets = 6 servings
5 pounds whole cleaned fish = 6 servings
2 pounds raw headless shrimp = 1 pound cooked =
6 servings
Jumbo shrimp = 0 to 15 per pound
Large shrimp = 16 to 20 per pound
Medium shrimp = 26 to 35 per pound
Small shrimp = 40 or more per pound
1 pound cleaned crabmeat = about 2 cups =
4 to 6 servings
1 pint shucked oysters = 1½ to 2 cups drained
oysters = 3 to 4 servings
1 pound bay scallops = 4 servings

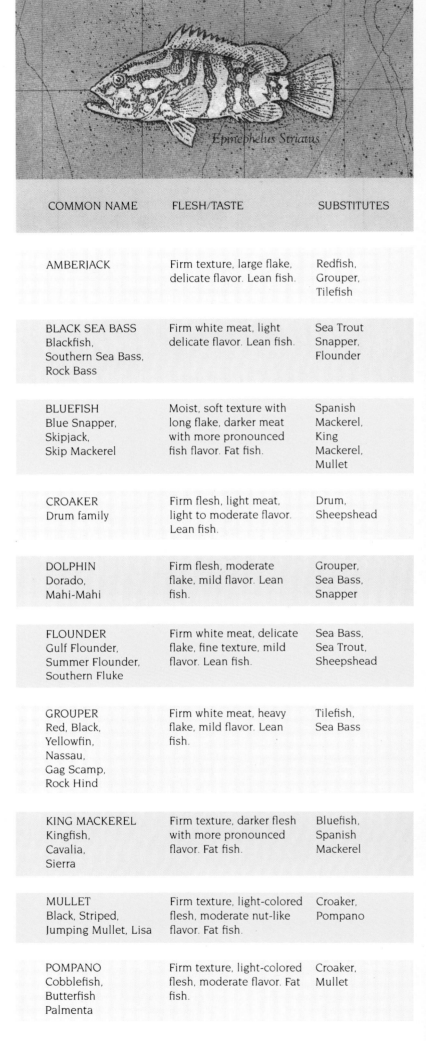

Epinephelus Striatus

COMMON NAME	FLESH/TASTE	SUBSTITUTES
AMBERJACK	Firm texture, large flake, delicate flavor. Lean fish.	Redfish, Grouper, Tilefish
BLACK SEA BASS Blackfish, Southern Sea Bass, Rock Bass	Firm white meat, light delicate flavor. Lean fish.	Sea Trout Snapper, Flounder
BLUEFISH Blue Snapper, Skipjack, Skip Mackerel	Moist, soft texture with long flake, darker meat with more pronounced fish flavor. Fat fish.	Spanish Mackerel, King Mackerel, Mullet
CROAKER Drum family	Firm flesh, light meat, light to moderate flavor. Lean fish.	Drum, Sheepshead
DOLPHIN Dorado, Mahi-Mahi	Firm flesh, moderate flake, mild flavor. Lean fish.	Grouper, Sea Bass, Snapper
FLOUNDER Gulf Flounder, Summer Flounder, Southern Fluke	Firm white meat, delicate flake, fine texture, mild flavor. Lean fish.	Sea Bass, Sea Trout, Sheepshead
GROUPER Red, Black, Yellowfin, Nassau, Gag Scamp, Rock Hind	Firm white meat, heavy flake, mild flavor. Lean fish.	Tilefish, Sea Bass
KING MACKEREL Kingfish, Cavalia, Sierra	Firm texture, darker flesh with more pronounced flavor. Fat fish.	Bluefish, Spanish Mackerel
MULLET Black, Striped, Jumping Mullet, Lisa	Firm texture, light-colored flesh, moderate nut-like flavor. Fat fish.	Croaker, Pompano
POMPANO Cobblefish, Butterfish Palmenta	Firm texture, light-colored flesh, moderate flavor. Fat fish.	Croaker, Mullet

Shells of all varieties are deposited along the lower Texas coast by the converging Caribbean and Mississippi currents.

FRYING FISH

COMMON NAME	FLESH/TASTE	SUBSTITUTES
REDFISH Sea Bass, Red Drum, Channel Bass, Red Sea Bass	Firm texture, moist white meat, heavy flake, mild flavor. Lean fish.	Grouper, Tilefish
RED SNAPPER Gulf Snapper, Pensacola Red Snapper	Tender, moist white meat, delicate sweet flavor. Lean fish.	Flounder, Sea Bass, Sea Trout
SEA TROUT Weakfish, Speckled Trout Gray, Spotted, "Specks"	Finely textured white flesh, mild sweet flavor. Lean fish.	Flounder, Sea Bass, Redfish
SHEEPSHEAD Convict Fish, Fathead	Light-colored meat, light to moderate flavor. Lean fish.	Sea Trout, Redfish
SHARK Mako, Blue, Blacktip, Angel, Hammerhead	Firm texture, white meat with very mild flavor, no bones. Lean fish.	Swordfish, Grouper, Redfish
SPANISH MACKEREL American, Atlantic Blue	Darker meat, more delicately flavored than other mackerels. Fat fish.	King Mackerel, Pompano, Mullet
SWORDFISH Billfish, Broadbill Swordfish	Firm flesh, light meat, light to moderate flavor. Lean fish.	Shark, Grouper
TILEFISH Golden, Grey, Blueline	Firm yet tender flesh, comparable to lobster or scallop, mild, sweet flavor. Lean fish.	Grouper, Redfish
TUNA	Firm flesh, darker meat, pronounced flavor. Lean fish.	Swordfish

*S*urely the most popular way to prepare fish is to fry it! In my travels around the Gulf Coast this method was the common denominator of every seafood restaurant. Coatings differed; fish were sometimes small whole ones, fillets, strips, or throats; shrimp were butterflied or not; sauces, if served, reflected the cuisines of the region. But basically the seafood was coated with something and fried in hot fat. When it is done well, it is superb. And this depends on three factors: the freshness of the fish (always the first factor), the integrity of the coating, and the temperature of the oil or fat.

A satisfactory average temperature is 375 degrees, with a 5-degree tolerance on either side. The oil for deep-frying should fill no more than half the pot. For pan-frying, the oil should be about ½ inch deep since the food will be turned to cook each side separately (as in empanadas or turnovers). A thermometer is the safest way to test the temperature, but a popular method is to drop a cube of bread in the hot oil. If the oil foams without immediately browning the bread, the oil is ready.

Herb Barranger, an expert on fish fries from his years of living in Florida, tells of an interesting way to test the oil's temperature. When he and his friends gathered for fish fries in Pensacola, they put the oil in a large iron kettle over the coals and floated a strike-anywhere match on top of the oil. When the match ignited, the oil was ready. Tongs were used to lift out the match.

COATINGS FOR FRIED SEAFOODS

Beat an egg and add water or milk to thin. Dip the dry fish into the egg wash and then into one of the following coatings:

flour seasoned with salt and pepper
seasoned corn meal
seasoned chickpea flour
masa harina seasoned with salt and cayenne pepper
or ground cumin seed
cracker crumbs
flour mixed with fine-chopped nuts or sesame seeds
crushed cornflakes

Or you can omit the egg wash and dip the fish into a mixture of equal parts of flour and fine dry bread crumbs seasoned with salt and pepper.

The folks at McIlhenny Company, makers of Tabasco Pepper Sauce, have this suggestion: Mix ½ cup lemon juice with 2 teaspoons Tabasco sauce. Toss seafood in this mixture, coating well, and marinate 1 hour. Dip in a mixture of cornmeal and flour, then fry.

The Chinese have developed batters to a fine art: Mix ½ cup cornstarch with ½ cup flour, ½ teaspoon salt, and 2 teaspoons baking powder. Stir in ¼ cup oil and ½ cup water to make a smooth paste. Dip the seafood into the batter and then fry in hot oil.

And, finally, here is a batter from Nora Scheers Schorp of San Antonio: Mix together ½ cup flour, ¼ cup cornmeal, ½ teaspoon salt, and ½ teaspoon baking soda and set aside. Mix together 1 beaten egg, ½ cup ice water, and 1 tablespoon oil. Stir the liquid into the dry ingredients to make a smooth batter. Dip the seafood into the batter and then fry in hot oil.

MARINADES FOR SHRIMP OR FISH FILLETS

*T*he weather down in the Florida Keys is usually ideal for outdoor cooking (if the mosquitoes aren't out). Raymond Huffman, chef at Duck Key Lodge, has developed various marinades for grilled seafood dishes. Here are two of his most popular marinades. Dijon Mustard Marinade is particularly delicious on grouper or mahi-mahi. Cuban Creole Marinade contains mojo criollo, a bottled sauce used in Cuban cuisine and available in the specialty section of most supermarkets. The Garlic-Ginger Marinade is excellent for not only shrimp but also cubes of dense-textured fish such as swordfish or wahoo as well as chicken or turkey breast.

DIJON MUSTARD MARINADE

½ cup butter, melted
6 tablespoons Dijon mustard or to taste
½ cup dry white wine
½ teaspoon dried tarragon
¼ teaspoon salt
¼ teaspoon ground white pepper

CUBAN CREOLE MARINADE

½ cup mojo criollo
½ cup vegetable oil
juice of 1 lime
1 tablespoon grated onion
⅛ teaspoon ground cumin
dash of cayenne pepper or Tabasco Pepper Sauce
¼ teaspoon salt

GARLIC-GINGER MARINADE

1 cup vegetable oil, divided
6 tablespoons lemon juice
1 large onion, chopped
6 cloves garlic, chopped
2½-inch piece fresh ginger root, chopped
2 or 3 fresh hot green chilies, seeded and sliced
1½ teaspoons salt
½ teaspoon pepper

To make marinades, mix all ingredients well. Marinate shelled and deveined shrimp or fish fillets for several hours. Baste with marinade while grilling.

SEAFOOD MADNESS SEASONING POWDER

Makes 1 cup

*P*eter Harman has been a professional chef in Florida's Gulf Coast resorts for over ten years. He is currently at the Sundial Beach and Tennis Resort on Sanibel Island, where he prepares delectable seafood dishes for a discerning clientele. His Seafood Madness is a great homemade seasoning for meats and poultry as well as fish. It will stay fresh indefinitely in a tightly capped bottle.

2 tablespoons salt
1 tablespoon coarse-ground black pepper
1 tablespoon ground white pepper
1 tablespoon cayenne pepper
1 tablespoon garlic powder
1 tablespoon garlic flakes
1 tablespoon onion powder
2 tablespoons paprika
2 tablespoons sugar
2 tablespoons ground oregano
2 tablespoons ground thyme

Mix all ingredients together well and store in an airtight container.

BRENNAN'S CREOLE SEASONING FOR FISH

Makes 2 cups

*T*his seasoning keeps indefinitely in a tightly sealed jar. Brennan's of Houston uses it to flavor seafood dishes, sometimes as a marinade and sometimes as one of the ingredients in the dish.

⅓ cup salt
¼ cup powdered or granulated garlic
¼ cup ground black pepper
2 tablespoons cayenne pepper
3 tablespoons ground thyme
2 tablespoons ground oregano
⅓ cup paprika
3 tablespoons powdered or flaked onion

Combine all ingredients and mix well. Store in a well-sealed glass jar.

Steamed and lightly salted prawns are bagged with fresh limes for sale at the docks of Veracruz.

COURT-BOUILLON

*T*he following liquid is used for poaching fish, either whole or fillets. Cool the court-bouillon, add the fish to be poached, and increase the heat gradually, especially for whole fish or large pieces.

1 carrot, sliced
1 small rib celery, sliced
½ small onion, sliced
1 bay leaf
1 teaspoon white peppercorns
2 sprigs of parsley
1 cup white wine
2 quarts water

Mix all ingredients in a stainless steel or enamel saucepan. Bring to a boil, reduce heat, and simmer 10 minutes. Cool and strain.

CRAB OR SHRIMP BOIL

*W*hen boiling shrimp or crab I use this recipe rather than a packaged version because the seasonings can be altered to suit the dish. Sometimes I add celery leaves, occasionally oregano or thyme. Using seasoned water also gives steamed lobsters or fish fillets extra snap.

2 quarts water
½ lemon, including rind
1 slice onion or 1 whole scallion
2 bay leaves
6 peppercorns
4 allspice berries
1 or 2 dried hot red peppers or ⅛ teaspoon cayenne pepper
1 teaspoon salt

Mix all ingredients together in a large pot. Bring to a boil. Reduce heat and simmer, covered, 5 to 10 minutes.

SEAFOOD STOCK

*H*omemade stocks are simple to make. They do not contain the salt and preservatives of commercially prepared bases and can therefore be reduced to concentrate the flavor. If using stock in a shrimp dish, add the shells and heads (if available) of the shrimp used in the recipe. If stock is needed for a lobster dish, add the lobster shells to the stock.

2 pounds fish heads, tails, and bones
½ onion, sliced
1 small carrot, sliced
1 clove garlic, optional
3 to 4 peppercorns
1 bay leaf
1 large sprig of parsley
1 sprig of thyme (or ⅛ teaspoon dried thyme)
½ cup dry white wine or vermouth
water

Combine all ingredients in a large kettle; add water to cover and bring to a boil. Reduce heat immediately and simmer for about 30 minutes. Remove from heat and let cool. Strain and salt to taste if desired. If reducing the stock to concentrate flavor or to prepare a glacé, do not salt.

STOCK USING CLAM JUICE

Makes about 1 pint

*W*hile it may not have quite the pizazz of made-from-scratch fish stock, this is an acceptable substitute. The secret is to enhance the bottled clam juice with some of the same ingredients of a homemade stock. If using the stock for a shrimp-based dish, add the shrimp shells and a few whole shrimp to the kettle at the beginning. The recipe can be increased by multiplying the ingredients for the desired amount. Remember that this is an unsalted stock and can be reduced to concentrate the flavor.

1 cup bottled clam juice
1 cup water
½ cup dry white wine
1 2-inch piece of carrot, sliced
1 2-inch piece of celery, sliced
1 bay leaf
1 small wedge of onion
shrimp shells and several shrimp (optional)

Combine all ingredients in a heavy saucepan and bring to a boil. Reduce heat immediately and simmer over low heat for about 10 minutes. Remove from heat and cool. Strain.

Peppers ripen in the sun of a Mexican market day.

ROUX-BASED SAUCES

*T*he most famous roux-based sauce is béchamel, which is used as a base for many other sauces. The method for making all roux-based sauces is basically the same. Proportions of flour and butter to liquid produces sauces of various thicknesses and amounts. The basic proportions are as follows:

FOR SOUPS

1 tablespoon flour + 1 tablespoon butter + 1 cup liquid

FOR SAUCES

2 tablespoons flour + 2 tablespoons butter + 1 cup liquid

FOR SOUFFLÉS

3 tablespoons flour + 3 tablespoons butter + 1 cup liquid

BÉCHAMEL SAUCE

1 cup milk
1 bay leaf
1 slice onion
2 cloves
2 tablespoons butter
2 tablespoons flour
salt and pepper to taste

In a small saucepan, heat milk with bay leaf, onion, and cloves. Bring to a boil and remove from heat. Cool to lukewarm.

In a heavy pan melt butter. Add flour and cook 2 minutes, stirring constantly. Pour milk mixture through a strainer into the roux. Stir until the mixture thickens; season with salt and pepper.

BROWN ROUX FOR CREOLE AND CAJUN COOKING

The roux used in the cooking of Louisiana has its own personality. Basically it is the combination of equal parts of flour and vegetable oil, heated in a heavy iron skillet and browned very slowly while stirring. A good roux will take nearly 45 minutes to brown properly so that it acquires its characteristic nutty taste without burning.

GAIDO'S TARTAR SAUCE

Makes 1 quart

*T*he most popular sauce requested with seafood dishes at this Galveston restaurant is tartar sauce. It's easy to make and will keep a week or so in the refrigerator if you rinse the onion slices in hot water before grinding them. This will help keep the onion fresh as well as remove most of the compound that causes discoloration.

2 cups mayonnaise
¾ teaspoon hot mustard
¼ teaspoon ground white pepper
¼ teaspoon salt
½ cup dill pickle relish, drained
1 cup sliced yellow onions
½ cup parsley leaves
2 tablespoons capers

Mix together mayonnaise, mustard, pepper, salt, and pickle relish.

Grind together onions, parsley, and capers. Add to mayonnaise mixture and mix well. Refrigerate until ready to use.

COCKTAIL SAUCE FOR SHRIMP OR OYSTERS

Makes about 4 cups

*T*his sauce from my brother Gib Thompson is better made one day in advance. It can also be frozen in plastic pouches, thawed in cool water, and served while still cold. It keeps several months and is convenient to have on hand when unexpected guests drop by at cocktail time.

3 cups tomato catsup
⅓ cup fine-chopped onion
⅓ cup fine-chopped celery
1 teaspoon salt
1 teaspoon cracked black pepper
3 tablespoons horseradish
juice of 1 lemon
½ hard-cooked egg, chopped fine (optional)
Tabasco Pepper Sauce to taste

Mix all ingredients well and chill thoroughly before serving.

These female crabs are returned to the water as part of a conservation effort.

JANET ROBINSON'S HOLLANDAISE SAUCE

2 tablespoons butter
4 teaspoons flour
1 cup boiling water
1 teaspoon salt
juice of ½ lemon
2 egg yolks, beaten

Mix together butter, flour, water, salt, and lemon juice. Cook over medium heat until thickened slightly. Remove from heat, cool slightly, and stir in egg yolks, mixing thoroughly.

SEASONED MAYONNAISES FOR BROILED FISH

*M*ost home cooks like to broil fish fillets because it's easy and quick. So Bruce Molzan and Gary Mercer, chefs at Ruggles Grill in Houston, came up with these ideas for broiling fillets with seasoned mayonnaise. The technique is simple: place the fillet on an oiled or nonstick baking pan. Spread a thin layer of mayonnaise over the fish, covering the entire surface well. Broil in a very hot oven about 3 to 5 minutes or until the mayonnaise starts to brown and bubble. The fish is done! These mayonnaises could also be used to dress grilled fish or to bind seafood salads.

SAFFRON AND CUCUMBER MAYONNAISE

Makes about 1½ cups

3 to 4 threads of saffron
1 tablespoon white wine, warmed
2 egg yolks
3 cloves garlic
1 cup olive oil
¼ cup grated cucumber, squeezed dry
¼ cup loosely packed chopped mint leaves
1 tablespoon lemon juice
dash of Tabasco Pepper Sauce or to taste
salt and pepper to taste

Soften saffron in wine. Set aside. Combine egg yolks and garlic and process in a food processor to make a paste. Slowly drizzle olive oil into the paste to form an emulsion. Do not overprocess. Transfer to a bowl.

Stir in reserved saffron and wine, grated cucumber, mint, and lemon juice. Season with Tabasco sauce, salt, and pepper.

WALNUT AND PARSLEY MAYONNAISE

Makes about 1½ cups

2 egg yolks
¼ cup walnut pieces, roasted in 275-degree oven until lightly browned
5 cloves garlic
⅓ cup loosely packed Italian (flat-leaf) parsley (or curly parsley, which is less flavorful)
1 cup olive oil
juice of 1 lemon
salt and pepper to taste

Combine egg yolks, walnuts, garlic, and parsley and process in food processor to make a smooth paste.

Slowly drizzle in olive oil to form an emulsion. Continue to add olive oil slowly. Do not overprocess or the emulsion will break down.

Season with lemon juice, salt, and pepper.

ANCHOVY MAYONNAISE

Makes about 1¼ cups

2 egg yolks
9 anchovy fillets, rinsed and patted dry
6 cloves garlic
1 cup olive oil
chopped fresh basil (optional)
juice of 1 lemon
salt and pepper to taste

Combine egg yolks, anchovies, and garlic and process in a food processor to make a smooth paste. Slowly drizzle olive oil into the paste to form an emulsion. Do not overprocess. Add basil and season with lemon juice, salt, and pepper.

BRENNAN'S HOMEMADE MAYONNAISE

Makes 1¼ cups

1 whole egg
2 tablespoons lemon juice or red wine vinegar
¼ teaspoon dry mustard
⅛ teaspoon salt
1 teaspoon Worcestershire sauce
1 cup vegetable oil (part olive oil is excellent), divided

Combine all ingredients except oil in a blender container. Add ¼ cup oil. Cover and blend at low speed. Remove cover and immediately pour in all remaining oil in a steady stream. Blend. (Do not add oil drop by drop, or the blender will liquefy the egg and the mayonnaise will not thicken.)

BRENNAN'S OF HOUSTON RAVIGOTE SAUCE

Makes 2 cups

*T*his piquant sauce is wonderful served over cold lump crabmeat, cold boiled shrimp, cold smoked amberjack, or just about anything that swims.

¼ cup minced parsley
4 teaspoons drained and chopped capers
¼ cup homemade mayonnaise
½ cup plus 2 tablespoons Creole or coarse-grained Dijon mustard
1 teaspoon dry mustard
juice of ½ lemon
1 tablespoon Worcestershire sauce
1 tablespoon prepared cream-style horseradish
salt and pepper to taste
2 hard-cooked eggs, chopped

Combine all ingredients except salt, pepper, and eggs. Mix well and season to taste with salt and pepper. Fold in chopped eggs. Chill.

COMMANDER'S REMOULADE SAUCE

Makes 2½ cups

*T*his classic sauce is updated in this version using Creole mustard. It is a delicious enhancement to any cold seafood.

3 eggs (at room temperature)
¼ cup Creole mustard or coarse-grained Dijon mustard
½ cup prepared mustard
2 tablespoons paprika
1 teaspoon cayenne pepper
1 teaspoon salt
1 cup chopped scallions
½ cup chopped celery
½ cup chopped parsley
2 cloves garlic, chopped
½ cup catsup
½ cup white vinegar
juice of 1 lemon
1⅓ cups vegetable oil

Combine all ingredients except oil in a blender container. Cover and mix at high speed until well blended. Remove cover and add oil in a steady stream. Sauce will thicken to a mayonnaise-like consistency. Chill.

Papantla's market overflows with the fresh produce grown in volcanic soil of the surrounding hills.

CAPER SAUCE

Makes about 2 cups

6 tablespoons butter, divided
2 tablespoons flour
1 cup hot water
2 egg yolks, beaten
half of 2½-ounce jar capers, undrained
salt and pepper to taste

Melt 2 tablespoons butter in the top of a double boiler over boiling water. Stir in flour, mixing well. Add hot water and stir until smooth and creamy. Add beaten egg yolks slowly, having first warmed them with a bit of the hot sauce. When sauce is thick and creamy, remove from heat and add remaining butter. Add capers, salt, and pepper and taste to adjust seasonings. Drain some of the vinegar from the capers for a milder taste.

CREOLE-STYLE MUSTARD SAUCE

½ cup heavy cream
½ cup dry white wine
½ cup chicken stock
1 cup butter (unsalted if using salted stock)
⅓ cup Creole mustard or other coarse-grained mustard
salt to taste
ground white pepper to taste

Combine cream, wine, and stock in a saucepan and cook over medium heat until reduced by half. Remove from heat and whisk in butter a piece at a time. Add mustard and seasonings. Keep warm.

A Tampico garlic vendor weighs in for Saturday street sales.

BASIC VINAIGRETTE DRESSING

*T*his dressing covers a multitude of greens—and other viands as well. It is a basic oil and vinegar dressing seasoned variously according to the taste of the cook and the use for which it is intended. The combinations are endless. A very good vinaigrette is made with Balsamic vinegar, a honey-sweetened hot mustard, and vegetable oil. Try wine vinegars with a variety of mustards and olive oil and the herb of your choice. Substitute dry vermouth for part of the acid content—its herbs add a delicate flavor to the dressing. If less acidity is desired, dilute the acid with a little water.

1 part acid (vinegar, lemon or lime juice, wine,
or a combination)
salt to taste
Dijon mustard
garlic
herbs such as basil, oregano, tarragon (optional)
3 parts oil (olive oil, vegetable oil, walnut oil, etc.)

In a bottle, jar, or bowl combine acid, salt, and any seasonings and herbs. Shake or whisk to dissolve salt. Add oil, shaking or whisking to form an emulsion. If allowed to stand for any length of time, it will separate. Simply shake or whisk to re-emulsify.

PETER HARMAN'S GRAPEFRUIT VINAIGRETTE

Makes about 2 cups

*T*ry this vinaigrette with a salad of mixed green lettuces, arugula, thin-sliced fennel, and radishes, with about ½ cup of lump crabmeat in the center of the plate.

1 whole egg
½ cup fresh basil leaves
2 cloves garlic, crushed
1 teaspoon cracked black pepper
1 teaspoon salt
3 tablespoons red wine vinegar
1½ cups vegetable oil
¾ cup fresh grapefruit juice

In a food processor combine egg, basil, garlic, pepper, salt, and vinegar. Process about 30 seconds. Slowly add oil in a constant stream to make a mayonnaise. Thin with grapefruit juice to give dressing a pouring consistency.

SKINNY-DIP DRESSING

Makes 1 cup

*U*sing their herb know-how, Madalene Hill and Gwen Barclay of Hilltop Herb Farm near Houston created this deliciously flavored low-calorie dressing. It contains about 15 calories per tablespoon when prepared with low-fat yogurt, even less with the nonfat type. Other herbs or the seeds of celery, coriander, comino, or fennel can be substituted for the basil and Mexican mint marigold.

1 cup buttermilk
1 clove garlic
1 tablespoon Dijon mustard
2 tablespoons each of fresh basil, parsley, and
Mexican mint marigold or tarragon
¼ teaspoon Tabasco Pepper Sauce (or ½-inch slice
jalapeño pepper)
½ teaspoon salt
⅛ teaspoon ground white pepper
1 cup low-fat yogurt

Combine all ingredients except yogurt in a blender and blend until smooth. Transfer to a bowl and fold in yogurt. Taste to adjust seasonings. If extra sharpness is desired, add 1 tablespoon white wine vinegar.

CREPES FOR SAVORY DISHES

Makes 16 to 18 crepes

*W*hen added to a basic béchamel sauce, extra cooked fish or leftovers from a fish dish can make an excellent filling for a crepe dish. Some of the fillings in the empanada and quesadilla recipes can be used as crepe fillings and will be good topped with cheese and a flavored béchamel sauce. Let your palate tell you what combinations might be pleasing to the diners at your house.

1½ cups flour
½ teaspoon salt
pinch of sugar
3 eggs
1 cup milk
½ cup water
3 tablespoons melted butter
1 tablespoon dry vermouth

Sift together flour, salt, and sugar..Beat eggs, milk, and water together. Add to dry ingredients, mixing well. Add butter and vermouth. The batter should be the consistency of thick cream. Let rest for 2 hours.

Oil a crepe pan lightly and heat until a drop of water "dances" on the pan. Pour a scant ¼ cup batter into the pan, tilting it to spread evenly. Pour out any excess batter. When the crepe has set, turn it over to seal the other side. Stack crepes between sheets of waxed paper until ready to use.

Spoon a generous amount of the filling of your choice into the crepe and roll it, placing the filled crepes side by side in a shallow casserole dish. Top with Béchamel Sauce (p. 204) and cheese, if desired. Preheat oven to 350 degrees and bake, uncovered, until heated through.

BASIC FISH SOUFFLÉ

Serves 4 to 6

A good way to use any leftover cooked fish or shrimp is to make a soufflé. This basic recipe is quick and easy to adapt to any seafood and seasoning you wish to use.

3 eggs, separated
1 cup thick Béchamel Sauce (p. 204)
1½ cups cooked flaked fish or chopped shellfish
3 tablespoons fine-chopped scallions
1 teaspoon chopped parsley
⅛ teaspoon paprika
¼ teaspoon dry mustard
salt and pepper to taste
herb or spice to taste

Beat egg yolks well and add to Béchamel Sauce. Fold in seafood, scallions, parsley, and seasonings. Beat egg whites stiff and gently fold into the fish mixture. Spoon into a 4-cup mold and set in a pan of warm water about 1½ inches deep. Preheat oven to 350 degrees and bake for about 1 hour or until a knife inserted in the center comes out clean.

Note: For a lighter dish, add 2 extra egg whites. Proceed as above, using a 6-cup mold.

BASIC PASTRY

Makes 2 9-inch pastry shells or
about 20 2-inch tartlets

*P*astry shells are easy to make if you keep in mind a few simple rules. First, use all-purpose or pastry flour with a low gluten content. Do not overwork the dough; it makes a tough crust. Allow at least 30 minutes for the dough to rest before rolling it out. Prebaking a crust seals it from the filling and helps keep it from becoming soggy. For greater interest and variety, try adding a touch of spice or citrus zest to a crust for sweet pies and tarts. For savory crusts try cracked black pepper, cayenne pepper, or an appropriate ground or dried herb.

3 cups all-purpose flour
1 teaspoon salt
¾ cup cold butter, cut into thin slices
6 tablespoons solid vegetable shortening
6 tablespoons ice water
1 teaspoon lemon juice or white vinegar

In a chilled bowl combine flour, salt, butter, and shortening and blend with a pastry cutter or two knives until the mixture resembles oatmeal flakes. Mix the ice water and lemon juice together and add, a tablespoon at a time, to the flour mixture. Mix dough to form a ball. If necessary, add additional water a little at a time. Do not overwork the dough.

Wrap dough in waxed paper or plastic wrap and refrigerate at least 30 minutes.

Roll out dough on a lightly floured board or between two sheets of waxed paper.

For uncooked fillings: Prick bottom of crust with a fork. Refrigerate 1 hour. Cover crust with aluminum foil cut to fit bottom and fill with dried beans. Preheat oven to 425 degrees and bake for 8 minutes. Remove beans and foil and continue baking another 4 to 5 minutes or until lightly browned. Cool and fill as desired.

For cooked fillings: Prebake crust 3 to 4 minutes. Cool, fill, and continue baking according to recipe directions.

The golden waters of Natula beckon an early fisherman.

INDEX

White pelicans feast in the wake of boat traffic across the Port
Aransas channel.

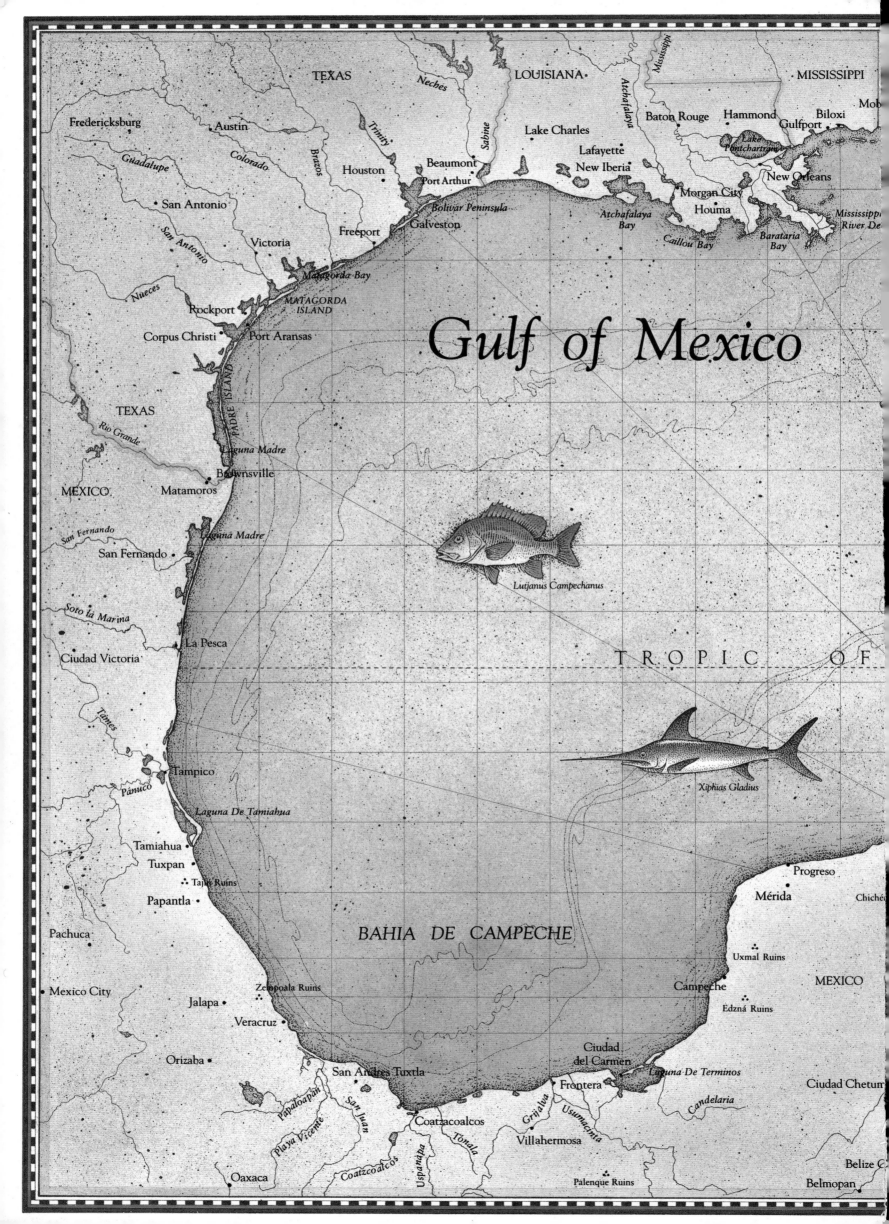

TEXAS   Neches   LOUISIANA   MISSISSIPPI

Fredericksburg   Baton Rouge   Hammond   Mob
                                                                    Atchafalaya   Gulfport   Biloxi
                    Austin   Lake Charles   Lake
                                   Trinity   Sabine   Lafayette   Pontchartrain   New Orleans
Guadalupe   Colorado   New Iberia
                                Brazos   Beaumont
        San Antonio   Morgan City
                            Houston   Port Arthur   Houma
    Victoria   Atchafalaya   Mississippi
San Antonio   Bolivar Peninsula   Bay   Barataria   River De
                                            Galveston   Caillou Bay   Bay
            Freeport
Nueces
                    Matagorda Bay

        Rockport   MATAGORDA
                        ISLAND
Corpus Christi   Port Aransas

                                                    # Gulf of Mexico
        TEXAS

Rio Grande

            Laguna Madre
            Brownsville
MEXICO   Matamoros   *Lutjanus Campechanus*

San Fernando

    San Fernando   TROPIC OF

Soto la Marina

        La Pesca
Ciudad Victoria   *Xiphias Gladius*

Tames

                                                                                Progreso

Tampico   Mérida   Chiché

        Laguna De Tamiahua

Tamiahua   Uxmal Ruins
    Tuxpan
        Tajin Ruins   MEXICO
    Papantla   Campeche
Pachuca   BAHIA DE CAMPECHE   Edzná Ruins

Mexico City   Zempoala Ruins
        Jalapa
    Veracruz   Ciudad
                                                                del Carmen
Orizaba   Laguna De Terminos
                San Andres Tuxtla   Frontera   Ciudad Chetum
Pánuco   Candelaria
                Papaloapan   San Juan   Coatzacoalcos   Tonala   Grijalva   Usumacinta   Belize C
    Oaxaca   Playa Vicente   Coatzcoalcos   Villahermosa
                                        Palenque Ruins   Belmopan